H
Love you, you.
Smooch,
Roz
Rom 8:28

HIS WORD IS TRUE!

ROZ MITAKIDES

xulon PRESS

DEDICATION

This book is dedicated to Jesus and my CancerHope family. He has so powerfully and lovingly orchestrated the things in my life to bring me to this point. This was never something I aspired to do. It was only brought about by His planting a seed and watering it through so many. These devotionals were written as weekly encouragement to those who struggle with cancer and the ones who lovingly support them. The intention was always to point them to Jesus, the Healer, Lover of our souls and the Author and Perfecter of our faith. May this be pleasing in Your sight, my King. To You be all glory and praise.

A special thank you to:

My beloved husband, Drew, who's generosity and
love is such an example of Christ.
You have my heart forever.

My sons, Steve and Nick. You both are my inspiration
and motivation. I am so very proud and thankful to be
your mom. Looking forward to our "reunion"
−1 Thes. 4:16.

My "extended" kids: Kim, Jody, Monica, Missi, Shannon, Eric, Angie, and Beckie. You are mine! I love you.

My grandchildren, Nikki and Quentin. You are my delight and joy! Cling to Jesus always and share your blessings.

and...my dad. Your walk of faith points the way home. Thank you.

Check us out at <u>CancerHope@Southbrook.org</u>.

ABOUT THE AUTHOR:

I was raised by parents who loved the Lord. My dad was a preacher that travelled around and taught on the book of Revelation. He would take a portable blackboard and draw it out! He was amazing. He was the most devout praying, God-fearing man I've ever known. When I was 8, he was diagnosed with pancreatic cancer and given 6 months to live. He lived 5 years, but was in terrible pain for some of it. At those times, a special lady would come and lay hands on him and pray. The pain would completely leave him! I was so amazed by that. When my dad died, I misunderstood it completely and turned away from God. Thankfully, He kept his hand on me and led me back to His heart. After 2 kids and a failed marriage, I knew I needed help. He was my answer. I was baptized and recommitted my life to Christ at age 30. The Lord brought me a wonderful husband and father to my boys. My faith continued to grow through bible studies and life experiences. Then, a date came that changed me forever. November 20, 1995. My youngest son, Nick, was killed in a car crash. He was 16. Nick had been attending bible studies with me for awhile and had given his heart to the Lord. I am so thankful for that! He was ready! God knew what was coming and had prepared him......and me. I was able to see that my dad's suffering had been *for me*. God knew what was coming in my life and gave me an example of strong faith, *no matter what*, in my dad. That realization brought me to my knees. This has been a journey of great sacrifice and grief, but I wouldn't change it for <u>anything</u>. I *know* the Father in a way that is not possible without pain. I trust Him with my all. Through Nick's home-going, my whole family has come to accept Christ. His plan is perfect and He is faithful to complete it. HIS WORD is True! By the way, the lady that prayed over my dad.....the day after my son was killed, she called my mom and told her she "saw Nick walking on streets of gold". I had not seen her since I was a teenager. Only God. He is good!

CONTENTS

I hope you felt the presence of Christ in a powerful way over the holidays. As we begin a new year, I am praying that you are filled with hope and faith for what God will do! Fear not, God is not at all anxious over the fiasco that tops our headlines! He is not "waiting to see how it will go" to enact His plan....*His plan* is not at all contingent on us. "For I know the plans *I have for you*, declares the Lord, plans for welfare and not for calamity *to give you a future and a hope.*" (Jer.29:11) But isn't it **wonderful**...that His plan *includes* us?! So, our role is to leave anxiousness / worry behind and look forward with *anticipation and excitement*. I know there will be times of difficulty (2 Tim 3:1), but God has gone before us! It's **HIS** plan!! We can forget that, can't we?? We are **in** HIS plan....we are the *center* of HIS plan. He died that we could live! No matter what is going on in your life or what will come in the new year...**HIS** plan is to "*give you a future and a hope*"! And *that* plan is secure! Glory! I'm praying that you will grasp how secure you are in His plan. May "the eyes of your heart be enlightened, so that you may <u>know</u> the hope of His calling,... the riches of the glory of <u>His inheritance</u> in the saints, and what is the *surpassing greatness* of <u>His power</u> toward us <u>who believe</u>." (Eph.1:18,19) "Now may the God of hope fill you with *all joy and peace in believing*, that you may **abound in hope** by the power of the Holy Spirit"! (Rom.15:13)

JANUARY   Week 2

I am praying that you will grasp the power and significance of John 14:16..."And *I will pray* the Father, and
He *shall give you* *another* **Helper**, that He may *abide*
with you *forever*." This is Jesus Himself talking and
sharing with His disciples that He will be leaving them.
Imagine...being there and believing that He is the One...
the Messiah! You've seen Him perform miracles and
experienced His incredible teaching and incomprehen-
sible love. And now, after 3 years of living life together
....He tells you He is leaving. You are staying......He is
going. That is some *really* hard news....isn't it?? If you
or someone you love has received some really hard
news....this is the message for you! Jesus has much to
say in *all* of John 14 that will just bless your socks off....
it's worth reading it over and over for at least a week....
"listen" to Him speak comfort and truth to you. In verse
16, He gives a very personal truth (notice the "you") when
we face significant uncertainty and some very difficult,
unexpected... news. He says that *He personally* is asking
the Father and Father **will** respond. To this point, Jesus
has been their complete focal point...they have looked
to Him for *everything.* They have been through hardships, but *He has always* been with them. Now, He's
leaving...imagine what's going through their mind..."what
are *we* going to do *without* Him??" Personally, I'd be
having a panic attack! I'm almost having one just putting
myself in their shoes for a moment! Jesus speaks directly
to their fear...I've asked Father and "He is giving you
another *Helper*" and not just that...but... "He *will abide*
with you **forever**"!! The Helper that is coming...that the

10

Father is sending...will <u>never</u> leave...He will *live with <u>you</u>* **always**! The word for "Helper" is *Paracletos*...it means "one called alongside to help", or "intercessor". The Holy Spirit (Helper) brings power and authority to *help and comfort* <u>you</u> just as if Jesus was personally standing beside you. Greater really, because that power is <u>*within*</u> you. (John 16:7) It is enacted by your faith (belief)! Notice John 11:40 where Jesus says "if you **believe**, you <u>will</u> <u>see</u> the glory of God"! 2 Cor. 5:7 says "for we walk by *faith* and <u>not by sight</u>". There will be bad news....we live in a fallen world of sin and disease. But the Helper will never leave you. He is in the moment....have faith! As we begin the year, I'm encouraged by being reminded of the <u>*ending*</u>....Rev. 21....."And I saw a **new** heaven and a **new** earth; for the *first heaven and earth <u>passed</u> <u>away</u>*, and there is no longer any sea. And I saw the holy city...coming down out of heaven <u>from God</u>, made ready as a bride adorned for her husband. And I heard a loud voice <u>from the throne</u>, saying, "Behold, the *dwelling of God is among men* and He shall dwell among them, and they shall be His people, and *God Himself shall be among them*, and He shall *wipe away <u>every tear</u>* from their eyes; and there shall **no longer** be any *death*; there shall **no longe**r be any *mourning*, or *crying*, or *pain*; the first things *have passed away*." And He who sits <u>on the throne</u> said, "Behold, I am making ***all*** *things <u>new</u>*." Oh glory!!! You just *have* to go and read the rest for yourself!!

I am praying for your faith to be strong and for the truth of His word to empower you to stand firm this year! The Helper is present...will you enact His power?

Come, Lord Jesus!

JANUARY   Week 3

I know many of you are facing some difficult days. I pray for your heart to be encouraged and your faith strengthened. The Lord knows and you are so precious to Him, that He captures your tears in His bottle. (Ps. 56:8) I love the picture of that in my mind.......the Father saving our tears for He *knows* the pain in each one, and He is close enough to touch my face with His hand. He is gentle and longs for us to *know* He is <u>with</u> us. (Deut. 31:6) He is *with* you. He will <u>never</u> leave you or forsake you. He nailed His beloved Son to a cross, so you could be *with* Him.......forever. (2Cor. 5:21) We may have some tough days, but God has a plan that *will be* fulfilled. He will see us through all the days and His incredible promise is: "He will *cause* <u>all things</u> to work together for the *good*, for <u>those who love Him</u> and are called according to His purpose." (Rom. 8:28) If you are in Christ, this promise is for *you*. <u>Nothing</u> can happen to you that God won't use for your *good*!

I am celebrating my son's birthday this week. The last one we celebrated together was 19 years ago....he was 16. As I have been contemplating that, I see clearly that my circumstances–<u>all of them</u>–are well *in the hand* of God. They *always* have been, when I've realized it.... and when I haven't. He is working <u>all things</u> for my good.

I can truly say..."it is *well* with my soul". My prayer is that you will get to that place... just believing Him, regardless of any circumstance that comes your way. Knowing He is close enough to touch your face....... saving your tears because you are that precious to Him.

"I will cry to God Most High, to God who accomplishes *all things* <u>for</u> me." (Ps.57:2) He is *for* you, dear one. And......He is *with* you. May you be filled with His peace and presence.

JANUARY   Week 4

1 *P*eter 1:3 tells us that God has "caused us to be born again to a living hope through the resurrection of Jesus.., to obtain an inheritance which is imperishable and undefiled and will not fade away, reserved in heaven for you, who are protected by the power of God through faith..." Our hope is ALIVE! He lives! We do not hope in something that cannot respond or does not hear. Our Hope is intimately acquainted with us–He knows our needs. He provides an inheritance that is reserved for you specifically–it has your name on it! Did you know that no-one else can get your inheritance? :) We are protected by the power of God.... amazing Resurrection power! There is nothing that can come against this power–the enemy has been defeated, the Victor has been proclaimed & it is final.....Jesus is Lord! Because we know our Hope is the Resurrected One, we can continue "rejoicing in hope, persevering in tribulation, devoted to prayer.." (Rom. 12:12). That is our task, isn't it? Rejoice in hope, persevere, be devoted to prayer.

Thank you for your devotion to Him and to prayer, dear one. May He bless you with His presence and peace, filling you with the "knowledge of His will in all spiritual wisdom and understanding, so that you may walk in a manner worthy of the Lord, pleasing Him in all respects, bearing fruit in every good work" (Eph.1:9, 10).

His abundance to you!

JANUARY   Week 5

I've been contemplating suffering from God's per-spective this week and thought I'd share with you. We are created in the image of God–so as our hearts go out to those who suffer.....how much more does God's?! Our focus, however, can mostly center around praying for relief and healing from suffering. God's focus seems to be on endurance and outcome (Ps.119:71–"It is good for me that I have been afflicted, that I may learn Your stat-utes"). It is *IN* suffering then, that we learn God's truths and His character. He uses our suffering in accordance with His divine plan–1 Tim. 2:4 "Who desires all men to be saved and to come to the knowledge of the truth."; John 8:32 "and you will know the truth and the truth will make you free". So God's heart is on much bigger things than our comfort....He is focused on our freedom for all eternity. When Jesus walked the earth, the sick and afflicted were brought to Him and He healed them. But, even though they were healed of that affliction.... they still died later on. Their "physical healing" was only temporary from the Master–the "forever healing" came later. So it is for us and those we lift before the Father.... as we continue to pray for comfort and healing....let us also pray for God's eternal purpose to be fulfilled–for the "forever freedom" that comes only through Christ.

Our hope is in You, Lord and You, alone. Keep our minds centered on Your great purpose and use us, Father, for Your glory. Remind us that physical healing is always only temporary at best and our "forever healing" awaits.

May the peace of Christ dwell in you richly!!

FEBRUARY   **Week 1**

I pray for your strength and endurance. I'm asking
our great God to stir the Holy Spirit within you to a
consuming fire....that He would consume all weariness,
doubt and fear–building you up strong in His might, filling
you with resurrection power that has conquered death.
Be reminded, dear one, that Jesus has completed
His work...it IS finished! While we still labor here and
encounter hardship and disease....keep focused that
the war is already won and Christ is victorious over ALL
things! Every knee WILL bow and every tongue confess
that Jesus is Lord of all! Just think about that....abso-
lutely everything answers to Him. But yet, He invites us
to participate with Him in loving, praying, and encouraging one-another. Rom. 8:26 tells us that the "Spirit
helps our weakness; for we do not know how to pray as
we should, but the Spirit Himself intercedes for us with
groanings to deep for words; and He who searches the
hearts knows what the mind of the Spirit is, because He
intercedes *for the saints* according to the will of God."
And then, my favorite / life verse–28: "And we know that
God causes ALL things to work together for good to
those who love God, to those who are called according
to His purpose." !! God's amazing promise to us is that
no matter what it "looks like or feels like"....HE is IN
control and HE will use *everything* for our good.....all of
it. AND, the Spirit of Christ prays FOR us!! Oh, Praise
God!! There is nothing like that anywhere on the planet!
I'm asking the Holy Spirit to infuse that promise to the
core of your being....may we believe it and live it more

each day–to the glory of His great Name! Let's just lift our hands and praise Him right now!! All praise and glory and honor to Jesus–our King!!!! If the Spirit of God is leaping in your chest right now...feel free to let you feet join in!! Glory!

Amen!!

FEBRUARY   **Week 2**

B rrr....it's cold! I gotta confess....I am praying for snow! :) I know...all ya'll don't get excited by that....but for those who do...feel free to join me! Now, for what I **really** want to share with you today..look at Gen. 17:1 with me. "Now when Abram was *99 years old*, the Lord appeared to Abram and said to him, "*I am* <u>God Almighty</u>; walk before Me, and be blameless." God was about to make a covenant with Abram, to give him a son by Sarah (*she was 90*!) and to make him a "father of a multitude of nations". Before God told him the promise, He gave Abram some information about Who He Is. Note how God introduces Himself..."*I am God Almighty*". He actually used the Hebrew word of "**El Shaddai**", which means "*all sufficient, most powerful*".... think a minute about what all that means. *All sufficient....* to be possessed of <u>unfailing strength</u>. *Most powerful....* nothing else needed, <u>enough</u>! Why do you think God gave Abram that information <u>before</u> He told him *what* He was going to do? He wanted Abram to *believe* Him....to *trust* Him to accomplish what Abram could not do. Abram even said in his heart, "will a child be born to a man 100 years old? And will Sarah, who is 90, bear a child?" But, God showed him the reality about Himself. The next year, Abraham and Sarah gave birth to a son....Isaac. And...He showed *us*. Now, go to 2 Cor. 12:9. Paul was suffering significantly with an ailment in his body, and he had gone to the Lord 3 times requesting healing. Notice God's response..."And He has said to me, "My grace is **sufficient** for you, for **power** is perfected in weakness."

El Shaddai (the <u>all sufficient</u>, <u>most powerful</u> One), says "My *grace* (goodwill, lovingkindness, favour) *is* sufficient for <u>*you*</u>.." It's enough. It's all you need. Certainly, He tells us to "ask" all through the Scriptures, but He also says....know Who I am! Know Who you're asking! "I am El Shaddai"! Then....trust....that He is sufficient. He is all you need.

I am praying for you...for whatever you may be going through...that your heart will embrace and believe *El Shaddai*, the all sufficient One! He knows you inside and out, He knows all that you need....may you rest in His sufficiency.

To Him Who is able,

*I*s there a song in your heart, today? I'm doing a Precept study in Ephesians and we're in chapter 5. God (through Paul) is telling us to be "careful how you walk, not as unwise, but as wise" men and women. He warns us to "not be foolish", but to understand His will for us. Let's look together at vs. 18; "And do not get drunk with wine, for that is dissipation, <u>but</u> *be filled with the Spirit.*" Drinking too much wine causes us to be *controlled* by the alcohol and to think <u>only</u> of *ourself.* "Dissipation" means a complete waste. "**But**", He says, "be *filled* with the Spirit." We can learn a lot from the original Greek language of this text. This is a command, and it is in the present tense....which means "keep on" being filled. Interestingly, it is also in the "passive voice", which means I don't "fill" myself, but I "allow or surrender" so the Holy Spirit can fill me. Cool, huh? There are 3 things that follow that show what it <u>looks like</u> when I am *filled with the Holy Spirit:* (vs.19–21)

   1) ..."singing and making melody with your heart to the Lord"–a song or music that <u>exalts Christ</u> fills your heart! When that is happening, you can *know* you are being filled with the Spirit! It's why music is so powerful and can take us from sorrow to praise....it is the power of the Holy Spirit!

   2) "*always* giving thanks for <u>all</u> things in the name of our Lord Jesus Christ to God". Thanksgiving is a complete work of the Spirit. It is a supernatural act that my *surrender* allows to happen <u>in</u> me. Being obedient with my mouth is a huge

act of surrender.....have your verbally "thanked" Him today?

3) "be subject to one another in reverence to Christ". The power of the Spirit causes me to be focused on others instead of myself. It is literally the *Spirit of Christ* that changes my attitude to be like His, which is always "*self*-sacrificing". Amazing!

So, now that we know what it looks like....let's surrender to the work of the Spirit and "be filled"! Rejoicing in song with you!

FEBRUARY   Week 4

The sun is shining and it looks to be a beautiful day.....but that can change quickly...can't it? We never know what the future will bring. We tend to get comfortable in a routine and then seemingly out of the blue, our whole world can be rocked. While that is true for us....it is never true for our great God. He is never surprised at what we encounter. He knows it all before it ever comes to pass. (Ps. 139) My devotional time over the last few days has focused on "trust". God simply asks us to "trust Him"–He is over all and knows all and loves us more than we can fathom. Ps. 37:5 says "Commit your way to the Lord, trust also in Him, and He will bring it to pass." Committing our way means offering today and all that comes with it to the Lord for His purpose (not my own) and then trusting Him to get me through it.... (even though I can't see how). Worry is an expression of a lack of faith. Rick Warren of Saddleback Church says "Worry is really just a form of atheism, because every time you worry, you're saying "it all depends on me". He goes on to say "You must trust God with your life. As long as you love anything more than God, that thing or person or item will become a source of anxiety." Anxiety is all around us...we live in very uncertain times. However, our God IS certain! He has provided a way for us to live with Him forever–through His own Son. I need to be reminded that His intention is to get us home–where we will live in holiness forever–**not** to make this life comfortable.

Prov. 3:5,6–"Trust in the Lord with *all* your heart, and do not lean on your own understanding. In *all* your ways acknowledge Him, and **He will make your paths straight**."

Let's offer Him our whole heart and all of our day—especially the part we just don't understand—let's *trust* our great God to make the way straight for us! It is His promise and He cannot lie.

I am praying for your heart this week—that you hold nothing back and offer Him all of it. I'm praying for our trust in Him to grow into a mountain. May He bless your heart and home with His peace.

MARCH   Week 1

As I write this, a storm approaches....thunder, lightening, wind, rain. I'm remembering the song by Casting Crowns–"Praise You in The Storm"..... the lyrics declare the tenderness, faithfulness, and authority of God:

"And I'll praise You in this storm
And I will lift my hands
For You are who You are
No matter where I am
And every tear I've cried
You hold in Your hand
You never left my side
And though my heart is torn
I will praise You in this storm"

The storms of life rage...but we can praise and offer thanks because God is on the throne! Our thankfulness opens the door to His presence (I just read that today in Jesus Calling). He tells us to express our faith through thanksgiving: "in everything *give thanks*; for this is God's will for you in Christ Jesus" (1Thes.5:18)– "whatever you do in word or deed, do ALL in the name of the Lord Jesus, *giving thanks* through Him to God the Father" (Col.3:17)–"*always giving thanks* for all things in the name of our Lord Jesus Christ to God, the Father" (Eph.5:20).

Let us join in lifting our hands and voice...right now... and offer praise to our great God. Thank You, Father–for

Jesus! Whose blood cleanses us from all sin, Who is at Your right hand interceding on our behalf, Who is over <u>all</u> things and is working <u>all things</u> according to Your plan. Thank You for a voice and hands to praise You. As long as we have breath, may we never cease to thank You. Life is tough, storms are tough....but You, Father...are always good...ALL the time! Thank You, for how much You love us! Thank You for never letting go of us! Thank You, for the season we are in...we know You are here with us. We exercise our faith in You, during this storm, by saying Thank You!!!!

May thanksgiving flow from your heart every day... all day! May the Holy Spirit flood you with resurrection power to rise up and praise....even during the storm.

MARCH   Week 2

*I*sn't God good?! He gave us snow *and* 65 degrees all in one week!!! Honestly, I was doing the "happy dance" for both! :)

Spring is right around the corner...when we get a "taste", we are reminded that it's coming. Do you *believe* Spring is coming? Is your faith strong that it is coming *for sure*? If it came _according to your belief_, what would that look like...and when?

I've been in Mathew 9:29 this week and captivated by it. Listen to Jesus speaking..."Be it done to you *according to your faith*." Let that sink it for a moment. The context is 2 blind men have been following Him, crying out "have mercy on us". Jesus then asked them (v 28) "Do you **believe** that I am able to do this?" They said "yes, Lord." He then touched their eyes, saying "Be it done to you *according to your faith*." If you had been one of them, how would you have felt just then....excited... scared...??? This response is not at all uncommon for Jesus. Notice Math. 9:22, His response to the woman who had reached out to "touch His garment"..."Daughter, take courage; _your faith_ has made you well." Math. 8:13, with the Roman centurion requesting healing of his ser-vant..."Go your way; let it be done to you _as you have believed_." Note also...John 11:40 (one of my favorites!). Jesus is at the tomb of Lazarus and He is speaking to Martha, who has resisted His command to move the stone covering the grave. Jesus _said to her_ "Did I not say to you, _if you believe_, you **will see** the glory of God?" While Grace is unconditional, (Eph. 2:8,9), the depth of our walk with Christ is dependent _on our belief_. Now, I'm not a "name it and claim it" fan....God is not a genie at my whim. But, He is *completely faithful* to His word. The question is...is that enough for us? Will we simply take Him at His word? That is where peace lives, dear one! May our belief in Him grow each day! I am praying that for you, this week. May your heart **believe** what Jesus wants you to _receive_!

In His most precious Name!

MARCH   Week 3

*P*s. 34:7 says "The angel of the Lord encamps *all around* those who fear Him, and He **delivers** them." I don't know all that you are going thru right now, but Jesus has you surrounded!!!! He is before you–He knows what is coming and He leads you!! He is not at all surprised by your circumstances (even though you may be!). He is beside you–both sides!! He is alongside–He is IN the moment–with you!! He will NEVER leave you or forsake you–you are not alone. He is behind you–He has your back! Nothing can sneak up on you, He pro-tects your blind-side. He sees all and knows all....you may not see it, but He does. I think we will be amazed at what we see in heaven, the times He thwarted evil and we didn't even know it was there! Thank You, Lord!!!!!

One of the most important things we can do today–is realize He is very near. He promises to deliver us! Our great God and King is faithful. Let us trust Him com-pletely to bring us through and take us home....we are forever secure. Enjoy His presence...now. Thank Him for it. His deliverance is coming!

"Oh, fear the Lord, you His saints! There is no want to those who fear Him." Ps.34:9

*C*ol. 4:2 says to "devote yourselves to prayer; keeping alert in it with an attitude of thanksgiving;". As we pray and lift up precious names entrusted to us, we can do so with thankful hearts....thankful that our God hears, thankful that we can carry the burdens that others cannot carry for themselves, thankful to be partners with those struggling, and thankful that our God cares and moves with compassion and power!

Col. 4:3 goes on..."praying at the same time for us as well, that God may open up a door for the word, so that we may speak forth the mystery of Christ..." Let us pray not only for healing and comfort, but that God would open a door for His word to be spoken and Christ to be shared—that whatever circumstances those we pray for are going through, that God would use it powerfully for someone to know Jesus! Isa. 56:11 gives us the promise that God's word will "not return to Him empty"...but it "will accomplish His desire and will succeed in the matter for which He sent it". What an incredible promise! His word has great power...it is "living and active and sharper than any 2-edged sword, piercing between soul and spirit, joint and marrow, and is able to judge the thoughts and intentions of the heart". (Heb. 4:12)

May the word of the Lord go forth!! May He raise you up to be mighty in prayer and thanksgiving! My prayer for you is Col 4:6 & 12—"that your speech always be with grace, seasoned with salt, so that you may know how you should respond to each one, and that you may stand perfect and fully assured in all the will of God". Amen.

MARCH   Week 5

*W*ell...another week of 60 / sunny _and_ snow! I'm just giddy! Ok, so I'm also a little cold....somehow, the bit of warm, made the cold....well, colder! Hmmm, as I just wrote that, I sensed it was spiritual. So, in my reflection, I'm thinking that as we draw closer to Jesus and begin to look/act more and more like Him (taking on His robe of "holy"), sin becomes "darker"....it's no longer a "little sin". We recognize that it grieves the heart of God and required the death of His Son. As that happens in us, it can serve a useful purpose to actually "repel" us from sin. (Thank You, Lord!) However, we must be very careful that it doesn't repel us _from sinners_! Jesus LOVED sinners, they (we) are why He came. As He begins to clean us (from the inside) and we begin to have a different view of sin, let us never forget from where we came. Let's go to Eph. 2 (it's not where I was headed when I began, but let's go with it!). "And you _were dead_ in your trespasses and sins, in which you _formerly_ walked according to the course of this world, according to the prince of the power of the air, of the spirit that is _now working_ in the sons of disobedience. Among them we too **all** formerly lived in the lusts of our flesh, indulging the desires of the flesh and of the mind, and were by nature children of wrath, even as the rest." We did not come from pretty! Ugh! As I reflect on _my_ former way....I am disgusted! Notice however, vs. 4..."**BUT GOD**, being rich in mercy, because of His _great love_ with which He loved us, _even when we were dead_ in our transgressions, made us alive together _with_

Christ (by grace you have been saved), and <u>raised us up</u> *with* **Him**, and <u>seated us</u> *with* **Him** in the heavenly places, in Christ Jesus,.."

Wow...that will get your head on straight! I'm grabbed by a couple of things....first, if I'm disgusted by the view of my former life (because Jesus is growing in me)...imagine how it looks from the perspective of "pure holiness"!! Yet, that is exactly <u>when</u> He "made us alive together with Christ"....that really helps me view sinners from a different perspective....it increases my desire to love them right where they are. (that can *only* be His Spirit in me!)

Secondly, did you realize that we have already been <u>*dead*</u>? That is truly very liberating to me. If I *was dead,* but now have been "*<u>made alive</u>*", and not just alive, but "*raised up* and *seated* <u>with</u> Christ"....for eternity! Exactly what, then, do we have to fear? Death? I don't think so...I've been there! I "was dead" in my sin...but no more! Whoop!! I have been made *alive* with Christ. Would you let that ruminate for while? I am praying the absolute truth of that would go deep in your heart and give you the power to be "done" with fear. You have been "raised up and seated with Christ"! You have power in the name of Jesus! You are "one" with Him! You *were dead,* but <u>now</u> you are alive! Hallelujah!! Also, I am praying that our hearts will be filled with compassion and love towards those who do not yet know they *are dead,* but can be "<u>made alive</u>".

APRIL   Week 1

As we approach Holy Week that leads up to Easter, I've been contemplating the Scriptures that document Jesus' triumphal entry into Jerusalem on what is now called "Palm Sunday". In preparation for this, Jesus sent 2 of his disciples to find a donkey and her colt (that no one had ever ridden; Mark 11:2) that were tied up and to bring them to Him. Not much is written about this, but it speaks volumes! Jesus describes to the disciples what to look for, they find it *exactly* the way He describes and when they untie the animals to bring them to Jesus, the owners ask "why are you untying the colt?" They simply respond "the Lord has need of it". Luke 19:34

That's it....the owners release the donkey completely. It's as if they *knew* that colt had been born specifically for that purpose and that time. There was great significance of a "king" riding on a "donkey"....it meant he was coming in peace. This also fulfilled the prophecy by Zechariah (9:9) "Behold, your king is coming to you; He is just and endowed with salvation, humble, and mounted on a donkey, even on a colt, the foal of a donkey." And this was spoken about 500 years *before* Jesus rode that colt into Jerusalem! So, that colt was *not* a coincidence. God's plan was for that colt to be right in the place it was supposed to be and He had prepared the owners to *immediately* accept His use of it. This is just one small detail.....yet, it was perfectly performed. Amazing. (The donkey's owner is on my priority list of people to meet in Heaven....I want to ask "how did you know??") :)

This is also the time when Jesus weeps over Jerusalem. (Luke 19:41) He lets them know their city will be taken siege and destroyed because they "did not recognize the time of your visitation". God was among them, yet they had blinded eyes and hearts of stone.

Our Lord wept over them. Our God grieves *for us* and *with us*. Immanuel...."God *with* us". My prayer is for you to have "fresh eyes" for this upcoming week. May all our hearts be aware of His walk during that week, 2000 years ago. I encourage you to read the accounts of Matthew, Mark, Luke and John; journey with Jesus as one of His disciples...experience it. Let us be changed by it.

APRIL   Week 2

*J*am in beautiful Lake Tahoe this week, where the scenery is breathtaking. The blue of the 1600ft deep lake with snow covered mountains on every side, and the sky is so blue it can almost cause your heart to leap from your chest! I am in awe of the majesty and splendor of our great God!! As I've been contemplating Him, a verse in Daniel caught my heart......"But the saints of the most High shall take the kingdom, and possess the kingdom for ever, even for ever and ever." I just can't put into words how that blesses the deepest part of my soul. Here's the background: Daniel has just received a vision from the Lord about the future. It is a terribly frightful vision filled with slavery, tragedy, and horrors for Daniel's people (the Jews) and all of humankind. But then, he is given these words of great encouragement and it begins with....."But". Notice there is a change of course at hand. Regardless of what has happened....it is in the past! Do you need to hear that today? If you have experienced a horrific year or are in the middle of a tough event....there is a change of course coming!! And just let that change of course sink in... "the saints of the most High shall take the kingdom, and **possess the kingdom** *for ever*, **even** *for ever and ever*"! This change of course not only changes your view (location)...it changes your status to royalty....and take notice of how long this change will last!!!! Whoop!!! This is your future, dear one! Be encouraged....it is **for sure**....and it's **coming**!!! I am praying this reality sinks deep in your heart, may you receive this promise of the Lord and embrace it as yours, this day!

*H*ello, child of the Most High God!! Do you know that you are loved with an _everlasting_ love that is not based on *how you perform*?! You are *so very loved* that the King of the universe took your place, so that you could be **completely and forever** *released* from your sin (Ps.103:12). Regardless of what you may be facing today, the Lord has completed His work on your behalf....you are redeemed! Your eternal destiny has been secured! Jesus says "I give eternal life to them, (My sheep), and they shall **never perish**; and *no one* is able to snatch them out of My hand. My Father, who has given them to Me, *is greater than all*; and *no one* is able to snatch them out of the Father's hand. I and the Father _are one_." (John 10:28-30) Our great God has once and for all, defeated death! We truly have nothing to fear. Today's "Jesus Calling" devotional says "Anxiety is a result of envisioning the future without Me (Jesus)". Think about that for a minute.....is that not the absolute truth??!! Our anxiousness comes from looking ahead to our circumstances and "what if's" and not at all seeing Jesus and His sovereignty there with us. *How do we let that happen*???!!! Ugh! I'm so done with that! How about you? The devotional gave 2 rules to follow...."If you must think about upcoming events......1) Do not linger in the future (anxieties sprout like mushrooms there) and 2) Remember the promise of Jesus' con-tinual Presence", (and I would add....love). Include Him in any imagery that comes to mind. As you see things that are not what you would choose...also look at the image of Jesus overshadowing it all.....just as you are "in His hand", all that you are going thru is in His hand as well. And *no one* can take you out! I just may have to get down on my face for a moment.......join me if you need to praise Him for that!!

K, I'm back. Spontaneous worship is soooo sweet!. I encourage you to go with it, whenever it wells up in you. It changes your outlook! Let's commit to always "see" the image of Jesus holding us (and our circumstance) in His hand, which is also in His Father's hand. That's a game-changer! Zeph. 3:17 says "The Lord your God is in your midst, a victorious warrior. He will exult over you with joy, He will renew you in His love, He will rejoice over you with singing." Picture that, dear one. The King of Glory singing over you! I am praying that picture stays with you, ...quiets your spirit and removes all anxiety. May you feel His amazing Presence.

s I write this, my door is open, the birds are singing, yellow daffodils are blooming, and the trees are beginning to bud. What was dead and bare a few weeks ago, is greening up and showing life! I LOVE Spring! It truly is the season of resurrection, rebirth! I'm so thankful God gave us this season as a symbol of the hope we have for heaven in Christ. As God gives us the physical example...let us receive it from Him with grateful hearts and joy! "Therefore we do **not** lose heart, but though our outer man *is decaying*, yet our inner man is **being renewed** day by day. For momentary, light affliction is producing for us an eternal weight of glory *far beyond* all comparison, while we look not at the things which are seen, but at the things which are not seen; *for the things which are seen are temporal*, but the things which are not seen *are eternal*." (2 Cor. 4:16-18) I know that many of you are dealing with major life events...and they certainly don't seem "momentary" or "light". But please note that Paul is saying *"by comparison"* to the **glory it is producing**.... it is momentary and light. He goes on to say it is "temporal"....temporary. The glory it produces is eternal. Our bodies are decaying...we are reminded, this is not our home. Note chapt. 5:6-8..."Therefore, being always of good courage, and knowing that *while we are at home in the body*, we are absent from the Lord–for we walk by **faith**, *not by sight*–we are of good courage, I say, and *prefer rather to be absent from the body* and to be at home with the Lord."

This is why we can suffer and grieve with hope....it is the promise of the resurrection! Life has conquered death! Jesus is the victor! We can be of good courage, no matter what we may experience. We must renew ourselves, day by day, feeding our spirit on Truth and looking for the signs God has given all around us. I am praying this for you. That you will have fresh eyes for what God wants to show you. That you will hear His voice in the birds singing, see His beauty in all the different shades of green, and be reminded of what is coming in the bursting forth of life from the ground. May all the earth praise Him for His goodness!

rov. 13: 1

"A wise son accepts his father's discipline, but a scoffer does not listen to rebuke". We would just rather *not* "be disciplined" or hear a word of "rebuke". In Rev. 3:19, Jesus says "Those whom I love, I reprove and discipline.." Hebrews 12:5 tells us; "My son, do not regard lightly the discipline of the Lord, nor faint when you are reproved by Him; for those whom the Lord *loves* He **disciplines**, and He scourges *every* son whom He *receives.*" Ok, how many of you are actually *looking* for the Lord to discipline you??? Did you get up and say "Lord, show me Your love today.....give me some strong discipline!" (me neither!)

But did you get what He said in Rev. and Hebrews...."those whom the Lord *loves*....He disciplines", and "*every son*" gets "scourged"...ouch!

Verse 10 goes into more detail (Heb.12:10)..."He disciplines us for our *good*, that we may *share* **His holiness.**" As our Father, He corrects us; to keep us safe, for our protection, and to make us look more like Him. Similarly, as parents, we do the same to our own children. Depending on their "acceptance" of our correction, it dictates whether stronger discipline is necessary....doesn't it? Interesting....back to vs. 1 in Proverbs 13..

"A wise son *accepts* his father's discipline". When I first read it...I was focused on the wrong word...I was focused on *discipline* (and was ready to "move on"). As the Holy Spirit had me linger....I began to look at the significance of my role....."accept" and "listen". As I look for

His discipline and *accept* it, it dictates whether I move to a "scourging". The Father loves us completely and doesn't discipline for punishment (because He's mad)..... but, for us to *share* in His holiness. Seriously....that just takes all the "sting" out of it for me. I'm praying it does for you, as well. Will you join me in "*looking*" for the Father's discipline today (and every day)? Let us submit our heart for what He wants to do *in* us and then *through* us. Is there something you have not been "accepting" from the Lord? Repentance may be in order....it was for me.

"Father, forgive us for not being attentive to Your voice and for being focused on the wrong word....when our "flesh" is not in line with Your Spirit. Thank You for never letting us go and for Your amazing discipline that is for our good. I submit right here, right now to Your good work in me....that I may share in Your holiness. I *look* for Your discipline and *accept* it from the Hand of One Who loves me, Who died in my place.... that I may live with You forever. In the name of Jesus, my Redeemer."

Amen.

MAY   **Week 1**

*A*sking God to strengthen you for *this* day. This day...today...is really all we have. We have no idea what will happen tomorrow, but today is a gift from the Lord. Jesus says "Do not be anxious about tomorrow; for tomorrow will care for itself. Each day has enough trouble of its own." (Math.6:34) Ps. 118:24 says "*This* is the day the Lord has made, let us rejoice and be glad *in it*." So, where are your thoughts....are they in today.... or tomorrow? Jesus says don't bring tomorrow's trouble in today. I've been in Revelation, so that's where I'm taking you...:) You know what they say....once you go *in* Revelation, you *never* come out!! :) True that. Ready???

Jesus is speaking to the churches, (Rev. 2 & 3), and He is giving them praise, rebuke and instruction. I am captured by His message about "being an overcomer"... (2:7) "To him who overcomes, I will grant to eat of the tree of life, which is in the Paradise of God."

(2:11) "He who overcomes shall not be hurt by the second death."

(2:17) "To him who overcomes, to him I will give some of the hidden manna, and I will give him a white stone, and a new name written on the stone which no one knows but he who receives it."

(2:26) "And he who overcomes, and he who keeps My deeds until the end, to him I will give authority over the nations.....as I also have received authority from My Father; and I will give him the morning star."

(3:5) "He who overcomes shall thus be clothed in white garments; and I will not erase his name from the book of life, and I will confess his name before My Father, and before His angels."

(3:12) "He who overcomes, I will make him a pillar in the temple of My God, and he will not go out from it anymore; and I will write upon him the name of My God, and the name of the city of My God, the new Jerusalem, which comes down out of heaven from My God, and My new name."

(3:21) "He who overcomes, I will grant to him to sit down with Me on My throne, as I also overcame and sat down with My Father on His throne."

Wow! I want all that! Don't you? So, what does it take to be "an overcomer"? John gives us the answer in 1 John 5:4,5. "For *whatever* is born of God **overcomes** the world; and this is the victory that has **overcome** the world–*our faith*. And who is the one that **overcomes** the world, but he who *believes* that *Jesus is the Son of God*?" Whoop!! That is just good! When we *believe* that Jesus is the Son of God and receive His Lordship in our lives.... we are overcomers! Why?.... Because He overcame! He defeated death, sin and the enemy of our souls. Dear one, you can get through today because when you are in Christ, the enemy is under your feet. It is finished. Walk in that, today! No matter what may be going on in your life, walk in victory *today*! You are secure in His hand (John 10:27–30....look it up–you need to *know* this!). May your faith be strengthened and grow by the authority in His word and power of His Spirit. Receive it, then *believe* it. Be an overcomer!!!!

*W*ell, this week...2 Scriptures are forefront in my mind...Isa. 43:2–"When you pass through the waters, I will be with you; and through the rivers, they will not overflow you. When you walk through the fire, you will not be scorched, Nor will the flame burn you." This is an awesome promise of God! Notice the "*when*"..... not "if". Jesus said "in this world, you **will** have trouble" (John 16:33), but He also said "but take courage, I have overcome the world."!! So, while trouble will come, He is over it and His promise in Isa. gives us great hope... notice the "***pass through***"...we are to ***keep moving***! I can only do that, when I'm pointing to Christ and not my circumstance. Keep looking up, dear one! You are not alone. The Lord is with you, He says He "puts your tears in His bottle" (Ps.56:8). How much He loves us!!! Refuse the devil's temptation to make you feel "stuck". Jesus says "I *will be with* you" and He has overcome the world! Ps.56:9 says "this I know, that God is *for* me." Let that sink in......the sovereign God of the universe is *for* you!

The other verse that I've been contemplating is Rom.8:1–"There is therefore ***now*** no condemnation for those who are in Christ Jesus." If you're like me, you have days that you beat yourself up with self-talk. We need to know that Jesus has taken our sins (ALL) and removed them. Pastor Rick Warren said if you write all your sins down on a piece of paper and then stick that paper in a book and close it...all you see is the book. That's what Jesus did...He took our sins, and wrapped His righteousness around us. God sees Jesus (the book!) when He looks at us. Amazing, really. Look at the word "**now**" in that verse...."now" is forever moving to the present. I sooo love how God speaks to our heart! If there is "***now, no condemnation***" then, praise the Lord!!!!, there never, ever, will be!! Do you need to hear that, today? I do!!

You are precious and our Lord delights in you (Zeph.3:17)! May you receive His spoken word to your heart and be encouraged....that you remain focused on "things above" and that in ALL things, you point to Christ.

*I*t's finally time to do some outdoor planting! I love how the Father teaches us deep truths in simple things. Consider Math. 13:3-23; Jesus teaches on the parable of the sower. In the parable, He describes 4 types of soil and how it affects the seed:

1. seed that falls beside the road—hears, does not understand, devil snatches it away
2. seed that falls on rocky soil—no strong root; wilts in the heat
3. seed that falls among the thorns—worry and deceitfulness of riches choke the word
4. seed that falls on good soil—yields <u>much</u> fruit

Notice that the seed is the same (the Word)....it's the *soil* that makes a huge difference! There are 2 different ways to view this: what is the condition of *my* soil? The "good soil" that Jesus describes is "the man who hears the word and understands it" (v 23). It's time to do a "soil" check. Am I *seeking* God's word for the purpose of understanding <u>so it will *change* me</u>? Am I *devoted* to becoming more like Christ, <u>even through suffering</u>? Do I have "open hands" to offer Him *everything*?

The 2nd way to view it is: where am I *scattering* seed? While I am responsible for "sowing" everywhere.....am I giving enough effort to the "good soil"? Am I focused on cultivating the "good soil" people that God has planted in my life; those that are seeking to *know* Him, that are in a season of surrender, that desire to *be changed* from where they are? Those are the fruit bearers!

Let's pray for eyes to see the "good soil" people in our lives and the energy to pour into them. Let's also do a quick *soil check* in ourselves....are we truly "good soil" or is #3 creeping in? Ps. 43:3–"Send out Thy light and Thy truth, let them lead me".

Let's go plant something!! :)

I have been drawn to Ps. 23 the last few days. This Psalm is such a comfort to those who are struggling. Let's review it together:

"The *Lord* is my shepherd," This is a beautiful picture of Jesus, the One Who came to find the lost sheep and take them home.

"I shall not *want*." When I trust the Shepherd (instead of myself), I can truly be content. Are you content today? Who are you trusting?

"He makes me lie down in green pastures; He leads me beside quiet waters. He restores my soul; He guides me in the paths of righteousness for *His name's sake*." The Shepherd takes care of my every need. God's house is all about 'peace'. His Spirit does not bring "striving"....but 'peace'. Are you walking in His peace today? Gal.5:16 says if we "walk by the Spirit, you will not carry out the deeds of the flesh." We have a choice.... we can choose (through the power of Holy Spirit) to walk in His peace. He won't "make" us... we must choose. Did you notice that all of these things that He does for us.... He does for *His name's sake*... not ours. It's why we can count on Him to be faithful and fulfill His promise to us. It honors His name! I am so thankful for His character and His great name!!!

Now for some of the most encouraging words ever written....

"Even though I walk through the valley of the shadow of death," We all walk here at times, don't we?

"I will fear no evil; for Thou art with me;" No fear.... why? Because the Master of the universe is *with* me! The One who is *over* death.

"*Thy rod* and *Thy staff*, they comfort me." The "rod" reflects the unbending Word of God, and the "staff" reflects the Holy Spirit who lifts me and guards me. The two tools of the Shepherd.... they comfort me!

"Thou dost prepare a table before me in the presence of my enemies;" Again, I have no one to fear!

"Thou hast anointed my head with oil;" I am protected and covered!

"My cup *overflows*." Amen!!! As we understand our Shepherd and His promise to us... we cannot contain His blessing!

"Surely goodness and lovingkindness will follow me *all the days of my life*, and *I will dwell in the house of the Lord* **forever**."

Let's just praise Him with our heart and our lips. His word is true! He has us in His hand and no-one can take us out! (John 10:29) May you feel His amazing presence and invite His truth deep into your heart.

MAY   **Week 5**

I hope you had a relaxing and restorative Memorial Day weekend. I am so very thankful for those who have fought for our freedoms and have stood at the post to protect them. May the Lord bless and keep them!

I spent the weekend away with my family and it was so good! I am reminded of James 1:17 "Every **good thing** bestowed and every *perfect gift* is <u>from above</u>, coming down from the Father of lights, with whom there is no variation, or shifting shadow." As I think about it, there is sooo much good to be thankful for in my life... how about yours? It can be easy for us to focus our attention on the thing that is not going well and forget all about the "good" that the Father has all around us. When that happens, we are missing God. James says that **"every** good thing" is <u>from God</u>. Jesus said that "*no one is good*, except <u>God alone</u>". (Luke 18:19) So, naturally God blesses us with *good*, because He is *good*! When we lose sight of the "good", we lose sight of God! In Genesis, we see that as God created, He pronounced it all "good"! Sin changed what God created as good, but it didn't change God! **He is still good** and *He never changes!* He is *always* good, <u>all</u> the time....He cannot be anything but *good*. The <u>only</u> way I can be good, is when His Spirit lives in me. He brings His goodness wherever He goes. Thinking about *His goodness*, makes me thankful. Ps. 92:1 says "It is *good* to give thanks to the Lord". I'm inviting you to focus on the *good* this week... and let's give thanks to our <u>good</u> and faithful Father. I am praying that you will see *His goodness* all around you!

"for You, O Lord, have made me glad by what You have done, I will sing for joy at the works of Your hands."

JUNE   Week 1

*T*he power of the cross. Amazing, really. Death was conquered, sin was atoned for, the enemy was defeated, we were reconciled to the Father! Eph. 2 says "But *now* in Christ Jesus you who formerly *were far off* have been brought near by the blood of Christ. For He Himself is *our peace*, who made both groups *into one*, and broke down the barrier of the dividing wall, by abolishing **in His flesh** the enmity, which is the Law of commandments contained in ordinances, that in Himself He might make the two into one new man, *thus establishing peace*, and might *reconcile* them both in one body *to God* **through the cross**, by it having put to death the enmity." It *all* happened at the cross. Jesus said "It is finished" (John 19:30). The work planned from creation, to save us, was *finished*. "Therefore having been justified by faith, we have *peace with God* **through** our Lord Jesus Christ." (Rom. 5:1) We have been reconciled to the Father!

"He who did not spare His own Son, but delivered Him up for us all, how will He not also with Him freely give us all things?" (Rom. 8:32) "For I am convinced that neither death, nor life, nor angels, nor principalities, nor things present, nor things to come, nor powers, nor height, nor depth, nor any other created thing, *shall be able* to separate us from the *love of God*, which is in Christ Jesus our Lord." (Rom. 8:38, 39)

The power of the cross! "Therefore also God highly exalted Him, and bestowed on Him the name which is *above every name*, that at the name of Jesus *every knee* should bow, of those who are in heaven, and on the earth, and <u>under the earth</u>, and that *every tongue* should confess that Jesus Christ is Lord, to the glory of God the Father." (Phil. 2: 9-11) This *will* happen one day.... let's not wait. Let's exclaim to all that Jesus is Lord! I am praying that the power of the cross seeps deep into your soul and that your heart absorbs it's truth. Death is conquered! Your sin is removed! Satan is defeated! You are at peace with God! Thank You, Jesus!!

JUNE   Week 2

*N*ow, time is flying by! There are so many things that can distract us, we just don't realize how many days are passing...until we sit for a moment and look at the calendar....and then it hits us! I think that's also true for our spiritual journey. We can be distracted until one day we notice that we feel far from God...or we can't remember the last time we meditated on His word. We can wonder–"God, where did You go?". His answer will always be–I didn't move....*you* did. "I will never leave you nor will I ever forsake you." (Heb.13:5) The promise in that Scripture is amazing! When we surrender our life to Christ, the sovereign God of the universe promises to **ALWAYS** be near you and with you....even when you don't "feel" His presence–He *is* there! James 4:8 tells us to "Draw near to God and He will draw near to you." When I am feeling alone and don't understand my circumstances, I have a choice.....I can "go" with those feelings *OR* I can take God at His word and thank Him with my mouth that He is *always* with me, will *never* allow me to be alone AND will use **ALL** things for my good (Rom.8:28). I've learned that by thanking Him out loud with my mouth (when my heart just isn't in it) that I am exercising obedience. When you are obedient, God will do what *you can't* and change your heart to thank Him from it's depths! I have experienced this, personally...I can assure you–He will do it. When we are obedient and cling to His word, He **WILL do** what He says.

JUNE   **Week 3**

"*B*e very careful, then, how you live–not as unwise but as wise, making the most of every opportunity, because the days are evil." Eph. 5:15 We have seen this week that "the days are evil", haven't we? We can get lulled into thinking that we live in a safe place and forget that the enemy"prowls around like a roaring lion, seeking someone to devour" (1 Pet.5:8) We are to be careful...how we live...being cautious–yet intentional, making the *most* of _every_ opportunity....being *wise*. Peter tells us to be "firm in your faith"... *believe* God. Jesus tells us over and over again..."Do not be afraid". Fear is not living wisely. Believing God is how I live wisely. Trusting Him to do what He says. When He does not deliver me from adversity, He goes with me *through* it. He brings peace and strength. I truly can go through anything IF I *believe* Him! Jesus healed many people and would say to them "Let it be done to you according to your faith"....we have to *believe* it to get it! "The Lord sat as King at the flood; Yes, the Lord sits as King forever. The Lord will give strength to His people; The Lord will bless His people with peace." Ps.29:10, 11. That is my prayer for you this week. May you believe God more and more each day. Be firm in your faith!

JUNE

*P*s. 19 tells us "The law of the Lord is <u>perfect</u>, *restoring the soul*; the testimony of the Lord is <u>sure</u>, *making wise the simple*. The precepts of the Lord are <u>right</u>, *rejoicing the heart*; the commandment of the Lord is <u>pure</u>, *enlightening the eyes*." Have you been in the Word today? Do you by chance need your soul restored? Or perhaps you need wisdom, or your eyes enlightened? How long has it been since your heart rejoiced? Did you notice how to get those things??? It's all in the Word of the Lord! Hebrews 4:12 says "The word of God is living and active and sharper than any two-edged sword, and piercing as far as the division of soul and spirit, of both joints and marrow, and able to judge the thoughts and intentions of the heart." Think about where the soul and spirit divide...or joint and marrow.... the word of God is precise! As we take in God's word, we are actually taking in the Spirit of Christ! "The Word became flesh and dwelt among us" (John 1:14). It is alive and active! It will accomplish that for which God intends! So....have you been in the Word today?? Go and drink deeply of Him! He desires to fill you....so that you will look like Him in your words and your deeds. May He speak to you through His word....today!

$\mathcal{W}$hat a beautiful day!! No matter what you are facing today, may you take a moment and delight in the Lord. He is our sovereign God, the One who called light out of darkness, Who created all that we see by speaking it into existence! (Gen.1, Col. 1) The earth spins on its axis and rotates the sun because "in Him *all* things hold together"! (Col.1:17) Isa. 43:10,11 says "*You* are My witnesses," declares the Lord, "and *My servant* whom I have chosen, in order that you may **know and believe** Me, and understand that I am He. Before Me there was no God formed, and there will be none after Me. I, even I, am the Lord; and there is *no savior* **besides Me**." There is NONE other than our God! He is our perfect Redeemer! He chooses us and we are now His witnesses! Will you witness Him today? Will you walk in the great joy of *knowing and believing* Him? That is my prayer for you. That you will be a strong witness.

Isa. 43:1,2 provides a great promise for whatever you may be facing...."....Do not fear, for I have redeemed you; I have called you by name; you are Mine! When you *pass through* the waters, I will be with you; and through the rivers, they will not overflow you. When you *walk through* the fire, you will not be scorched, Nor will the flame burn you." Oh, how I love that He calls me His!!! Don't you love hearing Him say "you are Mine!"???? Notice that He says you will pass through the waters and the fire. It may not feel like it right now, but this will pass. That is His promise. Hold on to Him. He is enough to get you through. The universe responds to His voice.. **believe** Him! You are precious in His sight! (43:4)

JULY   Week 1

As we celebrate our country's "independence" and those who fought to provide it—let us also celebrate our complete "dependence" on the One who died to restore us to the Father and separate us from our own sin!

HE IS:

–the "author and perfecter of our faith";

–"far above ALL principality and power and might and dominion, and every name that is named, not only in this age but also the one to come"

–"the image of the invisible God, the firstborn over ALL creation. For by Him ALL things were created that are in heaven and that are on the earth, visible and invisible, whether thrones or dominions or principalities or powers. ALL things were created through Him and for Him. He is before ALL things, and in Him ALL things hold together."

–"He Who is and Who was and Who is to come, the Almighty"

–"the Faithful Witness"

–"the firstborn from the dead"

–"ruler over the kings of earth"

–"the Alpha and Omega, the Beginning and the End, the First and the Last"

–"the Amen, the Faithful and True Witness"

–our Savior, our Lord, our Redeemer!

Blessing to you as you celebrate HIM and may His Spirit fill you to overflowing!!

*A*s we celebrate Independence Day, we pause and remember those who gave their life and service that we could be free. We appreciate so much the men and women who sacrificed for those they didn't even know. We pray for those in service right now for their country, may God bless them and bring them home safely! At the top of the list of our gratitude is Jesus. Our *true freedom* is found <u>only</u> in Him. Notice what Jesus says: "Therefore, if the Son makes you free, you shall be free indeed." (John 8:36) So, how does Jesus make us free? Look at vs. 31–*If* <u>you abide</u> in My word, you are My disciples indeed. And you shall <u>know the truth</u>, and the *truth shall make you free.*" Freedom comes from knowing the truth and truth is found only in His word. Jesus says in John 14:6 "*I am* the way, *the truth*, and the life." So, if Jesus *is* truth, if something doesn't line with what He says, it's <u>not true!</u> We have a choice of what we feed our mind. We can either feed it Truth or we can diet on lies. Truth will produce peace and freedom. Lies produce worry, striving, and bondage. Which will you choose today? If you are facing something that the devil is whispering lies about.....kick him out right now! Feed your mind the words of Jesus and live in His peace and freedom. Hang out in John 14 and allow the Truth to saturate your mind. "For I am persuaded that neither death nor life, nor angels nor principalities nor powers, nor things present nor things to come, nor height nor depth, nor any other created thing, shall be able to separate us from the love of God which is in Christ Jesus our Lord."!! (Rom.8:38,39) Now, there's some Truth! Abide in it.

Happy and blessed 4th!!

JULY   Week 3

*W*ould you please join me today in just saying...."not <u>my will</u>, but *Thine* be done....Lord, have *Your* way." As I look around, there are so many things that I just wouldn't choose to be in my life....but yet—here they are. If I focus on them...it's not long before I feel anxious, sad, and disillusioned. It's why Col. 3:1,2 is critical for us to hear and obey—"If then you have been raised up with Christ, <u>*keep seeking*</u> the things **above**, where Christ is, seated at the right hand of God. ***Set your mind on the things above***, <u>not</u> on the things that are on earth."

Let's unpack this a bit....this scripture starts with "**if**" you are raised with Christ...which is simply, I have accepted Christ as Lord and Savior—His death, burial, and resurrection covers me. He took my sin on Himself (2 Cor. 5:21), bore God's judgement on my behalf (Rom.6:23) and gave me His righteousness to come before the Father (Col.1:22). He did what I could *never* do. Then...He sat down at the right hand of God (position of authority!). So...if all that happened for me...I am told to "*keep seeking the things above*". When I have received Christ...I am to keep seeking Him. It's no longer about salvation (where I will spend eternity), but about focus.... on Who has the authority over my life (Col. 2:6 says "as you therefore have received Christ Jesus the Lord, so <u>walk</u> in Him").

He then tells us how to do that—"***set your mind on the things above***, <u>not</u> on the <u>things that are on the earth</u>". So, what are things that are "on the earth"?? Death, disease, sin, chaos, disasters, godlessness, quarrels, wars, aging, etc.....you know, those things that are in my life and yours! It's the "<u>on the earth</u>" that sets it apart from **"things above"**. None of those things I just mentioned are in heaven! I am to set my mind (focus my thoughts) on things that are in heaven..... life, perfect health and bodies, no tears, no Dr. visits, the radiance of His glory, brilliance of His majesty, all things beautiful, holiness....what would you add???

As I practice this.....my spirit lifts and my soul begins to praise our great God! Fear and anxiety flee. Phil. 4:8 tells us to "think on things that are true, honorable, right, pure, lovely, excellent, worthy of praise"...to "let your mind dwell on these things". Vs. 9 says to "practice these things; and the peace of God shall be with you." Would you practice that with me this week? Go ahead and make your list of things that are "on the earth"–and then make your list of "things above". Then <u>*set your mind*</u> to think on the things above.

May God's peace that passes all understanding fill you and guard your heart and mind in Christ Jesus. May you have a distraction-free week!

JULY   Week 4

*J*am encouraged this week by Isa. 41:13–"For I am the Lord your God, who <u>upholds your right hand</u>, Who says to you, *Do not fear*, **I will help you**." I love that He speaks to exactly what we need. And...not just speak to what I need, but *does* what He says He will. Lots of times in my life, I have needed Him to hold my hand.... He has truly kept me from sinking. He says to you and I..."*do not fear*". Behind every fear is a *belief*. Often it's a lie. The enemy loves it when we fear....it causes us to live "small". God designed us to fulfill His plan–living small has no place in it! He tells us throughout the Bible to "not fear" and He gives us why.....because **He** is *with* us! The Authority of the universe is *with us*....He <u>prom-ises</u> to *help us*, and <u>then He does</u>! He has been com-pletely faithful, even when I have not. He has held my hand and He tells me that I am *in* His hand, securely! (John 10:28-30) Do you need to visualize that today? That not only is He holding your hand, but you (and everything you may be going through) are **in** *His hand*, and....... you are secure. He is with you. He will help you. He has promised and He cannot lie. (Heb. 6:18) I am praying that you are encouraged by His word today. That as you ponder Isa. 41:13, you will see yourself firmly in His hand. Lord, we thank You for Your promise! Thank You that You are *with us* and will <u>never leave us</u>! We truly are *secure*. Thank You, Lord! Help us *walk* in that security.

"*F*or I am confident of this very thing, that *He who began* a good work in you *will perfect it* until the day of Christ Jesus." Phil. 1:6 This is one of my favorite verses. Did you notice who **started** the good work in you.....it wasn't you. I so need that reminder! I did nothing to make myself "good". Jesus said in Luke 18:19 ...."**No one** is <u>good</u> except *God alone*." Did you catch that?? Maybe you need to read it again......I'll wait.

So, Jesus is responding to a ruler who asked Him..."*Good Teacher*, what shall I do to inherit eternal life?" And Jesus responds with a question..."Why do you call Me *good*?" I just love how Jesus changes the question! The ruler thought he was going to get a direct answer on how to "get in"....but Jesus knows that what he really needs is to realize "*Who*" he's talking to. That can be sooo true for me, too! I can be so fixated on what I think I need, and forget "*Who*" I'm talking to. If you really think about it....it changes the question, doesn't it? It also changes the posture. If I'm speaking to "God alone", my posture changes from "it's all about *me*" to "it's all about *Him*"! Back to Phil.1:6. If He began the good work, what in the world makes me think *I* will complete it????? We get that way, don't we? And it truly is the work of the devil....he wants us to strive and worry. It completely lessens Kingdom power and destroys our witness! Don't be confused, dear one. We didn't start the good work in us....we surely won't complete it. But, it will be completed! Jesus does it. My job is to surrender....

to just say, "yes, Lord". I'm praying you join me in that today! Full surrender. Nothing less. You ready?

"Lord, we give You our all! Have Your way completely in us and through us. Thy Kingdom come in us this day, that we may be strong witnesses of your glory and power. You alone are God! Finish the good work You started in us. Have Your way! In Jesus' Name."

AUGUST   Week 1

*I*s there something you need to believe God's word for today? "As the heavens are higher than the earth, so are My ways higher than your ways and My thoughts than your thoughts. For **as** the rain comes down, and the snow from heaven, and do not return there, but water the earth and *make it* bring forth and bud, that it may give seed to the sower and bread to the eater, *so shall* **My word be** that goes forth from My mouth; It shall <u>not return to Me void</u>, but it *shall accomplish* that for which <u>I sent</u> it." (Isa.55:9–11)

There is sooo much in here, I don't know where to start! I guess I start where He did.... reminding us of *Who* He is and His view of all that we are going through. He is higher and there is greater purpose than we can see! Then, He gives us <u>absolute surety</u> about what is to follow! Notice how He does that–*as the rain and snow come down from the heavens and cause the earth to seed and sprout*–does that happen? Is that for sure? Really?? How do you know that? (hint...we've *seen it!*) He starts with what we know because we have seen it over and over and can be absolutely confident in it. Then, He gives us a truth that we can either believe.....or not. My belief doesn't limit what God does, but it limits what I "receive". If I don't believe it, I won't receive it. So.....what do you need to believe God's word for today? Is He faithful? (Math.28:20) Has He limited your trial to what you can handle? (1 Cor.10:13) Can you have peace in the middle of the storm? (John 14:27) Am I forgiven? (Isa. 1:18, 1 John 1:8) Can I make it through this? (Isa. 43:2, 2 Cor. 12:9)

Trust Him, dear one! He is high and lifted up! He is good! He is able! He is almighty God! He is Abba, our Father! He loves you more than anyone could ever love you!

"Now to Him <u>who is able</u> to do *immeasurably more* than <u>all we ask or imagine</u>, *according to His power* that <u>is at work</u> *within us*" (Eph. 3:20)

AUGUST   Week 2

" $\mathcal{D}$ o all things without grumbling or complaining" (Phil. 2:14). Hmmmm....notice it doesn't say "do some things" or "do most things"...or even "except for when you're having a bad day!" Seriously....ouch! I think I'm doing pretty good, letting God's word rule in my heart..... then, I come across *that* verse! How about you? Are you letting God's word rule in your heart? Done any complaining lately?? Me, too!

So, we could feel all guilty and hopeless, but we also have to look at Rom. 8:1: "There is therefore *now no condemnation* for those who are in Christ Jesus." As God gets our attention through His word to teach us how to live, He says we are not to feel guilty, but to confess our sin and be done with it. (1 John 1:9) When we confess, that is simply calling it what God calls it–sin. I agree with Him, that no matter what my situation, I am out of line with Him.....disobedience.....sin. My bible teacher told me long ago that whenever I hear myself using the word "struggle".....like I'm "struggling with that"....to insert "delaying obedience" instead of struggle, because that is what it really is. I have found that to be so true. When we say "struggle", we are making excuses and even denying truth. The battle between the flesh and the Spirit is real! They are in opposition to one another (Gal.5:17) So, instead of complaining, God says to give thanks. Eph. 5:15 says to "be careful how you walk...". He has been talking about sin in the previous verses, but this letter is to believers–those "who are faithful in Christ Jesus." (1:1) Paul gives us great instruction direct from God for how to "be filled with the Spirit" (5:18). He tells us to watch the way we talk and to have a song of praise in our heart continually. What is a favorite song you could keep in your heart? Then, he caps it in verse 20, "*always* giving thanks for *all things* in the name of Lord Jesus Christ to God, even the Father;". There's that "all things" again! And in case we're not sure He means it, He starts it off with "always"! Are you getting that? Everything! When we are singing praise in our heart and thanking Him with our lips, we are inviting the fullness of the Spirit to reign in and through us. I am praying that for you this week. Even if you cannot thank Him with your heart, I am praying that you start with your lips.... just be obedient. He will do the rest. What do you need to thank Him for today?

"And whatever you do in word or deed, do *all* in the name of the Lord Jesus, *giving thanks* through Him to God the Father." (Col.3:17)

AUGUST   Week 3

*W*ow...it's hot! I'm not complaining....just stating a fact. I'm really paying attention to "grumbling or complaining"....how about you? :)

This week, Ps.139:23 and 24 is speaking to me. "Search me, O God, and know my heart; Try me and know my anxious thoughts; And see if there be any hurtful way in me, and lead me in the everlasting way." Have you ever asked God to "search you"? As I think about that, it is sooo against what our flesh wants to do! Our flesh wants to "hide" things and the enemy knows that where we have things "hidden", that can be a foot-hold for him. (Eph. 5:11) So, to ask God to "search me" and "know my heart" is to take a huge spiritual step. We are inviting the Father to look deeper than what I think I know about myself. It's asking Him to find my "blind spots" and then lead me "in the everlasting way"...... or the "path of life" (Ps.16:11). That *is* our goal isn't it? To walk in the *path of life*? The opposite of that is the path of death....that's certainly not appealing! I love how the psalmist just opens himself up to God. David is the author of Ps. 139 and we know he wasn't perfect....he made some HUGE mistakes (adultery, murder...etc). But, it's this attitude that makes him a "man after God's own heart" (Acts 13:22). That no matter how much he has failed, he asks the Father to search his heart and then lead him in the path of life. I love how that is pos-sible with our Father!!! We confess our failures to Him and then ask Him to "complete the good work He started in us" (Phil.1:6), and He does! His promises are true...

you can take Him at His word. Would you ask Him to "search you" today and then lead you in the "path of life"? I am praying that for you this week. May He take all of our imperfections and make us more in the image of Jesus.

AUGUST   Week 4

I truly love a vacation away, but it's always sooo good to come home. I'm convinced God put "home" in our heart, so we could have a "taste" of what's coming. As good as it feels here.....imagine when we are *truly* HOME! The Scriptures give much detail about "Home": God Himself will dwell among us, He shall wipe away every tear, no death EVER, no mourning, no crying, no pain...all of it–gone forever (Rev. 21). New, glorious bodies (Phil. 3), full knowledge (1 Cor. 13), no sin, no curse, no devil (Rev. 20). The Lamb is there...and we shall see His face (Rev.22). Makes you want to just get face down right now, doesn't it??!! God's plan is perfect. His desire is that we live *with* Him, sharing our hearts as well as the day. The first thing we wanted to do, on our way home, was to see our kids. That is God's heart. He designed us with that in mind....communing *fully* with Him. We just can't do that here.... no, that's yet to be experienced–physical, personal reunion with the Father.....that's Home. We shall see Him, face to face.... that is, if I can get mine off the ground! :)

Lord, turn up the heat for "Home" in our hearts. Help us to see Your plan through eyes of faith. Give us strength to rejoice in the "home-going" of our brothers and sisters. Be with us in our grief, remind us it is a temporary separation. Ignite our passion to tell others of Jesus. Deepen our love for You and each other. Come, Lord Jesus!

SEPTEMBER   **Week 1**

*W*ho's expectations are you trying to meet today? It's a path I often find myself on and it can be exhausting! We all certainly have roles that we play– spouse, parent, friend, worker, boss, neighbor, brother/ sister, son/daughter..... and they are important roles. The problem comes when we begin to get our identity from the role. When my identity–the "who I am"–comes from the Father, the "who am I trying to please?" gets very clear and it's amazing how straight my path gets! (Prov. 3:5,6) On the other hand, when my identity comes from the role I'm in.....I try to please everybody (but God), because I have become my own god. Altho disguised as someone else, *self* is really the one we are trying to please and it's a bottomless pit! Jesus said "No one can serve 2 masters..." (Math.6:24) You can't serve "self" *and* God! There's room for only 1 at the top.....so....who is that for you....right now, in the situation you are in? I invite you to spend some reflection time and invite the Father to "search" your heart. When I find I've pushed the Father from being the "One" I'm trying to please, I can *immediately* change that **by choice** *and without condemnation!* (Rom. 8:1) I simply renew my mind with His thoughts (Rom. 12:2)...who *He says I am* and what pleasing *Him* looks like in this situation. Jesus says to "***Seek first*** *the kingdom of God and His righteousness*" and we won't need to worry about a thing! (my inter-pretation of Math. 6:33) Seriously, it's as simple as that. "Self" makes it complicated.....it really isn't. I'm praying for you this week, that you get "uncomplicated" and lay down all "expectations" but serving the Father. Get ready for peace to carry you like a river!

"Now to Him *who is able* to <u>keep you from stumbling</u>, and to <u>present you faultless</u> before the *presence of His glory* with *exceeding joy*"!!!!!!! (Jude 24)

SEPTEMBER   Week 2

"*T*herefore, since we have *so great a cloud of witnesses* surrounding us, let us also <u>lay aside every encumbrance</u>, and the <u>sin which so easily entangles us</u>, and let us *run with endurance* the race that is set before us, ***fixing our eyes on Jesus***, the <u>author and perfecter of faith</u>, who for the ***joy*** set before Him *endured the cross*, despising the shame and has <u>sat down at the right hand of the throne of God</u>." (Heb. 12:1,2) I am often encouraged by this passage and just thinking about the "great cloud of witnesses". In Hebrews 11, we are given names of those that have gone before us and had great faith–Abraham, Moses, Rahab, Samson, David, Samuel and others. They certainly were not perfect, but they all "believed" God....they took Him at His word. They have been joined by many others, over time. Some recently. Some that have our heart.

Note that the "great cloud of witnesses" ***surrounds*** us....I love that! They are close and we are surrounded by them! As I contemplate that, I am greatly en*cour*ag*ed*. I receive courage to keep going...how about you? It gives me the desire to "lay aside every encumbrance" and to just do away with sin, "which so easily entangles us". We can "run the race with endurance" when we "fix our *eyes on Jesus*"! He is the *author and perfecter of faith*....He gives me faith to believe and He grows it! If we keep our eyes on Him, nothing can stop us! He sat down at the right hand of the throne of God–the position of power and authority. He will lift us up when we need it and keep us going. He does the work, we just *keep* *our eyes on Him.* Don't get distracted....don't look down. One day, I will join that great cloud of witnesses....and so will you. We will then get to cheer on those that follow. The hardships will be done, the pain will be gone, the race will be over. But for now, let's *run with endurance*! Keep your eyes on Jesus!!

SEPTEMBER   Week 3

What a crazy week! Who knew our government could just "shut down"?! Aren't you glad that they are not our <u>hope</u>?!! I am so thankful that our Father *never* "shuts down", in fact His promise is the exact opposite—"I will <u>never</u> desert you, nor will I <u>ever</u> forsake you" (Heb. 13:5) He loves us so and wants us to know that we are secure—so He put it in writing! Regardless of how this government debacle turns out.....we can confidently say...."The **Lord** is my helper, I *will not* be afraid." (Heb. 13:6) Ps. 118:8 says "it is better to take refuge in the Lord than to trust in man." How true and helpful is God's word! We live in uncertain times, but we belong to a certain God! And "His lovingkindness is great toward us and the truth of the Lord is <u>everlasting</u>"! (Ps.117:2) So, dear one, be firm of faith and refuse the tactics of the enemy to make you afraid. "Trust in the Lord with all your heart, and do not lean on your own understanding. In *all your ways* acknowledge Him and He *will make* your paths straight." (Prov. 3:5,6) We are in the Father's hand and it's the safest place to be! Jesus says, "<u>No one</u> can snatch (you) out of the Father's hand." (John 10:29) Great news! Be reminded of whose you are....refuse the worries of the world. Our hope is in the Lord and it is certain! I'm praying for you to be grounded in this truth.

SEPTEMBER   Week 4

*T*he Lord has great news for us today! Well......*every* day, really. In Math. 6:31-33, Jesus says *"Do not be **anxious**, saying, 'What shall we eat?' or 'What shall we drink?' or 'With what shall we clothe ourselves?' For* all these things *the Gentiles (unbelievers)* eagerly seek; *for* your heavenly Father *knows that* you need *all these things. But* seek **first** His kingdom *and* His righteousness; *and* all these things *shall be added to you."*

That's a promise from the mouth of Jesus. It sounds so comforting that we are drawn to it like a warm fire. But, do we *really* understand it??

Notice the comparison that Jesus gives–*before* we are in a relationship with Him, as an unbeliever, we *eagerly seek* after things to satisfy our*self*. We are consumed with worry about if we will have *enough*. As you think back on that time, and even now just looking at the world in which we live, was enough......well,....*enough*? Self is never satisfied, history proves that over and over. Anxiety over *enough* will keep us from seeing the abundance that God provides–daily.

Jesus says, we are to be *different*. As a *believer in Him*, I am to be assured that my heavenly Father *knows* my needs and will provide for me. My role is making sure my priorities are straight. I am to *seek Him first*. Is He first in my day.....or me? Is pleasing Him first in my thought......or me? Even if I'm trying to please someone else, if it's not Him....I'm out of order. And anxiety will surely follow. That sense of "striving" is a red flag for me. Whenever I feel it, I quickly ask–"Lord, who am I trying to please in this?" It becomes immediately obvious. I can then consciously make the choice to please the Father *first*. Peace replaces striving. And in **every** situation, God works out completely <u>all I need</u>. How about you? Are you feeling anxious? Who are you trying to please? "*Seek **first** <u>His kingdom</u> and <u>His righteousness</u> and all these things shall be added to you.*" The Father's house is a house of peace. I am praying that for you!

SEPTEMBER   Week 5

*Y*ou may not want to read this today. I really didn't want to write it. But, it's where the Lord has me, so it must be good for both of us. :) The book of James is short...only 5 chapters. But, it is so power-packed with truth, you can't go in there without coming out a little bruised.....at least I can't. I'm in James 3 and he is focusing on the tongue. Vs. 5, says "the tongue is a small part of the body, and yet it boasts of great things. Behold how great a forest is set aflame by such a small fire." And just so we don't miss the point–vs. 6 "And the tongue is a fire, the very world of iniquity; the tongue is set among our members as that which defiles the entire body, and sets on fire the course of our life, and is set on fire by hell." If you haven't been smacked yet, vs. 9 & 10 will take care of that–"With it (tongue) we bless our Lord and Father; and with it we curse men, who have been made in the likeness of God; from the same mouth come both blessing and cursing. My brethren, these things ought **not** to be this way." Oh, ouch!! Have you gotten short with someone recently? What kind of speech has been coming out of your mouth about our government? Have you lambasted someone who didn't serve you well? How about drivers that just shouldn't even be on the road?! The same mouth that gives thanks to our Father for this day and all He has blessed us with, can in the next breath tell someone to "shut up" or "I just don't even want to talk to you right now!" Now, in case you are like me....and think "well, that's not cursing". (we just love a way out, don't we??!!) Look at Eph. 4:29; "Let no

77

unwholesome word <u>proceed from your mouth</u>, but **only** such a word as is good for edification according to the need of the moment, that it may give <u>grace</u> to those who hear." Seriously......s-m-a-c-k!!! Do I really even need to break this out? I'm so convicted, I'm thinking you've got to be too....but that wouldn't be a wholesome word, would it??? See what I mean?! I almost just deleted all of that so you wouldn't know I thought it. But, Holy Spirit said leave it in. :)

I am only to allow words to leave my mouth that will "edify" which means "build up" the other person. So, even if I'm to correct someone's thinking, I must do it in a way that builds them, not tears them down. And to clarify even more, it must <u>give grace</u> to those that hear! Grace is **unearned favor.** It's what you and I received from the Father when Jesus took our sins on Himself and set us free. <u>That's</u> what my speech should give! I sooo need the power of the Holy Spirit to do this! There is no way in my own strength and will power that I can do this. The really <u>good news</u> is that we don't have to! James 4:8, says "Draw near to God and <u>He</u> will draw near to you." Eph. 4:23 tells us to "be renewed in the spirit of your mind, putting on the new self, which in the likeness of God has been created in righteousness and holiness of the truth." We simply confess our sin (1 John 1:9) and ask the Holy Spirit to change us—we offer Him our tongue. Another layer of surrender. Such a small part of the body.....such big impact for the glory of Jesus. Will you join me in surrendering that today? Lord, help us see the damage our tongue can do. Holy Spirit, put a guard on our mouth that no unwholesome word can escape. Choke us if you must. We confess the sin of our words / tone and ask for You to make us new.....in the image of Christ. May we give grace to those who hear. Amen.

*A*re you feeling secure?? Do you feel safe? Those words strike a chord deep within us, don't they? We long to be secure.....safe. I want to share some wonderful words of Jesus with you, today. I'm hoping these words will land deep in your heart and regardless of your circumstances, leave you feeling more secure and safe than you've ever felt. John 10:27....."My sheep hear My voice, and I *know* them, and they *follow* Me; and I give eternal life to them, and they shall <u>never</u> perish; and <u>no one</u> shall snatch them out of My hand." Notice He doesn't say "all sheep"....He says "**My** sheep". As a <u>believer</u>, you belong to Him. And I love that He says "and I know them"....I love that He knows me! He knows you and I to the core. There isn't one thing He doesn't know about us....not one....not even the secret that no one else knows...He knows! And yet, we <u>belong</u> to Him! Notice who gives "eternal life" to us.....He does! He is the giver of life....life forever without end. And not only do we "never perish", but He gives us extra security...."<u>no one</u> shall snatch them out of My hand." No one is....well..... no one! Nothing can change my belonging to Him. Are you feeling secure yet? Then He gives an extra dose of security....vs. 29–"My Father, who has given them to Me, is <u>greater than all</u>; and no one is <u>able</u> to snatch them out of the Father's hand." Now that's some security! But, hold on....He adds more! Vs 30–"I and the Father are one."!!! So, picture this! As a believer, you are in Christ's hand, He who defeated death and sin (Rom. 8:2) and is before all things and in Him all things hold together (Col.1:17). HIS hand! And if that's not enough, He says, you are also in the Father's hand....the One who is "greater than all", the sovereign ruler of the universe (Ps.103:19). Then to just cap it off, He reminds us of the strength of where we are....not just in Jesus' hand, not just the Father's hand, but both of them united. That is secure! There is no safer place. I am praying that this truth will sink deep within your heart, and when insecurity looms, you will be reminded of where you are..... and whose you are. You are secure.

Bless the Lord, O my soul!!

OCTOBER   Week 2

As we cry out to God for those enduring great hardships around the world, we can stand on His word of truth: Ps. 9:9, 10–"The Lord <u>will be</u> a strong-hold for the oppressed, a <u>stronghold </u>in times of trouble, and those <u>who know Thy name</u> will put their trust in Thee; for Thou, O Lord, hast not forsaken those who seek Thee." We talked about security and safety last week. Knowing His name is my security. Believing and relying on His word and His character keeps me safe. Jesus tells us clearly "Let not your heart be troubled; <u>believe</u> in God, believe also in Me." (John 14:1) As He was preparing the disciples for His departure, He gave them an incredible truth–"These things I have spoken to you, that <u>in Me</u> you may have peace. In the world you have tribulation, but <u>take courage</u>; **I have** overcome the world." (John 16:33) These words are just as important to us, today. The world is a troubling place....it has been since the Fall. But, Jesus has overcome the world! The trouble and tribulation of the world is temporary. Notice Rev. 21:4,5; "and He shall wipe away <u>every tear</u> from their eyes; and there shall<u> no longer</u> be any death; there shall <u>no longer</u> be any mourning, or crying, or pain; the first things have passed away. And He who sits on the throne said, "Behold, I am making all things <u>new</u>." There is a new day coming! Jesus has overcome the world, it is finished! The rescue mission was accomplished on the Cross. We will encounter some tough and trying times, but our destiny is secure, for all eternity! We have His word on it. I am praying for your heart to be lifted and your faith to be renewed. May you be refreshed by His Spirit.

OCTOBER   Week 3

ello, dear ones! I read something from Charles Stanley last weekend that I'm ruminating on and thought I'd pass along to you.... "Who among us can serve the living God? Truthfully, no one can. Genuine service occurs only when we allow the Almighty to pour Himself through us; we are mere vessels." As I have let that soak into my heart....an unveiling is happening. My "service" to God is simply offering myself to Him for whatever He wants to do in me and through me....whenever He wants. Jesus was sooo effective in His ministry because He did not speak or act on His own initiative but, rather, depended upon His Father abiding in Him to do the work (John 14:10). The same Father seeks to abide and work in and through you and I.

Sometimes, we can get so caught up in serving out of our abilities, intelligence, and own power....that we can forget that for true fruitfulness....I just need to be "a vessel".

So, my prayer for you this week–is that you would empty yourself before the Father and ask Him to fill you and work His amazing power through you! That you will become one of His most utilized vessels! As we lift up names before our Father, may He fill our mouth with prayers for what He wants to achieve in those precious lives and families. "His greatness is unsearchable....The Lord is gracious and merciful; slow to anger and great in lovingkindness. ...The Lord sustains all who fall, and raises up all who are bowed down.....The Lord is righteous in all His ways, and kind in all His deeds. He is near to all who call upon Him...He will fulfill the desire of those who fear Him; He will hear their cry and save them." Ps. 145. Our God saves and He is near! He alone sustains us and raises us up—He is completely right in all He does....and He is kind...melts your heart, doesn't it?

"I am confident of this very thing, that He who began a good work in you will perfect it until the day of Christ Jesus!" (Phil.1:6) May He bless you in abundance this week!

OCTOBER   **Week 4**

I love Jesus' final words to His followers just before He went up into the clouds..."I am with you always, even to the end of the age." (Math.28:20) He could not give them, or us, a more comforting promise. Imagine being there....you have seen Him crucified and then be buried. Final...the end! Your hope is gone and you just don't know what to do next. Then, miraculously....He is back–He is alive! You now understand that He had to die for you to be saved, reconciled to the Father. You are beginning to comprehend that He *is* Who <u>He says</u> He is! He is God in the flesh! He is over *all* things, He created all things, He is the author of life and He has defeated death! Your heart is soooo full of who He is...it seems as though it will burst....and then.....He is leaving again, He is returning to the Father. And as He goes, He gives us instruction of what do to *and* a promise to sustain us. Even though our eyes see Him leaving, He **promises** to be "<u>with us</u> *always*". My heart rejoices at this promise! He is here, He is with me. He will never leave me, no matter what. We can truly make it through <u>anything</u>, when He is *with* us. He tells us plainly–"I will *never* desert you, nor will I *ever* forsake you." (Heb. 13:5) Notice vs. 6–"so that we can confidently say, "The *Lord* is my helper, I will <u>not</u> be afraid." My prayer for you is that will be your confidence today–Jesus is *with* you! May your heart rejoice at His promise to you. His word is true!

*A*re you in the middle of a storm? Perhaps you see one brewing in the horizon....not sure when it's going to hit or how extensive it will be. It can make you shudder, can't it? A big and powerful storm can cause you to quiver and ask–"Lord, where are You??" You feel as though you are in a small boat and the waves will soon take you under. That's exactly what happened to the disciples beginning in Math. 8:23 "...He got into a boat and His disciples followed Him. And there arose a great storm in the sea, so that the boat was covered with the waves; but He Himself was asleep. And they came to Him, and awoke Him, saying, "save us, Lord; we are perishing!" I can so relate to them, can't you? They see the storm and they believe they are certain to drown. The waves will surely sink the boat. Notice what Jesus is doing in the midst of the storm. He is sleeping. Does He not know there is a storm...can He not feel the boat tossing about, or hear the roar of the waves crashing on it? Hmmm, let's see what He does.... "He said to them, "why are you timid, you men of <u>little faith</u>?" Then He arose, and rebuked <u>the winds</u> and <u>the sea</u>; and it became perfectly calm." Belief is another word for "faith". So, He asks them, "why do you believe so little?" Now, they respond with awe...saying "what kind of man <u>is this</u>, that even the winds and the sea obey Him?" The disciples have been with Him, seen Him heal, cast out demons, and perform miracles. Yet, when the storm hits them, they <u>see</u> the waves and the wind and draw the conclusion that they will surely perish. It hasn't even occurred to them, "Who" is in their boat. The God of the universe that spoke everything into existence, the maker of all things and <u>in</u> Him, all things hold together. (Col. 1:16, 17) Do we really think that the boat **that One** is in will sink?? Na. There is no way <u>that</u> boat is going down! It's ridiculous to even consider, isn't it? We can read that and shake our fingers at the disciples to say "you should have thought that through, dudes"! You guys should have known better! Yet, consider 1 Cor. 3:16–"Do you not know that you are a temple of God, and that the Spirit of God dwells <u>in</u> you?" Hello! Jesus is in my boat! He is in your boat! Just because He is quiet, doesn't mean He is not in control. The boat <u>cannot</u> sink! And He is quiet because He is <u>not</u> worried. He knows exactly "Who" is in control and when to command the wind and the sea to "be still"! Personally speaking, it's generally way beyond my comfort level, but I am intensely aware that He is doing something in me. He is working on my "little belief". It needs to grow.....how about you? I'm in the midst of a pretty powerful storm right now, as are some of you. Let's take our eyes off the wind and waves and focus instead on "Who" is in our boat. It will <u>not</u> sink. That is my prayer for us. Lord Jesus, grow our little faith. Help us to focus our eyes on You–Master of the wind, waves, and all things great and small. Thank You, that You are *in* my boat!

NOVEMBER   Week 1

I've been reflecting on Math. 28:18 the last few days, it has profound implications (as does ALL of God's word!). So much so, that I'm going to invite you to reflect on it. The scene is after the Resurrection, Jesus had given instructions for the 11 disciples to meet Him at a mountain in Galilee. Let's pick up in vs. 17..."and when they (the 11 disciples) saw Him, they worshipped Him; *but some were doubtful*." Can you imagine that?! Here they were *seeing* Jesus (*alive **after** He was dead*).... yet, some of them were *doubtful*..or put another way... full of doubt. Seriously??? Notice it says "some"...not "all". What do you think the difference was in the ones who doubted and the ones who didn't??? They were all experiencing the same thing (seeing, touching, hearing Jesus). ***Belief*** is the key. Believing is a <u>choice</u>, dear one, not a feeling you wait to "hit" you. You simply "choose" to believe God....or you don't. Those that were doubtful.... *wanted* to believe, or else they would not have been obedient. But, they *invited* doubt and *allowed* it to live in their mind. Ouch! Sometimes, that's ***us***, isn't it?! Notice what Jesus says to **all** of them.... "and Jesus came up and *spoke to them*, saying, "***All*** *authority* has been given to Me <u>in heaven and on earth</u>."

Whoa!!! That will put doubt on notice...won't it? He speaks directly to their belief and gives them exactly what they need to hear! He is <u>The King</u> (not "a" king) and *everything* is under His authority. So....does that include illness? death? demons? satan, himself? How about what you may be going thru right now, does it include that??? You bet it does!!! Often, when something undesirable happens, doubt begins to creep in and ask "why?" Instead, we can look to Jesus and say "this is under Your authority! Shine through me!" Those 11 disciples took what He said to heart—they kicked out doubt, even though it meant dying horrible deaths. The name of Jesus went forward in great power and authority. Are you ready to hear Him speak those words to you, today? "All authority has been given to Me in heaven and on earth." That's one to memorize.

May that go deep in your soul and give notice to doubt...be gone, in Jesus' Name!

NOVEMBER   Week 2

I heard something this week that really has me thinking, so..... I'm sharing it with you. :) The Scriptures tell us that God's plan is to "conform us to the image of His Son" (Rom. 8:29), so that we are "ambassadors for Christ" drawing others to Him. His desire is to use everything in our life to equip us so that when we are "squeezed".....the right thing comes out. When lemons are squeezed.....what comes out? Lemon juice. When limes are squeezed....what comes out? Yep, lime juice. Well......we are called "Christians". When we are "squeezed"......what should come out??? You got it.... Christ!! That really has me examining myself. God's purpose in our life on earth (once we are a believer)....is to reveal Christ in us, so His other kids want to know Him too. 2 Cor. 4:11 says "For we who live are constantly being delivered over to death for Jesus' sake, that the life of Jesus also may be manifested in our mortal flesh." The death he's referring to, is death to self....to "my own way". Having it the way "I think" it should go. Life just doesn't work that way, does it? And, honestly....that's the good news! Because "my way" is all about "me". God's way is all about His Son. Which is the point of life, really. Christ **is** life! (John 14:6) So, when I get squeezed and Jesus comes out.....it is beautiful, because that is life! It's my life pointing to **His** through death to my "self"! So, the question to ponder....who shows up when you get "squeezed"?? Self...or Jesus?

Praying for us to accurately reflect His Name.

NOVEMBER   **Week 3**

There is much written in the Scriptures about "giving thanks". As I've been reading and contemplating them, I'm struck anew by why. Let's begin with 1 Chron. 16:34–"O give thanks to the Lord, for He is good; For His lovingkindness is everlasting." Notice...the *why* we give thanks–"for He is good".... "for His lovingkindness is everlasting". Interesting...we are to give thanks because God is good! And His love and kindness toward us is forever! Our giving thanks has nothing to do with our own circumstances or situation. It is not dependent on how happy or content we are at the moment, or how much is "going right" for us. The Scripture suggests it's not about "us" at all! Look at Jesus' example in Math. 26:27, 28: "and when He had taken a cup and given thanks, He gave it to them (disciples), saying, "drink from it, all of you; for this is My blood of the covenant, which is poured out for many for forgiveness of sins." Jesus is going to the cross in a matter of hours and an excruciating death where His blood is required.....and what does He do?? He "gives thanks". Why? Because the Father is good and His lovingkindness is everlasting! Jesus is looking past what He sees and focusing on what He knows. That's the secret of a thankful heart! It's also the secret of Eph. 5:20– "always giving thanks for all things in the name of our Lord Jesus Christ to God." Do you see it? My "thanks" isn't about me or my stuff.....it's about the goodness and faithfulness of our God. I can thank Him no matter what is going on in my life, because His promise is to use it for my good (Rom.

8:28)...why? Because <u>He is good</u> and His <u>lovingkind-ness</u> to me is everlasting. I am praying this truth sinks to the deepest part of you and causes your heart to rejoice in thanksgiving. May you be lifted by His good-ness and lovingkindness. The Father loves you with an everlasting love! He gave His Son that you would be with Him forever. (John 3:16)

When I am feeling low, I will often turn to the book of Revelation and begin to meditate on how John describes the "new heaven and new earth". It is an immediate boost for my spirits. John has been shown an incredible view of the future. While it was communicated to him by an angel, the revelation was directly from Jesus to show His followers what is *for sure* coming. (Rev. 1:1) While much of the revelation is confusing and somewhat horrific, when he gets to the culmination of what God has planned for those who love Him.....it is comforting and tremendously uplifting. In Chapter 21, we find that from a world that has been tainted and filled with sin, God has made *all things* new! The holy city is described as huge and brilliantly beautiful–filled with the glory of God. "There is *no temple* in it, for the Lord God, the Almighty, and the Lamb are its temple. And the city has no need of the sun or moon to shine upon it, for the glory of God *has illumined it*, and its lamp *is the Lamb*." (v 22, 23) Imagine that! The physical presence of the Father and Jesus outshines the sun!! I'm just in awe of that. Close your eyes and imagine being there.....can you feel the warmth of His presence? There is so much that I love in these chapters, but look at 22:3, 4: "And there shall no longer be *any curse*; and the throne of God and of the Lamb shall be in it, and His bond-servants shall serve Him; and they shall see His face, and *His name* shall be on their foreheads." This just lifts my heart into the heavenlies! While we are here on the earth, we walk by faith...not by sight. We believe Him and take Him at His word. But a day is coming!! We shall see *His face*! And, we will be marked as *belonging to Him*! Seriously, I can hardly wait! May your heart be lifted by the thought of what He has planned for you, it is *for sure* coming! No matter what you may be facing now, He <u>will make</u> *all things new*!

"Come, Lord Jesus"!

DECEMBER   Week 1

tand firm, dear ones! Your Redeemer draws near! As hurricanes and chaos loom....let us be encouraged by Ps.46:

"God **is** our refuge **and strength**, *always* ready to help in times of trouble. So we will ***not fear, even if earthquakes come and the mountains crumble into the sea."*** Wow...I am struck by the *"even if".* It is to provide a context for the worst thing we can imagine....what would follow your "even if"? As we think about what that might be for each of us, we are reminded to stack that up against the first part–"God is our *refuge and strength".* We can only "not fear" when we realize God is over and bigger than all of it. Note vs. 6–"The nations are in an uproar, and kingdoms crumble! God thunders, and the earth melts! The Lord, Almighty is here among us; the God of Israel is our fortress." We seem to be in the midst of kingdoms crumbling....we could panic and lose heart...except for the next line–"The Lord, Almighty is *here among us*"! Vs.10 wraps it up beautifully–"**Be still**, and **know** that *I am* God!" No matter what follows the *"even if"*– we are instructed to keep our eyes on *Who He is* vs. on what we see. Only then, can we be without fear, because we KNOW that He is God and He is here, among us! I am praying this week for that truth to sink deep into your heart...that through the power of the Holy Spirit, your view of Him would become more and more accurate. That your *"even if"* would pale in comparison to His magnificence and power.

"Now to Him who is able to do *exceeding abundantly* beyond all that we ask or think, according to the power that works within us" (Eph.3:20)

DECEMBER   Week 2

*C*hristmas!! The season of joy!! I must confess, I am a Christmas girl. I am decked out in Christmas shirts, sweaters, socks and jewelry throughout the whole month of December.....my car is even decorated with antlers and a red nose! (yep....that's me!) However, our circumstances can make this an especially tough time to get through. I've experienced some of those seasons. I'm going to suggest that we can have deep joy, regardless of the tough situations we may be facing. Let's dig into the Word to see how...Luke 2:10–"and the angel said to them, "Do not be afraid; for behold, I bring you good news of a <u>great joy</u> which shall be for **all** the people;". What is that joy??? "today in the city of David there has been born for <u>you</u> a Savior, who is Christ the Lord." The great joy that abounds is that Jesus came for us! He did not leave us in our rebellion and sin. The Glory of Heaven, became a baby and put Himself in the hands of men, was tempted in everything that we are tempted– yet, did <u>not</u> sin! Why? That He would "destroy the works of the devil" (1 John 3:8) and "deliver us from the domain of darkness and transfer us to His kingdom". (Col. 1:13) Death would be **forever** defeated by His crucifixion. (1 Cor. 15:54) The war of good and evil was resolved at the cross. Jesus, the Savior, is the victor for all time! WE ARE FREE!!! The debt has been paid!! Oh, glory!!! Do you see why the angels were rejoicing at His birth? It is why we can rejoice even in the midst of sorrow.....we have a Savior!!! He has come! He has completed His work and "whoever believes in Him shall have eternal life". (John 11:26) Oh, come.....let us adore Him! Let us sing loudly and rejoice during this wonderful season of joy!! Let us say "Merry Christmas!" to all in our path! The world is singing "our songs".... let's put joy on our face so the world can see....Jesus has come!!!! I am praying for you to be infectious with joy this season. (and...if you see me, honk and wave!) :)

DECEMBER   Week 3

*C*hristmas is one week away....are you ready?? I don't mean the decorating, planning, baking, and shopping. I mean...is your *heart* ready? With all of the other activities of the season....if we're not intentional about preparing our heart...we could just miss it. We can get so distracted by the "doing", that we miss the "holy awe" of Christ being born......to die. I've been reflecting on that this week. His much awaited and celebrated birth was just as much about His *death*. It is, after all, His death that saves us (Eph. 1:7). I'm still amazed when I read John 3:16–"For God *so loved* the world, that He *gave* His only Son, that whoever believes in Him should not perish, but have everlasting life." The Son, the sinless One, was *given* <u>by God</u>.....to take the judgement of our sin, so we could live with God....forever. God's *Christmas tree* was the cross. He decorated *His* Christmas tree with the flesh and blood of His beloved Son....*because* <u>He loves us</u>! Love originates with God. He demonstrates His abundant love for us, through His Christmas gift to each of us.....Jesus. I am praying the Christmas story falls afresh on you. "She will give birth to a son, and you are to give him the name Jesus, because He will save His people from their sins." (Math. 1:21) Let us prepare our heart to receive this amazing gift. And may we *give* Christ our <u>whole heart</u> this Christmas. It's the perfect *birthday gift* for Him.

DECEMBER   **Week 4**

*A*re you getting enough "rest"?? I'm not just talking about sleep, altho that is part of rest. I'm talking about "rest of soul".....it comes from abiding in Christ. Jesus says "Come to Me, all who are weary and heavy-laden, and I will give you rest." (Math. 11:28) Notice the answer to being weary and carrying a heavy load..... "Come to Me". As I focus on coming to Jesus with what-ever I'm carrying, my burden begins to shrink as I intently "come" to Him. He continues to say, "Take My yoke upon you, and learn from Me, for I am gentle and humble in heart; and you shall find rest for your souls. For My yoke is easy, and My load is light." (29, 30). A "yoke" is always and only worn by 2. As we abide alongside Him, the yoke also keeps us in the right step.....not getting ahead or falling behind. Regardless of how heavy my burden is, His is "easy and light". Why??? Because of Who He is! He has conquered death! He is the Creator of all things! He is Master! So, when I yoke to Him, the strength of the universe picks up my burden. Aaahhh! I can rest. I don't rest from my burden.....I rest in my burden, because of Who has picked it up with me. "I can do all things through Christ who strengthens me." (Phil. 4:13) Whose yoke are you carrying today? Are you trying to carry your own? Jesus invites us to "Come to Me". I'm praying that for you.

Have a good rest!

DECEMBER   Week 5

 s we prepare to move into a new year, I'm reviewing last year and asking 2 questions..

Ready?? Do I *love* God? Raise your hand if your answer is, "Yes"!! The next question then, is "Do I *obey* God"?.....always? Is your hand still up?? Ok, maybe the breeze was from my own hand falling! :)

Let's look at what *God* says about love. We need the truth of His word to prepare our hearts to move into a new year. John 14:15, Jesus says "**If** you *love* Me, keep My commandments." And, because we rarely "get it" the first time...look down at vs. 23..."If anyone *loves* Me, he will keep My word". Then, just to make sure we really hear what He's saying...vs. 24–"He who does not love Me does not keep My words; and the word which you hear is not Mine *but the Father's* who sent Me." Soooo.... **God** defines *love* as *obedience*.......and not just sometimes, but all the time. "Sometime" or "partial" obedience... is really, *disobedience*. My heart *needs* to hear that, how about yours? The word corrects us and gets us back on track. (2 Tim. 3:16) It equips us and builds us up for obedience to whatever God calls us to do in 2014. And whatever He calls us to do, He gives us the power and ability to achieve it. But it all starts with *us* "choosing" to obey. (1 John 4:22) May next year be a tremendous year of obedience for all God's children! It will *then* be a year of great love!

Happy New Year!

CPSIA information can be obtained at www.ICGtesting.com
Printed in the USA
LVOW09s1148261014

410555LV00001B/240/P

I Didn't See It Coming

I Didn't

See It

Coming

William E. Jones

We Heard You Like Books • Los Angeles, California

PUBLISHED BY WE HEARD YOU LIKE BOOKS
A Division of U2603 LLC
5419 Hollywood Blvd, Ste C-231 Los Angeles CA 90027

http://weheardyoulikebooks.com/

Distributed by SCB Distributors

ISBN: 978-1-7378428-2-8

Cover image: still from *Fall into Ruin*
by William E. Jones, courtesy of the artist,
David Kordansky Gallery,
and The Modern Institute

April 2023

First Edition

10 9 8 7 6 5 4 3 2 1

I will not descend among professors and capitalists

– Walt Whitman, the Talbot Wilson notebook

ONE

As I lay in bed one night, I got a telephone call from my friend Daniel. I hadn't seen him in years. He told me how much he missed me and proposed we get together. We arranged to meet that coming Sunday.

On the day, I ate a late breakfast, trimmed and filed my nails, and packed a small bag. I wasn't sure if Daniel's visit would entail travel, so I prepared myself for any eventuality short of kidnapping.

Daniel arrived a few minutes before eleven AM. He had trouble parking his enormous pickup truck on my narrow street, so he blew his horn. I looked out, and he motioned for me to join him. I grabbed my bag and left. When I climbed into the passenger seat, I kissed him and asked, "Where are we going?"

He turned onto the northbound Hollywood Freeway and said, "Santa Clarita." As we drove through the traffic snarls where freeways merged, Daniel talked about what he had been doing. He had started a company with his boyfriend John, but it was Daniel who did all the work. Although John was obsessed with money, he often experienced difficulties finding employment, because he refused to do what he considered menial labor. The couple solved their financial

1

problems by finding a roommate to rent the extra bedroom (formerly, a playroom) in the house they owned in Sylmar. This arrangement put a strain on their relationship, and Daniel began to suspect that John and the roommate were carrying on an affair while he was at work. "I want to leave that guy sometimes," he said, "but I don't want to lose the house."

As his truck started to ascend the last grade before the Santa Clarita Valley, the entire system of roads narrowed to a single freeway going over a mountain pass. I looked to my right and saw the Los Angeles Aqueduct Cascades, the end of the pipes that carried water two hundred miles from the Owens Valley to the San Fernando Valley. Normally dry, the artificial waterfall was in full flow at that moment, to spectacular effect. On this spot in 1913, as the water that made Los Angeles's urban growth possible rushed down the slope for the first time, the project's chief engineer William Mulholland proclaimed, "There it is. Take it."

We exited the freeway at Magic Mountain Parkway and ended up at a building in an industrial park off Rye Canyon Road. As intense sun beat down on the parking lot, I remembered the extreme summer heat in the area. I was glad I no longer lived anywhere near there. Daniel unlocked the door to an office and turned on the lights and air conditioning. The entryway was cramped and bright, cluttered with paperwork and boxes of products about to be shipped. Beyond it was a large dark room, also cluttered, intended for storage, and in a couple of open areas, for assembling products. Less sympathetic souls would have called the place a sweatshop.

Daniel had set up a bed in the inner room, and beside it, a table with all the supplies he needed: poppers, tit clamps, his own special mixture of lube, and a baby bottle full of a combination of vodka and fruit punch. He turned on loud techno music so the neighbors wouldn't hear what we were about to do. He stripped off his clothes and got on all fours. He put plugs in his ears and blindfolded himself.

Just before he put a ball gag in his mouth, he said, "I'm ready. Pretend you're fisting Helen Keller." He stuck his ass in the air.

As my eyes became accustomed to the darkness, I spread lube on my hand and forearm and looked around. The business, DanielzCrypt, manufactured horror-themed novelties. To my left I saw a box labeled "small plastic skulls; color: fluorescent green." To my right, there were refrigerator magnets made from tiny portraits of famous serial killers. Behind me I noticed a jar containing fetal twins conjoined at the head and suspended in translucent liquid. I assumed that this was a sample of the sort of object the company could produce on demand for clients, but I wasn't entirely sure. If anyone would have had a pickled medical specimen in his workplace, it was Daniel. I laughed loudly enough for him to hear. He stirred from his position and asked, "What's so funny?"

"Oh, nothing. This must be the most peculiar place I've ever had sex."

"I doubt it," he said, and then replaced the gag in his mouth.

I decided to be gentle with Daniel; I felt his asshole carefully, and finger by finger, put my hand inside his rectum. There was little resistance. I gradually made my way inside him until I was elbow deep in his ass. At that point, my hand felt a tight bend. I delicately worked it open. My progress was only a tiny fraction of an inch every few minutes. Then suddenly, his colon opened up dramatically. I was able to make a fist and move it back and forth. I heard a muffled scream, and Daniel raised one hand—our usual signal for me to stop—so I began to pull out. I did this as slowly as I could, feeling each band of sphincter muscles caressing my fingers. He broke out in a cold sweat and began to tremble, but I continued at the same pace until my hand emerged little by little from his ass. When I was finished, he rose to a kneeling position, took off his gag, and kissed me. He said, "I love you," then returned to his prone position before I could respond.

After a few more plunges nearly elbow deep, I lubed up my other forearm and tried to fit both hands inside his ass. While one hand was fully inserted, I would place the other hand on top of my arm and slip it inside with the thinnest part of my wrist. By the end of the session I was able to insert both hands completely. He screamed into his pillow. His screams and the pink blood that had started to appear on my hands concerned me, so I stopped.

I wiped off the lube and collapsed on the bed next to him. He began to fondle me with slight grazing motions, and I soon had an erection. He swallowed my entire cock as his eyes watered. When I was about to come, I gave his sweaty face an affectionate slap. He took a deep breath and let me ejaculate down his throat. He lay down next to me and we dozed off briefly. I woke up first and went to the bathroom to scrub my arms.

We had lunch at a sushi restaurant around the corner. Daniel ate with messy abandon, stuffing himself to break what must have been a twelve hour fast. With a mouth full of food, he said, "That was the best session since the first time you fisted me. We have to do this more often."

"Maybe at my place. That way, you'll only be driving forty miles, rather than a hundred."

"I'd drive a thousand for your fist."

I smiled and asked, "Are you feeling well enough to take me home?"

"I don't know. You might have to drive my truck to your place."

"That giant thing? I'll try." After we paid the check, I did my best to negotiate the freeways on the route home. Fortunately, there was little traffic. Daniel quickly dozed off in the passenger seat and was asleep when I reached my street. I parked the truck in the only space on the block large enough to accommodate it.

As he woke up, he asked, "Is it okay if I come in and rest before I drive home?"

"Of course."

Once inside my apartment, he immediately took off his clothes and headed for the shower. I tidied up the bedroom a bit and turned back the covers. He staggered in dripping wet and sat down on the bed. I wiped off his back. He had gained weight since I had last seen him. He looked like a big, bald homeboy approaching middle age. We took a nap that lasted until dinnertime.

Not wanting to re-park the truck, I suggested we walk down the hill to my favorite neighborhood restaurant for a light dinner. Daniel made fun of the Peruvian food, saying it reminded him of a meal on *Pee Wee's Playhouse*. He imitated Paul Reubens's voice: "All we have is liver and noodles."

I said, "Hey, it's not like my experiences with Salvadoran cuisine have been exciting."

He grunted, "I don't like it too much either, but I grew up with it." In an absentminded way, as though he was reciting a slogan, he said, "*Recuerda a tu país, guanaco.*" It was the first time I had heard him utter a complete sentence in Spanish.

"I think Salvadoran food is too bland."

He laughed. "You've been trained by those Mexican fanatics to eat super spicy food. I can't handle it."

I shrugged. "I've gotten addicted to chili peppers."

"You'd reconsider if you had to bottom. A few hours later, it's fucking painful."

Daniel spent the night. I couldn't tell if he felt too groggy to drive home, if he wanted to punish his boyfriend for something, or if he considered this a rehearsal for a new domestic arrangement with me. He slept soundly, snoring while I slept fitfully. I wasn't accustomed to sharing my bed.

∞

5

Shortly after ten the next morning, my friend and coworker Bernie called while Daniel was in the bathroom. "I'm at the store, and there's a situation here." He sounded panicked.

I asked, "What's going on?"

He said, "I'm locked out."

"Do you need me to come over?"

"That would be helpful."

Daniel took me to Libros Revolución in Westlake, a drive that took all of five minutes. I kissed Daniel on the mouth and thanked him. He said, "I hope I see you soon."

As I got out of Daniel's truck, I heard a man dressed in filthy rags shouting, "Come on, I just want you to suck my dick!" Although Bernie had a powerful physique and could easily have defended himself, he shrank back from the aggressor until the wall of the building stopped him. I immediately understood why. A stench like hot garbage and dried piss came wafting my way.

The man didn't see me, and I surprised him by saying, "Get out of here *now*."

Startled, he wheeled around and limped away, muttering, "I didn't mean no harm. Why can't you give a horny man a break?"

Bernie laughed, more from relief than amusement, and said, "Thanks for scaring him off. I thought I was going to faint." He pointed to a chain and padlock across the entrance to the building and said, "Happy April Fool's Day."

I called the store manager Jim on my cell phone and said, "We're locked out. What the hell is going on?"

He answered, "I'll be there as soon as I can."

We went to a nearby doughnut shop to wait for Jim. Over coffee, Bernie told me, "I've seen that homeless guy before, but this was the most aggressive he's ever been. He thinks Libros Revolución is his own personal sex club."

"Why?"

"It's all Temo's doing." I felt my throat go dry at the mention of Cuauhtémoc. I must have had a worried expression on my face, because Bernie peered at me and asked, "Exactly how well did you know him before he disappeared?"

I looked down at my coffee, took a sip, and winced. Even with cream and sugar, it was almost undrinkable. I preferred tea, but the doughnut shop didn't have any. I tried to frame the proper response to Bernie's question. "Well, Temo and I had an affair for a while."

He raised his eyebrows. "How did that work out?"

"Terribly." I drank a bit more and said, "You know Temo got married, right?" Bernie looked surprised. "Someone named Julieta in Mexico City. From the best of families, I'm sure. There was an annulment."

Even though the place was empty, Bernie lowered his voice. "Temo is the most extreme pervert I've ever met, and I lived in New York before AIDS had a name."

I leaned forward and asked, "What do you know?"

Bernie took a breath. "After Temo left town, random men started to show up at the store asking for him—all kinds of guys from Macarthur Park, the office buildings downtown, Skid Row. They weren't shopping for books, that's for sure. Some of them propositioned me. They looked like the clientele of a bathhouse, and a lowdown one at that. I thought the action was over until today. That guy couldn't take a hint."

The news of this array of characters populating Temo's sex life wasn't entirely surprising. Trying to hide my dismay, I said tentatively, "To be honest with you, I took a liking to Temo. He was such a degenerate that I couldn't resist." I paused and thought about my oldest friend's interactions with him. I said, "Poor Moira got tricked into acting as his beard for a while, but he never proposed to her." I drank the last of my coffee and added, "Every time I learn something new about him, I tell myself this can't be possible. And yet it is."

Bernie asked, "Do you think he was doing a lot of drugs? Some of his tricks looked like tweakers."

I shook my head. "I never saw any evidence of it. But then, he kept the different parts of his life as separate as possible."

"I'm not sure I should tell you this, but whenever you came up in conversation, he went crazy. He'd go on these jags and ask a lot of questions. Moira told me that he might have been CIA, and I started to wonder what was really happening."

I said, "Yeah, we used to think his job at a communist bookstore might have been a cover for some surveillance operation, but I don't see how that's possible. In his imagination, we were probably building bombs on our days off." I tried to laugh nonchalantly at this remark, but I wasn't remotely convincing.

Bernie continued, "The questions were really personal. He wanted to know if you had a boyfriend and how promiscuous you were. The slightest indication that you were having sex provoked a response I can't describe. He'd launch into a tirade and say horrible, irrational things."

"About me?"

"Mainly about 'faggots' in general. If I were you, I'd forget that guy."

"Well, the last we heard from him, he was back in Mexico City. That was quite a while ago." I struggled to find the right words to continue. "Moira thinks he got murdered while cruising in the slums, and she sent me a newspaper article. I don't think it was actually about him. Anyway, if he's still alive, he's probably fifteen hundred miles away." That statement brought the conversation to an end, but I felt unsettled, as though Temo was looking over my shoulder. He had left me six years before, but forgetting him was the last thing I could do. In the absence of other partners, I clung to the notion that he was the only man I'd ever loved.

Bernie interrupted these thoughts when he said, "Jim must be waiting for us by now. We should get going."

∞

When Jim arrived at the store a few minutes after we did, he looked as though he had been sleeping off a binge. He stank of stale booze, and I kept my distance. He scoffed at the padlock on the front door. We walked to the alley behind the building, and he forced his way through a small door I had never noticed before. It had been painted over during one of many renovations undertaken by indifferent landlords. To our surprise, the lights still worked. The interior of the store hadn't been disturbed by the new landlord.

Jim was a local legend. His brother Peter, a well-known figure in the Los Angeles punk scene, looked almost exactly like him. Both had a permanent scowl, which served Pete well in performances with his band. The main differences between the two of them were Jim's hard-left politics and his more realistic attitude toward male pattern baldness—he simply shaved his head every week, whereas Pete grew a thinning patch of hair above his forehead to a preposterous length; along with a unibrow, this strange hairstyle became his trademark.

The brothers were Los Angeles natives with many connections in the city and had little motivation to leave. They were the ultimate provincials, occasionally surprising people with the depth of their knowledge on a wide range of topics. Pete knew more about film than almost anyone, including professional scholars, and Jim had read virtually every significant book by an American from Thoreau to John Reed. His program of reading veered to the east after the Russian Revolution. To contemporary Americans, his tastes were rather obscure. When the two brothers got together, they discussed their common interest, the Hollywood blacklist, and described in detail many films that sounded fascinating but which were simply unavailable—a testament to the continuing hold the Cold War exerted on American culture. Over the past couple of years, Jim had been involved in many Iraq War protests, which were well attended, and as far as anyone could tell, absolutely ineffectual. He looked beaten down.

Jim verified that the land line in the store no longer worked, then took out his cell phone, a reluctant concession to modern life he had recently made. He went into the back room and engaged in a heated conversation I wasn't meant to hear. At the end, he said, "Well, we're fucked. Nothing we can do. Legally, we're trespassing right now, so I have to move everything I can as quickly as possible. I brought my truck." He surveyed the shelves and said with a sigh, "I can't pay you for moving the stock. Who knows if your last paycheck will even clear the bank? I'm going to get some day laborers to do this and pay 'em with whatever cash is left in the register." He added, "I know, I'm exploiting the local immigrant population, but I have no choice. It's an emergency."

I asked, "Where will the books go?"

"We'll have to store them in our office in Koreatown until we can find a new location."

I wasn't entirely sure to whom "we" referred, because I had only ever dealt with Jim and Bernie after Moira and Temo quit working at the store. I asked, "Did you find out what happened? Are we getting evicted?"

"Yeah, it's been in the works for months."

"Who bought the building?"

"No way of knowing for sure. Some shell company with the words 'assets' and 'management' in the name."

I helped load books into the truck until I was sore and exhausted. When I could take no more, I said to Jim, "I guess I should go and call the unemployment office."

By way of a farewell he said, "Sorry it ended like this. If you need a reference, just let me know."

TWO

I walked home in a daze through a neighborhood I traversed regularly. The area hadn't been redeveloped yet, and I imagined that I was seeing what Los Angeles was like before Figueroa Street to the east became a canyon of skyscrapers and Wilshire Boulevard to the west was transformed into a Korean shopping and entertainment district. The architecture, much of it stucco construction from the 1920s, remained standing, but the population inhabiting the buildings had changed radically since then. Small businesses displaying signs emblazoned with pyramids, quetzal birds, and maps of El Salvador and Guatemala replaced elements of the cityscape that older Angelenos discussed with misty eyes.

I had worked at Libros Revolución since graduating from art school. The store was in a position to sell political books to the immigrants in the neighborhood, and the management undertook periodic rearrangements of the stock in an attempt to appeal to them, but the end result was always chaotic. I didn't take part in these renovation campaigns, except to do the physical work of moving books around, and I wasn't sure what I could have contributed anyway. Moira, whose politics were sincere and whose Spanish was fluent, had the best chance of making the store relevant to residents of Westlake, but ever since she left for a teaching job in Mexico, the place had been adrift. Expensive academic history, theory, and cultural studies books, all of which were in English, gradually replaced old communist texts, most of which were available on the internet. It was as though the store was preparing for a wave of left-leaning bohemians who never arrived.

My paychecks from Libros Revolución never bounced, but the source of the money to pay me was unclear; it certainly didn't come from sales. I found working there much more pleasant than working as a video store clerk, practically the only other job for which my Master of Fine Arts degree qualified me. Sometimes a whole shift would pass without me speaking to a single customer. On most days, my interactions were mainly with Bernie, who moonlighted to supplement his meager salary as an adjunct instructor at Otis College of Art and Design nearby, and with Jim, whom I hoped wouldn't notice me and lay me off. My wages from six hour shifts were barely adequate, but I managed to make ends meet somehow. Jim must have realized this and consequently asked little of me. I did some clerical tasks on slow days, and I spent a lot of time reading. As far as I could determine, my work at the store was the bare minimum necessary to show that the place wasn't abandoned. Paying me must have been cheaper than installing an alarm system.

As I walked, I did various calculations to confirm that I had enough money for April's rent and expenses. I didn't know if I'd be able to afford May. I was so preoccupied that as I cleared the crosswalk at Wilshire and Hoover, I ran right into Paul, an acquaintance from school. I hesitated to call him a friend. He was very entertaining company, but I didn't think he could be trusted. For a second, I imagined he didn't register my presence, but I was wrong.

"Girl, would you look at what the cat dragged in?" he asked no one in particular. "You're a sight for sore eyes, even if you're trying to avoid me."

"Sorry, it's been a strange day." I took a good look at Paul. I met him when I first arrived at art school. In those days, he projected the image of a preppy gone to seed, perhaps after a stay in a private mental hospital. Since then, he had changed his hairstyle—it was now slicked back severely and dyed an approximation of his natural color—and had taken to wearing all black clothing. He looked like a vampire searching for a neck to suck.

He brushed imaginary dust from his thrift store jacket and said, "Well, your mother will overlook the slight. I was only now emerging from my retreat atop the venerable Bryson Building to sup at HMS Bounty before the *hoi polloi* take all the booths. Care to come along?"

It was already late afternoon, and I realized that I had forgotten to eat lunch. I replied, "Yes, please."

Over greasy hamburgers, he asked me, "What have you been doing?"

"Until today, working at Libros Revolución. Some fucker bought the building and evicted the store. Now I'm unemployed."

"A minor annoyance for a brilliant young man such as yourself." Paul got impatient when a conversation strayed beyond his favorite topics: gossip, drugs, the pursuit of sex, and himself. He asked, "Do you ever hear from that glamorous art couple, Gregorio and Winston?"

"Not as often as I'd like," I said with downcast eyes.

My vaguely self-pitying answer didn't interest Paul in the slightest. He said, "Snap out of it, my dear. You need to revive your social life. Pining after those boys in Berlin will do you no good."

"By the way, he's called Andë now, not Winston."

"Child, what kind of name is that?"

"Albanian." With a tone of disapproval I said, "You really should take an interest in the nationalities of the cocks you suck."

He said, "Don't be bitter. You're better off not being a third wheel in their relationship, and Berlin is practically polar." He took a sip of gin and continued, "All those countries where they've been fucking their cousins for the last few hundred years are so tribal and inbred. Yes, they have national health plans and free education, but darling, the boredom is overwhelming. The last time I was in Berlin, it was an endless pub crawl with a dozen 'best friends' I no longer wished to socialize with after a half hour, or an ejaculation, whichever came first. I could hardly imagine spending a whole winter with them." He shuddered. "No amount of foreskin is worth putting up with a marathon of drunken blather. And when the cocaine comes out, it gets so very vicious."

I asked, "Did you get talked out of town?"

He looked up at the ceiling in a pose of mock piety. "Perhaps." He glanced around the room and waved someone over to our booth. "Darling, you're a sight for sore eyes," he said to Jerry, whom I hadn't seen since I graduated.

From what I could tell, Jerry felt more embarrassed than I did to be meeting again. He asked, "Is it okay if I sit here?" I nodded.

Paul asked, "Whatever is going on between you two? Are you former fuckbuddies? Spill."

I looked at Jerry. "Do you want to explain?"

He blushed and said, "I did some nasty things back when I was drinking a lot, and I'd like to apologize." He turned to Paul. "I took a shit on his thesis exhibition, and one night I pulled out my cock for him to suck. God, I was an asshole."

Paul was excited to hear news of unseemly art school hijinks that he hadn't instigated himself. "I must say, gentlemen, it's wonderful that I wasn't alone in acting a fool at our alma mater. I was beginning to feel like 'the voice of him that crieth in the wilderness,' to quote the good book with which my family used to bludgeon me."

Jerry said, "I hope you forgive me."

I shrugged. "Why not? As long as you don't expect that blow job."

He shook his head. "I don't know what got into me. I like women. Grad school makes you do funny things."

14

Paul asked, "Have you heard about Jerry's new career?"

Jerry said, "I'm working at vca Pictures in the Valley."

I remembered those initials but couldn't place them. I asked, "What are you doing there?"

He laughed. "Making porn."

Paul proposed a toast: "To that great refuge of errant art school alumni, the adult video industry."

A moment after we drained our glasses, I spotted Bernie across the room. His massive torso and shock of prematurely gray hair set him apart from the lithe and animated ephebes who usually propped up the bar at the Bounty. As I rose to go to him, I asked my companions what they were drinking. In his best imitation of Bette Davis, Paul blinked his eyes and said, "A martini, very dry."

"What'll you have?" I asked Jerry.

Paul couldn't resist continuing the scene. He said in a slightly demented tone of voice, "A milkshake?" Jerry, not knowing the dialogue of *All About Eve* by heart, asked for a ginger ale.

I walked over to Bernie and said, "Fancy meeting you here."

He responded with a mild chuckle and said, "I need a stiff drink, or three. Mind if I join you?"

"Not at all. I warn you, though, my drinking companions have already heard an earful from me, so Libros Revolución won't be the best topic of conversation."

He shrugged. "I'm not too upset. I was about to quit anyway."

I asked, "Did you get a raise at Otis?"

"Oh no, I'll be teaching full time at usc for the fall semester. A sabbatical replacement gig. I think I'll finally earn enough money to ditch this place and move back to New York." I tried and failed to look suitably happy for him. Seeing my distress, he said, "If you need to borrow any money, just call."

I smiled sadly and told him, "Thanks, but that won't be necessary. At least I don't think so."

After getting the drinks, I brought Bernie to the booth. From the moment we sat down, he started staring at Jerry. It was as though he had been overtaken by something he couldn't control. Jerry was his type: tall, dark, and handsome, with eccentric facial hair and the self-deprecating manner of a California native. The chance of Jerry reciprocating Bernie's interest was precisely zero. I admired Bernie's wide and eclectic body of knowledge, especially about photography, the subject he taught at art schools, but when it came to social interactions, he gave a painfully awkward impression. His tendency to become obsessed with men who didn't want a relationship with another man was his main weakness, and I had seen this pattern played out on a few unfortunate occasions. I tried to distract from Bernie's stare as best I could, but my efforts were in vain. When Bernie went to the men's room and Paul left to smoke a cigarette, Jerry said, "I should probably go soon."

I said, "I'm sorry. I didn't know Bernie would fixate on you."

"I'm sure he's a nice guy, but... wow."

I asked, "Do you want to slip out now?"

"No, I'll wait until he comes back. By the way, there's something I want to talk to you about." Jerry took out a business card and handed it to me. "Nothing creepy, I swear." He spotted Bernie returning to the booth and started to get up. He said, "See you later. I'll say goodbye to Paul on my way out."

I saw Bernie's dejected expression as he approached. After collapsing into the booth, he asked, "Jerry doesn't like me, does he?"

"I wouldn't put it that way. He probably has to get home to his girlfriend."

He asked, "What's she like?"

"Please, that's not a discussion for now. A certain little bitch is headed our way."

Paul sat down and blithely asked, "Did you know that our companion here, because of some cockamamie principles, once refused to suck Jerry's cock?" I thought Bernie might explode at hearing this, but Paul didn't quit. "What did his member look like, my dear? I couldn't stop thinking about it the whole time we were talking."

I said, "I respect your one track mind, but to be honest with you, I don't remember. It's all in the past anyway. I'm hoping Jerry can find me some work at VCA."

Intrigued by the thought of Jerry and me involved in the production of pornography, Bernie asked, "Do you think I could get a job there?"

Paul leaned over to Bernie and said, "Between us girls, I have to say you'd do a lot better at snagging trade if you were a little less obvious."

Bernie squirmed and mumbled a few incoherent things. He finally said, "Let's change the subject" with a whimper.

I said, "Happily," but could think of nothing else to say.

Not wanting to stick around until the conversation got maudlin, I made my excuses and left. Bernie followed me out. He caught a Vermont bus home, and I walked up Commonwealth Avenue. At Beverly Boulevard, I passed a bar with an open window. I looked in to see news about the war in Iraq. The report was in Spanish, and I didn't understand everything, but I gathered that several Americans had been lynched in a place called Fallujah. I saw images of blackened corpses hanging from a bridge, with people gathering around and cheering. I didn't have cable at home, so I'd need to ask a friend or wait until the next day's newspapers came out to get more details of the story. From what I could gather, the war was turning into an unexpected disaster less than a year after President Bush proclaimed, "Mission accomplished" on May 1, 2003.

THREE

The next day, I called the unemployment office and spent hours on hold. Just as I walked away from the phone to get a drink, someone answered and I rushed back to grab the receiver before I was cut off. Fortunately, the processing of my claim was straightforward, and the person on the other end of the line handled my case with as much pleasantness as anyone could expect from a worker who spent his days dealing with irate people waiting on hold for excruciating periods of time. I was told to expect a form in the mail within a month. I hoped that would happen before my money ran out. I needed another job, and quickly.

∞

Late that afternoon, I called Moira's office in Chiapas. She answered on the third ring.

"Hi, how are you?"

She said, "Well, the answering machine is broken, so I can't screen my calls. I ordered a replacement, but it hasn't arrived yet. Sorry, I don't mean to be rude, but it's been a busy day."

"Should I call back?"

"No, I have a free hour now." She got up and turned down the volume of an English language radio program in the background, then asked, "Have you been following the news?"

I said, "On television I saw some charred bodies hanging from a bridge in Fallujah. It looked horrific."

She asked, "Is that all they're showing?"

"Seems that way."

She let out an audible shudder. "There were suicide bombs in Baghdad and Karbala on the same day. Hundreds of Iraqis were killed. But the American media concentrates on the deaths of four Blackwater contractors. Those bastards operate with total impunity. When innocent people protest the US occupation, they just fire their automatic weapons into the crowds. The laws of Iraq don't apply to them. There's incredible resentment of these mercenaries, because that's what they are, and the American military force that supports them. No one in charge seems to have the slightest grasp of the history or politics of the Middle East."

I asked, "Do you?"

"I know more than George W. Bush. He's holding the whole world hostage to his Oedipus complex, waging the war his daddy never had the balls to fight in the 1990s. The ghouls supervising this carnage are leftovers from the Nixon era. Finally, they've got the war they always wanted—an imperialist power grab, with the nearly unanimous consent of the American electorate. If you ever needed an argument against representative democracy, here it is. Dissent had no effect whatsoever. The so-called opposition party lined up to support a war based on fabricated evidence. Disgusting."

I was about to say something when Moira, catching her breath, continued, "Before the war there were protests, the largest ones ever, all over the world. Then the war began, and what happened? The protests stopped. People were demoralized by the willfulness and indifference of political power. The United States has given itself over to a death cult." She paused and concluded, "I blame television and its relentless campaign to trivialize everything. I think if television transmitted not only images and sounds but also smells, all warfare would come to an end. If you're insulated from carnage, you can accept almost anything. How long would American voters tolerate a war if the odor of burning corpses invaded their living rooms every night?" Moira never said much about her past, but she spoke with the fervor of someone who had seen actual battlefields and smelled death. I struggled to find a response, and as I did, she calmed down and asked, "So why did you call? Probably not to hear a rant from me."

I said, "I saw Jim and Bernie yesterday, under unpleasant circumstances, I'm afraid. We were locked out by the new owner of the building on Eighth Street. Libros Revolución is over."

"That's a shame, but hardly a shock. Will you be okay for money?"

"I think so. I may have a lead about work in porn."

She laughed. "Your dream job."

"Maybe, but I don't know what it will entail." I paused and asked, "Do you ever wonder what you'd be doing if you had stayed in Los Angeles?"

In an offhand way she said, "Probably a PhD in comparative literature. I guess some people believe they're doing political work and changing people's lives in American academia. I'm not one of them. I belong here." She added casually, "Besides, I'm involved with someone."

"Oh, how long has this been going on?"

"A while. His name is Miguel. We teach at the same school. I love him. We'll get married one day, but it's complicated. He speaks Tzotzil and Spanish but no English. He wants to get a job teaching in his native language, but that hasn't happened yet. The situation for indigenous people in Mexico is changing, but slowly."

I asked, "What is Tzotzil?"

"A language spoken mostly in Chiapas. Linguists call it Mayan, but the people here use the specific name, because they can't understand the other languages in the family and don't see the connection."

"Do you speak it?"

"I'm learning. There are lots of clicking sounds. People give me funny looks. When I speak Spanish, no one bats an eye, because I could be a white Mexican, but when I say a few words in Tzotzil, they think I must be an anthropologist, or playing some kind of trick on them." She exhaled. "I suppose that amounts to the same thing." Almost as an afterthought, she added, "I've been meaning to tell you, I'm pregnant."

"What? I must say, you really know how to bury the lead." For a moment, I tried to picture Moira as a mother, but I couldn't. Perhaps she was experiencing a similar failure of imagination herself. I asked, "How far along are you?"

"Seven months."

"Have you told your parents?"

She sighed. "That's a whole story. They insist I come back to LA. They want their granddaughter to be born in the US. But I haven't renounced my citizenship, and she can get an American passport in Mexico."

"Ah, so you're having a girl."

"Yes, we'll call her Flor."

"I'm sure she'll be beautiful."

"And if my family wants to see her, they should come to Chiapas. It's too late in my pregnancy for me to fly safely, and there's no airport near San Cristóbal anyway. What annoys me is that my parents assume I'd drop everything here just to be with them. There's no way I'm going to try to smuggle Miguel across the border, and I'm not driving through northern Mexico alone and pregnant. They live in their own little world. We've had plenty of drama."

"You're having a baby, so of course there's drama. Congratulations."

"Thanks," she said. "I should be going."

"Take care. I'll try to call again closer to your due date."

"By that time I should have an answering machine that works."

∞

Next I called Jerry, and he answered right away. I asked, "Is this a good time?"

"Sure. I have a job for you. VCA is planning to release a line of gay adult compilations on DVD, and they could use your help."

I said, "I didn't tell you last night at the bar, but I just lost my job at the bookstore. Is there decent money in it?"

"I'm guessing there is, but you'll have to discuss the details with my boss. He goes by the name Antonio Passolini." He asked, "Are you available tomorrow? I have to go out there and I could take you with me."

"Yeah, what time?"

"I'll pick you up at ten."

The next morning, Jerry drove us to a part of the San Fernando Valley I had never visited. In the distance I saw giant rocks that looked like they belonged on another planet. Beyond them was a mountain pass leading to Simi Valley. I could hardly believe that we were still within the city limits of Los Angeles. I thought of the Manson family living in this area and asked Jerry, "Are we near Spahn Ranch?"

He said, "Not quite that far out. I never saw the place, because it burned down before I was born. You know I grew up in Simi, right?"

"That's serious suburbia."

"Yeah, really boring. I was in a metal band when I was sixteen, and we had a recording contract and toured and everything. It didn't really take off, but I'm still in touch with the guys. I'm the one who left town and got an education, now I'm living the dream as a pornographer with a goth girlfriend. How more LA can you get?"

"I think the city means something else to tourists."

He groaned, "Oh, like Venice Beach?"

"The gay bashing capital of Southern California."

"I didn't know that. Figures."

I asked, "What should I expect at this meeting?"

Jerry thought for a moment and said, "Tony's a good guy. After I worked for a couple of years at VCA, he's letting me do what I want, because the company is dying. He's willing to try anything to stimulate sales."

"So I'm part of an attempt to respond to market forces? That's hilarious."

"I don't think they're doing new all-male productions any time soon. The last one was a big budget turkey. You'll be dealing with the old stuff."

I said, "I guess my years of experience renting gay porn to the perverts of Silverlake will come in handy."

He chuckled. "I figure you know the field as well as anyone. Definitely better than the people at VCA. It's a very straight company. The editors are a bunch of football jocks, and some of the women in the office are retired performers. Try not to stare at the ones who've had a lot of work done."

I asked, "Is Tony a dumb jock?"

"Not at all. The rumor is he went to Harvard."

I rolled my eyes. "An Ivy League fuck up? I know the type well."

Jerry continued, "He got involved in the business in the 1980s, when it was really wild. He did a lot of drugs and they took a toll. I haven't seen him in while, because I've been doing pre-production and didn't need to go into the office. Let's just say that if he's fat, he's doing well, and if he's skinny…. Well, I hope he's not skinny. I've got to get him to sign off on my film."

We pulled up to a nondescript low-rise office building on De Soto Avenue in Chatsworth. Jerry had other things to do, so he introduced me to his boss and left. Tony was fairly chubby, which I took to be a good sign. He shook my hand and started telling me about VCA's plans, "We have this big library of all-male titles that we aren't really using, and I thought they could be a new revenue stream. But first I had to make sure our editors wouldn't refuse to work with the material. It's not like they never see cocks, so I don't know why they're so sensitive. One of them asked me, 'Are you coming out of the closet, Tony?' because to these dudes, the only reason I'd want to release a line of gay videos is if I were gay myself." I laughed uncomfortably. "Anyway, you may have seen our DVD compilations." He handed me a copy of something called *Big Black Cocks, Volume Four.* The design looked as crude and old-fashioned as advertisements for trusses or wigs in the back pages of a tabloid, but even more grotesque because the images were in color.

I said, "The main message I get from this package is that VCA doesn't care about its gay titles."

He said, "I want you to be part of changing that. Our line is called Tool Factory, and we release four-hour DVDs of excerpts from our gay movies, selling for ten bucks each. We need someone who can choose the best scenes, make edit decision lists, and give each compilation a snappy title. I always loved gay adult titles, they're way more fun than the straight ones. I think the first one I ever saw was *Logjammers*." He chuckled and asked, "Can you think of any off the top of your head?"

I realized that this was a test of how well I could think on my feet. I knew that parody was an established strategy in porn, and that simple, obvious descriptions also made good titles. I said tentatively, "*A River Runs Through It* could become *A Rimmer Runs Through It*." He raised his eyebrows, urging me to continue. "How about a Ramones tribute? *I Wanna Be Fellated.*" He clapped his hands. "And sometimes you just have to state the obvious: *Sleazy Dick Pigs.*"

This last title made Tony convulse with laughter. "Perfect," he said once he caught his breath. I thought it a little odd that he found the phrase so amusing, because it was simply how some people I knew described themselves. "I think you'll be great," he said, and shook my hand. He explained, "You can do this job from home. We'll send you VHS window dubs. They have time code numbers in a box superimposed at the bottom of the frame."

"Yes, I've seen those before."

He grabbed a thick stack of dot-matrix printouts from his desk and handed it to me. "These are all the titles it's okay for us to use. The list will be modified later, I'm sure. The legal department always has a say in things."

"Well, thanks."

Tony got up and we went to another office, where there were forms for me to fill out. He said, "Welcome to Video Company of America," and left me with a woman whose appearance I found extraordinary. She was about fifty years old, but her breasts were large and firm like a young woman's. Her face was smooth and a bit hard, as though she'd seen everything. I marveled at her hair: dyed brassy blonde, done up in pigtails tied with pink ribbons.

A nondescript male staff member came in to give me a tour of the place. First we went to the editing suites. The editors nodded to me but didn't shake my hand. I imagined this was because they didn't want to catch AIDS. Next we went to the vault where VCA stored artwork and original master tapes. The room was practically freezing. My guide asked if I'd like to look at images of a specific performer, so I requested Fred Halsted, whom I had met and whose films I admired. He found a binder of color slides and let me leaf through it for a moment. I found nothing from his best film, *L. A. Plays Itself*, but there were many images from his later films, all produced by VCA.

We went from the vault to the art department, where women of less startling appearance than the first woman I met prepared cover artwork and promotional materials. Someone who looked like a conventional San Fernando Valley mall shopper told me, "Do the best you can with identifying talent. Some of those all-male directors just pulled whores off the street to make their videos. We might have no information on them, but we'll see what we can find." She was careful to distinguish not only between gay and straight porn, but also between people who prostituted themselves and people who had sex on camera for money—a distinction that in practice hardly existed. Even in an environment as dubious as this one, I recognized an entrenched prejudice: homosexuals came from the gutter, and the gutter was exactly where homosexuals belonged. I felt a sense of relief that I could work from home.

I wouldn't receive a regular salary, but be paid per compilation. It was my job to devise four compilations and email instructions to the editors every month. I would need internet service in my apartment to do this work properly. I had been avoiding this expense for a long time. With what I would be paid, I could afford rent, utilities, and food, plus monthly telephone and internet bills, with a little bit left over. The popular stories of people making their fortunes in the porn industry clearly didn't apply to me.

I met Jerry in the hallway, and he said he could drive me back home. He went into an office and came out with an envelope full of money. He smiled and said, "I just got funding for my first feature. Let's leave before someone changes his mind."

Once we were on the freeway, I asked him, "What's the movie you're making?"

"*Art School Sluts*. It's alt.porn."

"'Alt' as in alternative?"

"Right. It'll have all my favorite things in one video: goth, punk, and emo girls in designer clothes getting fucked to the sound of drum and bass music. VCA is so desperate to make something profitable that they're willing to take a chance on me. It might even work."

"Congratulations. Is *Art School Sluts* based on your experience at Cal Arts?"

He laughed. "Loosely. The guys in the movie get laid a lot more than I ever did. But yeah, there'll be some things you recognize in it. I don't want to spoil any surprises." We rode in silence for a little while, then he asked, "Have you chosen a porn name yet?"

I smiled and said, "I've given the matter some thought. I'll be Hudson Wilcox."

"Like Rock Hudson?"

"Actually, the name refers to the old meat rack near the YMCA in Hollywood. During the '60s and early '70s, if you wanted a hustler, you went to Selma Avenue between Hudson and Wilcox."

"Nice. I'm Eon McKai." I laughed. Although it would be spelled differently to avoid a lawsuit, it sounded exactly like the name of the singer of Minor Threat and Fugazi, Ian MacKaye, a man known for his "straight edge" lifestyle and activist politics. He was probably the last person in the world who would direct a porn film. Jerry had devised a new porn aesthetic and a persona to go with it, and all of this was designed to get maximum publicity. I was sure he'd be a big success.

FOUR

When I was growing up in the Midwest, I never expected I would work in adult video. The industry in Southern California was a distant realm of activity that, if not technically illegal, brought permanent opprobrium down upon its workers. Once a porn star, always a porn star—or so America's moral entrepreneurs wished us to believe.

Before the internet made sexually explicit material almost universally available, anyone who wanted to see pornography had to make an effort, overcome internalized shame and disapproval, and pay money. My parents didn't live near an adult movie theater and would never have discussed such a place. Visits to adult bookstores offered my only glimpses of the industry's products, because home videos were far too expensive for me to collect. A porn magazine was a special artifact to be enjoyed furtively. Even though this material was difficult to get, it was still easier to come by than sex in my hometown, which I escaped at the first opportunity.

When I moved to Los Angeles, all of this changed, to my great relief. I found a neighborhood with gay bars and adult bookstores, though there were hardly any porn theaters left by then. I worked at a video store that depended on renting porn to make a profit. I became an avid consumer, making up for lost time.

I also had sex with men in many different situations. I maintained a few relationships but had never lived with a lover. It was difficult to find things in common with the men I met. Most expressed themselves in a vernacular drawn from television and shopping. In recent years that had changed; now there was a third ingredient: the internet. I cared about conversation and sought out interesting people, but in the atmosphere of commercialized surveillance and conformity that had developed in the early twenty-first century, I often felt discouraged. My main romantic attachments were to Daniel, who was living with a boyfriend, and to Temo, a difficult man with whom I fell deeply in love before he vanished from my life. Both men acted and spoke in ways that bore a resemblance to porn, though how life imitated art was something that we had difficulty examining or analyzing.

In the last few years, I felt less need for sex and lost much of my interest in porn. I didn't harbor the slightest ambition to be an adult video producer, and yet I had recently become one. It was my job to sift through historical gay porn with the aim of recycling the choicest bits, and in doing so, to help keep a bloated and sclerotic company alive.

∞

Video Company of America owned the rights to an extensive library of all-male movies, the core of which was the HIS Video collection. Whether the letters HIS stood for anything specific I wasn't able to determine. Everyone referred to it as "his video." VCA released most of the HIS library on VHS in the early 1990s, and titles remained in print until the supply of tapes in the warehouse was exhausted.

The compilations I was hired to produce would consist of scenes from the vca's back catalogue. vhs window dubs would be delivered to me at home. I would watch the tapes and log the time code numbers, noting the beginning and end of each scene. I would also describe the location and the action, and whenever possible, identify the cast. Based on my notes, I'd make edit decision lists and email them to the post-production coordinator. He would send these lists to the guardian of records, who verified that all performers were over eighteen years of age at the time of production. The Child Protection and Obscenity Act, passed in 1988 and finally enforced in 1995, mandated that no sexually explicit material could be commercially released without proof of age on file for all performers. The ostensible intent of what the industry called 2257 regulations (after the section number of the federal statute) was to prevent minors from being sexually exploited. The real intent—never completely realized—was to harass the adult video business out of existence. Once the guardian of records vetted my edit decision lists, they would go to the editors, who would assemble masters for the compilations, and to the art directors, who would design the packaging. I was told the whole process would take about two months from my initial email to the release, or street date, of the DVDs. I received the first shipment of window dubs a week after I was hired. There was no further need to show up at the offices in Chatsworth.

When I requested titles from the HIS library, vca was often obliged to make new copies of them so that the movies could be digitized. In some cases, the master tapes were three-quarter inch U-Matic, vhs, or some other long-obsolete production format. Many of these originals had begun to suffer significant deterioration. A number of vca's earlier titles were on the verge of being completely unusable, so in a sense, I was saving them by causing them to be duplicated. I indulged the thought that I served as an archivist of sorts, although that was not my job title, and I never handled the physical masters themselves. There were hundreds of movies to watch, and I saw the project as an opportunity to learn something about film history, not the official version, but the far vaster subaltern version.

It quickly became clear to me that I wouldn't be able to produce compilations based on strictly defined themes. Most of the VCA titles had been intended for the widest possible release, and they exhibited the sameness of industrial products. I found the most extreme uniformity in the work of the director Sam Abdul. His taste in men was what I called "West Hollywood generic." In one of his videos, the white guys in the cast were virtually impossible to tell apart. I could only distinguish one from another by the color of their tank tops. I wondered if the men in the videos ever had this problem among themselves in real life. I thought to myself, if I wanted to see cousins fuck each other, I never would have left Appalachia. While attempting to identify performers, I looked for the sort of distinguishing marks (moles, birthmarks, tattoos) that police officers used to identify suspects. I welcomed the sight of relatively uncommon traits like a hairy back or a tattooed penis, because they made my work easier. Partly for practical reasons and partly out of boredom, I developed succinct shorthand to describe the types of men I saw. Phrases such as "haggard blonde" or "twink with poofy hair" were not kind, but they served their purpose.

In the midst of a veritable avalanche of gay porn, I began to suffer from the malaise of a consumer stupefied by superficial variation within profound sameness. In the 1980s, standardization worked well for mass production and marketing, but during the 1990s, the industry changed. Many small companies specialized in niche markets and catered to specific fetishes. By contrast, mainstream corporate adult video had come to seem like a shop offering many different colors of ice cream in only one flavor: vanilla.

∞

On one lonely Sunday during a period when I was waiting for more tapes to arrive from VCA, I went to a used bookstore and found something I'd never seen before, a novel called *Antics*, marked down to $2.00. The press that published it was well respected but moribund. Their books had a dated look, featuring vibrantly colored and busy covers, the work of graphic designers who had recently discovered computers. Some of the writers published under this imprint went on to better things, or at least had names known to me, but not this one. I was curious enough about the book that I brought it home and started reading right away. The novel was short, more of a novella, and I finished it that afternoon. The plot of madcap adventures—mostly public sex between men—seemed familiar, but at first I didn't understand why. I checked the back of the book and saw no photograph of the author. The climax of the narrative, a camper set on fire by a jealous lover, seemed to come directly from the life of someone I knew, so I called him.

"Hello, Paul."

"A thousand apologies, but I can't tarry. I'm absolutely famished, and I'm about to go to dinner at my habitual spot. Would you like to join me?"

"Yes, please."

He said, "See you in twenty."

I said, "It'll be more like thirty. Please grab a booth for us." Paul could talk for hours on the phone, and I was relieved that we could discuss my recent purchase over a meal. I arrived at HMS Bounty to see Paul with a gin and tonic and a dish of fluorescent macaroni and cheese in front of him. I ordered a hamburger and fries with a lemonade.

As soon as my food arrived, Paul started dishing dirt. "Child, have you heard the news? Our friend Carmen has reinvented herself yet again. She's now a gallerist in this fair city." He explained, "Apparently, some elderly moneybags in her family keeled over and bequeathed her a building near Macarthur Park. It used to be a quaint communist bookstore."

I sat there aghast. "Libros Revolución? Bernie and I worked there until recently. Haven't you been paying attention?"

With a look of exaggerated disdain, he said, "Since liberating myself from the typing pool many moons ago, I pay no mind to stories about regular employment. Perhaps you told me and it didn't sink in. Are you, as they say in merry old England, skint?"

"No, I got a job at VCA, producing. The janitor probably makes more money, but I'm not complaining."

Paul waited for me to stop talking so he could continue. "I saw Carmen in the flesh only recently, and there's less flesh. She's slimmed down and become a fashion plate. The hair has returned to her natural shade of mousy brown, and it's grown long. She looks ever so professional, and not dykey at all. I also heard that she's married. I can't imagine why Carmen would take up with a man. Frances, from what ones hears, is an earthshattering lay. Perhaps the laying is still going on, as our dear friend has the first solo show at the new gallery."

I smiled. "Is Frances in town?"

"I believe she is, but I'm not in direct contact with either of them since our last falling out."

I asked, "What now?"

"Carmen probably sees me as unreliable and prone to disclosing her voluptuous lesbian past to all and sundry, which of course I am."

I asked, "Is she one of those legendary creatures, a bisexual?"

He leaned toward me. "Frankly, I'm an agnostic when it comes to heterosexuality, bisexuality, and other such perversions. I'll believe it when I see it. There must be a practical aspect to the arrangement, knowing her. She must want to bear a child before her lady parts dry up."

I said, "You have such a way with words."

"Why the fuck else would she get married? She's got money, and if she wants companionship, there are loads of adorable puppies languishing at shelters."

I asked, "What about true love?"

He harrumphed, "California is a community property state, darling. You don't get hitched unless you mean business."

I said, "I'd love to see the two of them. Do you have Frances's number? All I've got is a land line in Williamsburg."

I took out my phone, and Paul, amused by the simplicity of the instrument, cooed, "Baby's first cell phone." He put his BlackBerry on the table and shared Frances's latest contact information.

"By the way, I have some questions," I said, wiping the grease from French fries off my hands. I reached into my jacket pocket and handed him a copy of *Antics*. I asked, "Do you know this book?"

"Know it? I wrote it. Under a pseudonym, *bien sûr*, back when I had faith in the ability of the cultural establishment to recognize…" he cleared his throat, "my unique voice, as writing instructors are wont to say."

"I've read it."

He peered at the book like a scientist examining a strange specimen and said, "You and approximately one dozen other readers. Some of the print run was remaindered, and the rest was pulped to avoid warehouse fees."

I said, "I'm sorry."

"For what? It all happened eons ago. The risk-taking press that published my literary début was acquired by one of the 'majors,' a corporation concerning itself exclusively with the bottom line. No-account authors like yours truly got purged from the list. My editor—I can't believe I'm using that phrase in the twenty-first century—lost her job, and my agent, bless his benighted soul, moved to Montana to raise sheep. Or fuck them, I don't remember which."

"Are you still writing?"

He smoothed his hair and said, "From time to time, I do pound the keyboard. I really can't say to what end. If only to keep a record of my tricks, I produce a few thousand unpublishable words per year."

I didn't tell him that I had been writing more or less seriously for the last decade, never publishing anything, but still holding out some hope. I asked, "Any advice to aspiring writers?"

"In a word, don't." He drained the last of his glass and motioned to the waitress for another. "They don't tell you this in school, but commercial publishing is the most conservative part of American culture this side of a Klan rally. The only readers the publishing industry wishes to reach these days are moms: upper-middle class women of a certain age, bitter about their divorces, fighting tooth and nail for tenure, nagging junior to apply to Stanford, awaiting the magical transformation of menopause. These valiant women are the guardians of propriety. They want beautiful prose by respectable, deep-thinking bitches who deliver uplift, or so the corporate twats and their stooges in the critical establishment tell us. I'm not so sure. I'd wager that these readers are as horny as Tennessee Williams heroines. In any event, no one in a position of influence saw any use for a drug-crazed homosexual scribbler." The liquor was hitting him and he was on a roll. He picked up the book. "This product of my blood and sweat got precisely one review, in which the anonymous critic called my novel 'breezy and superficial.' That's code for homosexual, in case you didn't know. You might as well say the book has a lisp!"

"Well, I enjoyed it. I wanted more."

"Because you have an appreciation for the finer points of sodomy. All I have to say is that if you harbor ambitions of a literary career in your breast…." His voice broke and he seemed to be fighting back tears. "I took my art school education and tried to become a writer. Don't make the same mistake I did. Take your art school education and make art. Talk to Carmen. She's ambitious. I bet she can sell your work."

I protested, "But I haven't made any for a while."

"Tsk-tsk, I won't hear of it. The art market is booming. Get a piece of the action for yourself. Rid yourself forthwith of the illusions that hampered your mother, who is reduced to selling various chemicals from a bachelor apartment in Westlake." He shook his head emphatically, then changed the subject. "So how do you like your new job? You see, here I am, taking an interest."

"I notice the halo forming above your head already." I looked down at my messy plate and said, "I don't know, I thought I'd be living the life promised by spam emails—'watch porn; make money'—but it's incredibly boring."

"Looking at hour after hour of sex bores you?" He slammed his fist down on the table. "You don't know how good you've got it." He looked around to see if anyone had been disturbed by his outburst.

I asked, "Do you think you'll ever publish another book?"

He said, "That's not a realistic possibility. I'm not a private school educated sociopath who looks like a supermodel, striving for a piece of Brooklyn real estate as the reward for well-behaved mediocrity. I'm incapable of producing next year's version of the campus novel, the marital infidelity novel, the dead faggot novel, the age of anxiety novel, the holocaust novel—whatever mewling, passive-aggressive, self-righteous navel gazing passes for literature these days. What the intelligentsia calls literary fiction is a mere distraction from the naked lunch at the end of everyone's fork: corporate publishing makes all its money from right-wing political slush. Literature is—how shall I put it?—a tax write-off." He looked off in the distance. "If you marry well, become a fixture on the residency circuit and teach creative writing, then you've done more than enough. Your podiatrist father and hedge fund husband can be proud." Paul had an exhausted look on his face, and asked, "How bitter did that sound?"

I said, "Somewhere between art school faculty member and Roman Catholic priest."

He nodded. "Not bad. When I descend to the level of middle-aged video store clerk, you have permission to slit my throat."

"You say the most romantic things."

FIVE

The next day I called Frances, and she said, "Sweetheart, I'm in LA now, been here for a few days, and Carmen is letting me use her gallery space as a studio."

I said, "Paul told me."

"That nutty queen. Did he tell you she's married?"

I laughed. "I heard that, too."

"After what went on between us, I thought she'd be a dagger forever."

I asked, "Does she want a kid?"

"Maybe. She doesn't discuss it with me. She's all business now. I don't mind, I need a gallery."

"I want to come over and see this place."

"Sure. I'm here all the time." She began to give me the address, and I interrupted, "I know exactly where it is. I used to work in that building."

"Really?"

I said, "It was once Libros Revolución."

"That's terrible."

"The eviction was inevitable. I was surprised the store lasted as long as it did. Anyway, I can be there in forty-five minutes."

As I approached my old workplace, I noticed a new sign reading "Blanco Projects" in large black letters. Carmen had used her surname for the gallery, an obvious choice, but it was impossible to ignore that this was a new business emblazoned with the word "white" in the midst of a neighborhood of immigrants mainly from Central America. I rang the bell, and Frances came to open the door a moment after I took my finger off the button. "Welcome to my studio," she said.

I looked around to see blank walls cleaner than when I had worked there, with no traces of bookshelves or counter. The furnishings consisted of a rolling office chair and two folding tables covered with brushes, tubes of paint, and piles of newspapers. The only word I could manage to say was "impressive."

"Only temporary, but for now, such a luxury."

Frances had placed a large easel in the brightest part of the room. Off to one side, there was a small television, a VCR, and a video projector. Cable news was playing in the background. She found a remote and muted the sound. One painting looked nearly finished: an image of the destroyed hulk of a car body consumed in bright orange flames. No human carnage was visible, only a beautiful glowing object. "Is it done?" I asked.

"Almost. I'm working differently now." Frances's earlier paintings were loose and sensual, and part of the pleasure of looking at them was making sense of the riot of colorful forms. The new work was more smoothly and precisely executed. She had developed a way of suggesting that the source images came from television without resorting to imitating the look of video pixels.

I asked, "Will the whole show be based on news reports about Iraq?"

"I don't know yet." She paused. "It looks like the biggest disaster of our lifetimes. I'm too young to remember much about the Vietnam War. The Iraq War seems like one more endless, bloody television show."

I said, "My main memory of the Vietnam War was being angry when news bulletins interrupted my cartoons. What a little idiot I was. I wish I'd paid more attention. When I was learning to read, I'd see names that weren't pronounced the way I expected, like Hue, and those numbers that appeared above Walter Cronkite's head when he read the news—a casualty count."

Frances became distracted by a CNN report, turned up the volume on the television set, and asked, "Have you seen this?" She quickly pressed the record button on the VHS deck, and we watched in silence. It was my first exposure to the tortures at the Abu Ghraib prison. The photographs were shocking, even though they had been blurred for presentation on the news: a human pyramid of hooded, naked prisoners with a man and a woman, American military personnel, standing over them and smiling broadly; another woman in army fatigues holding a leash attached to the neck of a prone, naked man; a man wearing a poncho and pointed hood standing on a box with outstretched arms to which wires had been attached. The last picture, the only one that contained no nudity, served as an emblem of the whole sordid episode, and was shown repeatedly.

After a few minutes' coverage of this latest human depravity, there was a cut to a dog food commercial, and Frances stopped the recording. I said, "I think this must be the beginning of the end of the American empire."

She asked, "Is that something to celebrate or something to mourn?"

"First one, then the other. What does Carmen think about your current subject matter?"

"She's getting used to it. Compared to movie stars and naked boys, the work will be a harder sell, but I need to paint these things. Everything else seems trivial by comparison."

"I wonder if Winston is making paintings based on war images, too."

She asked, "Have you heard from him?"

"Not in a while. I want to stay in touch more often, but it's easier to communicate with Gregorio."

I wandered off to look at copies of the *New York Times* she had stacked on the table. Several front-page images were smeared with paint, and a couple of them were marked with pencil lines. The pictures were beautiful enough to make luscious paintings. She said, "The warmongering fucks at the *Times* were so busy sucking the asses of the powerful that they didn't bother fact checking the 'weapons of mass destruction' story. Now they're pretending that they weren't partly responsible for this mess. I only trust pictures now. Those photographers really risk something. They can't just hang around hotel bars, go to press conferences, and then make up a lie."

I asked, "Do you think you're glamorizing war?"

There was a long pause. Looking sadder than I had ever seen her, Frances answered, "I don't know."

∞

The main advantage of my new job was the freedom it gave me. As soon as I finished a month's worth of compilations—a task that came easier once I had logged a lot of material—I could do more or less whatever I wanted. I took long walks, often all the way to downtown. One evening, I decided to pay a visit to Jerry, who lived in an apartment building next to the Million Dollar Theater, a former movie palace transformed into a church. I managed to reach him on the intercom and he buzzed me in.

I said, "Sorry to drop by unannounced, but I was in the neighborhood, and I haven't seen you in months."

Jerry said, "It's a nice surprise. I can take a break." A non-linear digital editing suite dominated what passed for a living room in the open plan apartment. The walls and floor were concrete, and whatever sounds we made echoed, as street noise undoubtedly did, though on the evening I saw the place, the neighborhood was quiet.

We sipped soft drinks and looked out on Broadway. I asked, "How is *Art School Sluts* going?"

"Pretty well. We had a delay because one of the men I lined up for the cast tested positive for HIV and left the country. You can't work unless you have a negative test result and the paperwork to prove it."

I said, "In the straight industry. For gay films it's condoms only, unless you're Paul Morris."

Jerry asked, "Who's he?"

"Treasure Island Media, all bareback all the time. His competitors hate his guts, because he makes money hand over fist."

"Does he require tests?"

I scoffed, "Are you kidding? His performers are all positive, or soon will be."

"Wow, he's hardcore."

"That's one way to put it."

Jerry sighed and said, "I don't know what it is about the porn business, it's so much more dramatic and cut-throat than regular entertainment." He shook his head. "It's a box of broken toys."

"I'm glad to be Hudson Wilcox, the homebody producer."

"Yeah, you're out of the line of fire. Anyway, I have a rough cut, but no music yet. Do you want to see it?"

"Yes, please."

"I'll show you the in-between stuff, because you're not going to care about the sex, I'm sure."

The cut of *Art School Sluts* I saw had an artfully amateurish look, with shaky camera work, glitchy video shot from the monitor, and a desaturated, blown-out color palette I'd never seen intentionally used in a porn video before. The female lead, Keiko, playing an art student named Mia, narrates the beginning. She says in her languid and contemptuous way, "Every single person in my classroom is a fucking pervert." The students, bored and casually dressed, have trouble staying awake during their critique class.

Over a shot of an older man continuously licking his lips, Keiko delivers a scathing appraisal of a faculty member named Mr. Davis: "I'm totally convinced the only reason he teaches is for the pussy. He never really had an art career to speak of. If you type his name into Google, all you get is a long list of boring post-hippy art showings." This man paws the face of another female student and asks if he can photograph her. She slaps him and exits the scene.

Later, Keiko holds up a "Canoga Park Institute of the Arts" diploma and delivers a realistic assessment of her prospects: "The only thing worth less than one of your paintings is your art degree, so the only job you can keep after art school is pornography."

The other performers don't acquit themselves as well as the charismatic female lead. Jerry explained, "That's on purpose. Keiko was the only one who learned all her lines." He pointed to a man on the screen. "I didn't give Dominick a script until he arrived on set." With an impressively high Mohawk and ratty punk-style clothing, he claims to be "the number one S&M performance artist in the country." He presents a hastily improvised piece of sculpture—a condom over a dildo—and reads his lines from the script. His main point, "This condom is a cage of oppression," draws disgusted looks from fellow students. After the cum shot, he takes a wad of semen and rubs it into his hair.

Jerry fast-forwarded to the final scene between Keiko and James Deen. As she fondles Deen's crotch, Keiko asks him, "So why didn't you show any work in school today?"

He responds, "Um, I'm kind of just a slacker, you know? I mean I have a trust fund and do a lot of drugs. It's kind of hard to get artistically motivated."

As Jerry was about to press the space bar to pause the video, I said, "Let it run. I want to see a little sex."

Jerry said, "Some of the people at VCA freaked when they found out this was James Deen's first scene ever. He's only eighteen."

I said, "I can't tell that he's new."

"Oh, I can. His ass is totally hairy, see?" I looked at his ass crack, which was even hairier than his legs. "He hasn't gotten a porn star haircut yet. Only his cock and balls are shaved."

When the video was over, I said, "I think you should be proud. You've encapsulated the art school experience quite successfully."

"Thanks. The press has shown an interest already. I've done two interviews, and I'm not even done editing."

"Congratulations. What's the street date?"

He said, "A few days after the election, November ninth. I bet people will want to drown their sorrows in porn."

I asked, "Do you think George W. Bush will be reelected?"

"Absolutely."

"You're probably right." Jerry was much better at figuring out the zeitgeist than I. "Have you been following the war?"

He said, "I can't believe that stuff from Abu Ghraib. The army is literally making porn."

I asked, "Do you think VCA will start producing parodies?"

"No way, man, it's too controversial. First Amendment politics are fine, but I don't think we could get away with it."

"The original material outstrips anything the studios can do. It's so vicious. I bet straight porn movies will get rougher from now on."

He said, "Probably. We have to keep up with the US Military."

∞

I began visiting Frances's studio in the afternoon. By that time of day, she was ready for a break. Often I found her listening to *The New Real Fall Album (Formerly Country on the Click)*, an astonishing recent release, full blast. It sometimes took a while to gain access to the studio, as she didn't hear the doorbell. I took her to restaurants in a neighborhood I'd gotten to know well over the years. After lunch I would see how her work was taking shape.

I returned again and again to look at one particular painting based on a photograph of an inmate at Abu Ghraib. Against an acid green background, the subject seems to jut out from the picture plane. He is alone in a close up. The photographer (in all likelihood also the torturer) used a flash, and the resulting shadow creates a subtle double image. No obvious marks of torture mar the young man's smooth brown skin. He has tilted his face down slightly, as if to ask defiantly, "Do you really want to take my picture?" The tilt also reveals a wound partially obscured by his closely cropped black hair. Coagulating blood drips from the wound in rivulets. Two lines of dark red flow from a spot just below his eye and almost reach his thin goatee, giving the impression that he is crying tears of blood. His eyes, the most riveting part of the photograph, are as green as the wall behind him. His mouth, tightly closed, seems poised to snarl, while his gaze from under prominent eyebrows pierces the spectator. With a face frozen in an expression that is nothing short of feral, the man has been utterly dehumanized. His posture suggests a Renaissance painting of Jesus's flagellation.

Frances had captured the brutality and menace of the scene, and it was obvious that she struggled a bit to represent the expression on the subject's face. Her technique for replicating a digital image depended on thin applications of paint; any substantial buildup of impasto would have wrecked the effect. Among the works in the studio, the portrait of the young man in Abu Ghraib stuck out as unresolved. I was reluctant to talk to Frances about it, for fear of saying something that would ruin what had the potential to become my favorite of all her paintings.

SIX

The next time I fisted Daniel, he came to my place. I managed to get my hand inside him as far as the bend in his colon, but once again, I wasn't sure how to go deeper than my elbow. It was a very hot day, and all the windows were open. Daniel sweated profusely. He insisted on being blindfolded but went without the gag. I lived in the upper right apartment of a four unit building, and the building manager was in the lower left. The tenants of the other units were a rotating cast of aspiring white professionals. I didn't care if the sound of Daniel screaming with my hand up his ass offended them. The manager heard little of the commotion, but the people below and beside me heard a whole performance.

After we finished and I was getting dressed in the bedroom, I noticed a text on my cell phone: "Hoedown at the Bounty. Join us." It was from Paul and had arrived only a couple of minutes before.

I asked Daniel if he wanted to go, and he agreed. As always, he was ravenous after a fisting session. He insisted on driving. I said, "With that beast of a truck, we might spend half an hour looking for parking in Koreatown."

He grunted, "Leave it to me."

The drive took five minutes, during which I texted back, "Be there soon. Bringing a trick, so behave."

I had fretted for nothing. Daniel found a space directly in front of the Gaylord Building. He said, "After six, this beast can park in a loading zone and not get a ticket."

As we were about to reach Paul's booth, Daniel whispered in my ear, "I fucked that faggot." There was no time for me to respond, and I was blushing when we sat down.

Paul asked, "Aren't you going to introduce me to the friend who's making you turn that delightful shade of crimson?" While I stammered, he took the initiative. "I'm Paul, like the great villain of the New Testament."

"I'm Daniel."

It occurred to me that even though they had fucked, they might not know each other's names. I thought of the Venetian noblewoman who once said about a lover beneath her station, "Penetration does not constitute an introduction."

Bernie, whom I hadn't seen at the bar, came over with drinks. He asked Daniel and me what we wanted, and after he left, Daniel whispered, "I fucked that one, too."

I seized upon the paranoid notion that Daniel, wanting to stir up trouble, had had sex with both of them because they were my friends. I chose to keep quiet, though I suspected Paul knew what was happening. He proposed a toast with the drinks Bernie brought: "To hoedowns, with emphasis on the 'ho.'"

For a moment, no one could think of what to say, and Bernie, the most uncomfortable among us, tactlessly asked me, "How do you two know each other?"

Daniel replied, "His arm was up my ass an hour ago."

Paul said to him, "I admire your fortitude, but personally, I don't want my asshole to look like a bundt cake."

Daniel smiled and asked, "Are you sure it doesn't already?" We all laughed.

Paul, not wanting to discuss his anatomy, turned to Bernie and asked, "How's your teaching job?"

I found Paul's sudden interest in academia more shocking than any discussion of assholes, but Bernie sighed and began his tale of woe. "I don't know why they hired me. I get no respect at all. The only knowledge they value is what they think will help them succeed in the art world of the moment. They're what Jack Smith called 'walking careers.'"

Daniel asked, "What are you talking about?"

Bernie said, "I'm a sabbatical replacement in the art department at USC. I have a full time position for the fall semester."

Paul, who was beginning to show his boredom, said, "Receiving paychecks from the University of Spoiled Children doesn't sound bad at all, dearie, and one can endure almost anything for twelve weeks."

Bernie said, "I'll put it this way—my colleagues are the most abject courtiers I've ever met. They're instrumental in all their human relations. It's suffocating. The master's program has only fifteen students, not exactly an interesting mix, and one of them is a Kermode. He's the son of famous art collectors. He got the best education money can buy, but if he had an original idea, his head would explode. He takes up space and makes no actual work. His only role seems to be crushing the dreams of anyone naïve enough to have convictions or feelings. He's as cynical as an embittered gay guy, but I've been told there's a girlfriend somewhere in the background."

I said, "We've all heard that one before."

Bernie imitated him in a whine, "Dad, I *really* need some extra money to pay the writer of the catalogue essay. He said he wouldn't do it for less than ten thousand. Don't be such a *dick*."

Paul remained unmoved. "Darling, if I'd met a sap like him years ago, I might still be a writer. Bless."

Bernie continued, "You don't know the half of it. The creepiest thing is that the other faculty members are falling all over themselves to kiss his ass. They love him, can't get enough of his bullshit. At first I thought it was a case of people with art school educations being deferential to a smart-mouthed Ivy Leaguer, but then it hit me: my colleagues want him to put in a good word with his parents so the Kermode Family Collection of Santa Monica will acquire their work."

I laughed, but Paul was not amused. With a dismissive look, he said, "I'm sure that child will go far in this common world." He turned to me and asked, "What's new with our porn producer?"

I said, "I recently saw a rough cut of Jerry's first feature, *Art School Sluts*."

Daniel asked, "Straight porn?" I nodded. "Get me a copy, please. I love watching guys' asses while they fuck a pussy."

'I'll see what I can do." I asked Bernie, "Will you finally be able to move to New York?"

He answered, "I want to leave as soon as possible, but I don't want to drive through snow storms."

I said, "Damn, I thought you'd be a lifer. Once you spend ten years in this town, it becomes almost impossible to leave, and your anniversary must be coming up."

Daniel nudged. "We should go. I have work tomorrow."

As soon as we were outside, I asked Daniel, "Did you really fuck both of them?"

"Oh yeah, they wanted some homeboy cock, and I gave it to them. I can play that game when I want to. That's not who I am, but they don't know the difference. Only you know my story."

I asked, "How are things with John?"

"Good. We're working things out. We got rid of the roommate. He turned out to be a crystal meth addict."

His truck pulled up to my apartment building and we kissed. He held my hand and said, "I hope I see you soon."

"Of course. I love seeing you."

He said, "You mean you love destroying my ass."

I laughed. "Was it okay to have drinks with my friends?"

"No problem."

I asked, "How did you meet them?"

He said, "I fucked that queen Paul in a sling at Slammer. The gray-haired muscle-bound guy? I forget. Maybe Recon."

I asked, "What's Recon?"

"It's a fetish website. Lots of fisters on there. You should join." He paused. "But there's a new one—Asspig.com. Not as many guys, but all of them are into fisting."

"Hmm." We were interrupted by a car horn, because Daniel's truck was blocking the street. I kissed him again and said, "I'd better go."

When I got inside, I turned on the computer and searched the internet for Asspig.com. I joined the site and looked for Daniel's profile. I saw a picture of him wearing wraparound sunglasses and looking tough. Other, more intimate pictures had been blurred. I didn't pay for a membership to see them clearly because I could have the real Daniel in my bed whenever I wished. I sent him a message on the site and added him as a "buddy," then signed off.

∞

Buffy the Vampire Slayer had become available on DVD, and I dutifully bought each season's box set as it came out. This was made easier with the credit card I finally managed to obtain after repairing my post-bankruptcy credit. I found I enjoyed the show playing in the background while I did things around the house. It kept me company, and I especially appreciated this when I worked on porn compilations. Once I had logged over a hundred tapes, I began to rearrange the scenes in different combinations without looking at any of them. The content and order of the scenes didn't matter as long as the running time of each disc totaled exactly four hours. The process was like assembling a puzzle and involved no aesthetic decisions by me. I generally completed four compilations in an afternoon. At the rate I was paid, I earned as much per hour as an attorney, but I only worked one day a month. I developed a ritual: I would put a disc of *Buffy* into the DVD player, and while watching, I would do my month's work. I had refined my technique to such an extent that I could finish before reaching the end of the last episode on the disc. Once I emailed the edit decision list and invoice to VCA, I was free until the next deadline. There was only one lingering responsibility: inventing titles for the compilations. I frequently wrote down inspirations on index cards and placed them on the refrigerator door using serial killer magnets from DanielzCrypt. When the time came to do my monthly job, I grabbed a few cards from the fridge and assigned names arbitrarily to the compilations. Occasionally, a title would be rejected. I quickly learned that according to company policy, no porn title could contain words of more than three syllables, not even one like "ejaculation," which was perfectly germane to the project. I was disappointed that VCA also rejected any phrase they had already used for straight porn titles, for example, *Weapons of Ass Destruction*.

I faced the question of what to do with the remaining one hundred and fifty hours per month during which people with regular jobs were occupied. Bernie encouraged me to apply for adjunct teaching work at Otis, but I wasn't successful. I eventually decided to adopt the most austere economies so I could subsist solely on the money that VCA paid me. I went back to the way I lived in my early twenties, with one crucial difference: I had found a group of friends with schedules as eccentric as mine.

∞

While I was preparing the October compilations, the land line in my apartment rang, something that happened less and less frequently since I started using a cell phone. I didn't bother to pick it up. The answering machine beeped, and I heard a woman speaking Spanish. She mentioned Moira, and I could tell that she wasn't aware that my friend had moved to Mexico and transferred her phone number to me. I was expected to take messages for Moira, but as it happened, she had only received boiler room calls and prerecorded solicitations until now. The woman knew Moira well enough to have her number, but obviously hadn't seen her in six years or more. I didn't recognize the voice, but as she hung up, it occurred to me that she might have been Temo's mother.

I called Moira's office with my cell phone and reached her answering machine. I said, "Congratulations on the birth of your daughter. If you have a chance, please give me a call. I'd love to talk to you." The machine cut me off, so I called back. This time I said, "You got a phone call today from a woman who left this message." I played the recording and hoped the sound was clear enough to be heard. I didn't understand everything, because the caller spoke quickly, but I gathered that her name was Graciela. When it was finished, I pressed "save" on my answering machine. I hoped Moira would hear the messages in a timely way, but since she was on maternity leave, I doubted it.

I was so distracted that I almost forgot to send documents to VCA. I went back to the computer and logged into my email account. The possibility of Temo's mother trying to contact Moira reminded me to check the academic account I used when I was a graduate student. Not wanting to see persistent requests for donations of money I didn't have, I hadn't checked that email in a long time. There was a huge backlog of unread messages waiting for me. Just as I was on the verge of consigning a whole page of them to the spam folder, I noticed bolsillodepayaso@aol.com, Temo's email address. I felt an immense sense of relief at seeing proof that Temo was still alive. I had never lent credence to Moira's theory that he had been shot in the back by rough trade. My doubts concerning what happened to him had never gone away, and they gnawed at me for years. I took a deep breath and opened the email:

> Payaso,
>
> Are you alive? You never answered. Do you still love me? This is my last attempt to reach you. You are breaking my heart.
>
> Temo

I noticed the date the message was sent, January 5, 2002, over a year and a half before I finally read it. I composed a response:

> Dear Temo,
>
> You have written to me at an email account I stopped using a while ago. I am very sorry you missed me. I think about you every day. I will send you a message from my new email account right away.
>
> Love,
>
> Payaso

I looked for more emails from him and found two. The first, dated Christmas 2000, was an apology and an attempt at reconciliation. The second, dated a few weeks later, was an angry denunciation. The third and most recent was the first message I read and the one to which I had responded. I printed out these emails and pored over them for clues as to Temo's whereabouts, but found none. I imagined that I was the only person who received messages from *bolsillo de payaso* (clown's pocket), and that when he got no replies from me, he stopped checking the account. In my inbox I saw no immediate notice that his email address had ceased to exist. I could only hope that one day he'd receive an old-fashioned notification in the insipid AOL voice, "You've got mail," and read my message.

∞

A few days later, Moira called. I asked, "How are you? How is the baby?"

She said, "We're fine. Getting very little rest. Flor is so hungry all the time that I let her sleep next to me in bed. The moment I turn over so I'm not facing her, she wakes up and cries. She wants easy access to the food source. Miguel is annoyed, but he doesn't have to feed her. I've ordered a breast pump, and the moment it arrives, I'm going to start working again. I'm really bored."

"Moira as a mother—you must send me pictures."

She laughed. "I will, I will."

I asked, "Did you hear the message I left on your machine?"

"I did. Graciela is Temo's mom, as you probably guessed. She gave me a Mexico City number, but I haven't gotten around to calling it yet. Something always comes up… mostly Flor's vomit."

I said, "Sorry if I'm being pushy."

"No, you're curious. Who wouldn't be? She didn't mention Temo, but I'm guessing she'll tell me everything when I get hold of her. She always liked me."

"Just call me when you have a chance. And good luck with Flor."

As soon as I hung up, I went to the drawer where I kept the only photograph of Temo I ever had, a gift from Moira. In the picture he looked like Alejandro Fernández, son of Vicente, one of the greatest stars of Mexican music. Temo probably would have been appalled by the comparison to a pop culture heartthrob, but it was inevitable in a city with so many fans of *ranchera* music, and the resemblance was close enough that he might have been mistaken for Chente's son in public. I placed the photo on the bed, and in the afternoon light, I took a picture of it with my phone. The image was small and not very sharp, but I could still make out his handsome face. Now I could look at it whenever I was away from home.

SEVEN

I picked up the phone just as Bernie started to leave a message on my answering machine. "Hello there."

He asked, "Is it okay if I come over? I have something to give you."

"Please do." I had wanted to see him since our recent night out.

When he arrived at my apartment, Bernie was carrying a large bag. He put it down and said, "I was planning to give some things to Goodwill. I thought I'd let you take a look first."

"That's great. Preparing for your departure already?"

"As best I can. So far I've only found a few books I want to get rid of, though." He knelt and retrieved one from the top of the pile. "I want to give you this." He handed me a hardback book with a plain black cover. He asked, "Do you know it?"

"I don't think so." I opened it and saw "The Olympia Press, 1959," and "This special edition of *The Black Diaries* (the only one to contain Roger Casement's diary for 1911), is limited to 1,500 numbered copies. This is copy no. 1105." It had been printed in France to evade censorship, and as I found out, the formal disapproval of the British security services. It was unclear why a publisher trading in "dirty books" would be interested in the text. I asked Bernie, "What do you know about this?"

He said, "Roger Casement was a Protestant Irishman who worked for the Foreign Office of Great Britain. He investigated the exploitation of the early rubber industry in the jungles of the Amazon and the Congo. He exposed incredible abuses: murder, slavery, kidnapping, mutilation, people dying of exhaustion and starvation from overwork—all so the first manufactured automobiles could have affordable tires. He was knighted for his efforts, but within a few years, he lost his knighthood and was executed for treason."

"How did that happen?"

"He involved himself in Ireland's independence movement. He negotiated with the Germans at a time when Great Britain was at war with them, to procure guns for an uprising in 1916. He was betrayed and arrested as soon as he landed in Ireland. Lots of people objected to his death sentence, but the British circulated his private diaries among influential figures to eliminate any sympathy for his cause. The diaries contained explicit notes about sex with many young men at home and abroad. I'm sure all the agents of colonialism fucked the natives, but he preferred to get fucked, and this was beyond the pale for his potential supporters. In the early twentieth century, hardly anyone would come to the defense of a passive homosexual. And he was a size queen, as you'll see. The Irish of the last century were simply unable to cope with the notion that such a person was a national hero. There is even a theory that the evil Brits concocted these documents themselves. Who would have had the skills to forge them, and how bureaucrats could have commanded the resources to commit such a complex fraud are questions the adherents of the theory have never answered. It's been about a hundred years since Casement first became well known, and he's still a controversial figure."

"I can't wait to read it. Thank you." I hugged Bernie, and he held me for longer than I expected. I wasn't sure how to react to his ardent embrace.

He composed himself but made no comment. Instead, he continued his story: "Casement was handsome and very tall, with a thick black beard. He must have been extremely conspicuous in South America and Africa. Joseph Conrad met Casement after *Heart of Darkness* came out, and Conrad told him the book was 'an awful fudge.' Conrad was a bit repelled by this mad Irishman, and told a friend that Casement was 'a man of no mind at all. He was all emotion.' People have understood this as Conrad expressing his skepticism about Casement's idealistic politics, but I've always thought that he was really expressing his distaste for a homosexual. Conrad led a life of travel and physical daring, but he never really stuck his neck out. He didn't have to, he was always the exiled Polish aristocrat. A cool customer." Bernie stared off into space for a while and we stood there in silence. He abruptly snapped out of it, grabbed his bag, and turned to leave. He said, "I should get to Goodwill before it closes," and made an uncomfortable exit.

After he left, I asked myself why a collector would give away such a valuable book. Bernie's hug was uncharacteristic, but he never said, "I'll miss you" or anything as straightforward as that. He experienced difficulty with emotions, and I gathered that he felt a lot of them around me. Until that moment, I had been oblivious to this. He trotted out long and fascinating discourses that he had probably rehearsed in advance, but he was unable to handle the sort of simple conversations that friends and lovers have between themselves every day. The book I held in my hands was a wonderful gift, but I couldn't give him anything in return, because he could never bring himself to ask for what he wanted. It was only just before his departure that an act of generosity happened to reveal his feelings, indirectly and too late.

∞

That evening, I looked carefully at *The Black Diaries*. In the "Cash Ledger of 1911," Casement made notes of expenses, some to be reimbursed by the Foreign Office, others more personal, like the amounts he paid for sex. The details were tantalizing, for example, "Enormous Dublin under 19 very fair—thin knickers & coat, white scarf, *blue* eyes & *huge* huge stiff long & thick one." The brevity of the entries made me wonder about Casement's emotions, which were so obvious to Conrad when meeting the man in person. The evidence of them in the book was extremely slim. I supposed no one would ever know what Casement thought about the males of almost every ethnic group and age with whom he had sex. Nor could anyone know to what extent his experiences were typical for the time, or if he was such an outrageous case that authority figures felt compelled to crush him. I couldn't help but think that some of the people who decided his fate—policemen, informers, judges, politicians, clerics—must have indulged in similar pleasures, but were not unlucky enough to have been prosecuted as traitors, with their private diaries (if they were courageous or foolhardy enough to write such texts) read by numerous strangers.

I reflected on the book that Bernie had given me, and I decided to find a way to make art based on what I found in it. On impulse, I walked to an art supply store across the street from the old Otis College of Art and Design campus and bought some fine paper and a few pencils. That night, I began to make drawings of Casement's diary entries. I wasn't satisfied with the results, so the next day I took the book to the library and made photocopied enlargements of the pages that particularly interested me. I envisioned a large series and planned to make at least one drawing per day until I ran out of text to draw.

∞

During an afternoon walk, I stopped by Libros Revolución/ Blanco Projects to see Frances. After a longer pause than usual, she opened the door and let me in. She wasn't alone and looked a bit frazzled. She said, "I'm wrapping up a meeting."

"Well, hello," I said to two distant figures in the studio. I recognized Carmen first. She was exactly as Paul had described her, lithe and professional, wearing a faintly absurd outfit. Her skirt looked like a full length dress with the top half taken off and gathered at the waist. It was a color I hardly ever saw in the inner city, ecru, a shade of nothing that suburbanites often chose to paint their houses. Her blouse, if such a word could be used to describe the garment, looked like an inside-out brown sweater with a white tag showing at the bottom. At the top it hung normally as a sleeveless shirt. I couldn't figure out how the garments had been constructed and gave her a puzzled look.

"Hello, silly, are you in space?" asked Carmen as she came over to hug me.

"Sorry, I was staring at your outfit."

She said, "I'll take that as a compliment. It's Margiela."

I had never heard the word—I assumed Margiela was the name of a designer, because that was what people with money to spend on fashionable clothes tended to talk about. She turned around to show me the whole look, and I noticed four diagonal white stitches on the back of the shirt, just below the nape of her neck. They appeared to be a mistake, but I was sure they weren't. I also saw that the back of the garment was a bit frayed at the bottom, since it had been cut but not hemmed. The outfit was made to self-destruct. I could only utter the words, "How perverse… and extraordinary."

She laughed and said, "I'm glad you're a fan. You know, I've been thinking about you. I always respected your eye and your ideas. I'd like to have a meeting with you some time soon." Her way of speaking was at once more formal and more casual than I remembered.

"That would be great." As soon as I said this, I noticed that her companion was Brad, whom I had known in art school. During those days, he cultivated a clique around himself, a bunch of kids who thought they were destined for art stardom. None of them had been heard from since, except Jerry, who became the celebrated porn director Eon McKai. Brad had gained a fair amount of weight and lost a lot of hair since I last saw him several years before. His apparel made him look as if he had just stepped off a sailboat at Kennebunkport, strangely contrasting with the setting—a former communist bookstore in Westlake, where he stood amid large paintings of war atrocities, in the company of three notorious inverts. He came over and shook my hand. I said, "It's been a while. I almost didn't recognize you."

"That's funny," he said. "You look exactly the same as you did in school." I couldn't tell if this was a compliment, an insult, or an expression of jealousy. I glanced down to see a wedding ring that matched the one on Carmen's hand. My eyes moved to his crotch, not as impressive as I remembered, and I considered the question of his sperm count. He waved to get my attention and said, "Anyway, these two talk about you a lot. I feel like you're in the room with us sometimes. And here you are."

I asked, "When did you get married?"

Brad went over to Carmen, held her around the waist, and said, "Our second anniversary is coming up soon."

I said, "Oh, congratulations, belatedly. I didn't know.'

He said, "We were in New York for a few years. This is only my third trip out here since I graduated. But we've taken the plunge. We bought an apartment in the Eastern Columbia Building, so we'll be living here full time."

I asked, "That's in the film *Zabriskie Point*, isn't it?"

"It is." Carmen was tickled that I knew the place, a distinguished Art Deco style office building faced with green ceramic tiles and topped with a giant clock under letters spelling the word "Eastern." I wasn't aware that it had been converted into residential spaces, but that made sense. Broadway in downtown Los Angeles had been gentrifying for years.

Extending his hand to me again, Brad said, "We need to get going. Furniture shopping. It was great seeing you." His tone made him sound like a character in a situation comedy. I expected canned laughter to accompany his attempt at bonhomie. I wondered if his ego allowed him to understand that I loathed him when we were students. Perhaps he enjoyed torturing me. He always struck me as a passive-aggressive little shit.

Carmen came over and asked for my cell phone number. She promised to call me once they had finished moving into their new apartment.

After they left, I asked Frances, "How was the studio visit?"

She said, "Fine, fine. Carmen's worried about opening her gallery with a bunch of Iraq War paintings. I reminded her that she has a way with rich masochists. They're her special niche. I tell you, she was a phenomenon in New York. Of course, she stole the mailing list of every gallery she worked for."

I said, "I have no doubt."

"I don't know Brad that well. I got the feeling he came along to keep an eye on Carmen, to check if we're having an affair. If only."

I asked, "Do you understand why they're a couple?"

"Your guess is as good as mine. Brad started his MFA after I left. Carmen said that he was a darling in the Art School."

"He had a certain magnetism, but I thought he was a total phony. The faculty might have been taken in. Flattery will get you everywhere with those people."

She said, "Carmen told me he was used to getting a lot of attention, but his first solo show after he graduated did nothing for him. No sales, no reviews. He decided he couldn't handle being an artist struggling for decades in obscurity. What he really cared about wasn't making work, but making money, so he went into real estate. Now he's flipping lofts downtown."

I said, "I guess that smarmy manner comes in handy."

"Hey, at least he didn't hug you," Frances said as she opened a beer. She offered one to me, and I shook my head. She said, "I'd do Carmen again. To be honest, I need a girlfriend. This is a lonely town."

I said, "I've gotten used to it somehow. I've been here for more years than I care to count." I asked, "Do you think Brad and Carmen have sex?"

"I guess so. When we were together, Carmen's sex drive was as high as mine. Maybe she's settled down."

"I bet she wants you to be her back door man."

"I could show her back door a few tricks," she said with a leer. "Could Brad be giving her what she really wants?"

I said, "Brad's a great person, if you've never actually met a person."

"That sounds about right." She sighed and said, "I can't imagine them in bed together."

"I can. Brad asks for a blow job, and Carmen says, 'I wouldn't suck your lousy dick if I was suffocating, and there was oxygen in your balls!'" We both laughed uncontrollably. At that moment, my cell phone started buzzing. Annoyed, I grabbed it and was on the verge of shouting an obscenity at the caller when I noticed that it was Moira. I caught my breath and said to Frances, "Sorry, I have to take this." I turned away and said, "Hello. How are you and the baby?"

Moira answered, "Oh, we're fine. I'm teaching again. Miguel's mother has started to help us with Flor." She paused and asked, "Are you sitting down?"

I pulled over a chair and said, "Now I am."

"Okay. I talked to Graciela."

I said, "Tell me everything."

There was a long pause. "Temo's alive, but his mother doesn't know where he is. Somewhere in the US, she thinks. She's been sending money to his account at a California bank, and the transfers go through. There's no way of knowing what happens with the funds after that."

I said, "I found an email from him recently, so I'm not surprised he's alive. I responded to it but haven't heard back. I bet that he's in Los Angeles. I've never seen him, though."

"Graciela thinks his green card is about to expire. That would be a reason for him to show himself or return to Mexico if he doesn't want the undocumented immigrant experience."

I asked, "When's the last time he spoke to his mother?"

"Christmas. She's going crazy with worry. You see, the family situation has changed. Pedro—that's Temo's father—had a stroke, and he's incapacitated. Their assets are in disarray. Graciela was always kept in the dark about money. She's trying not to get ripped off, but it's difficult."

"The poor woman."

"It's not all bad. Pedro can't abuse her anymore. Graciela didn't go into details, but she told me she feels free now. She said, 'When I finish meeting with bankers and signing papers, that old bastard can die.'"

"And Temo knows nothing about this?"

"Not unless he's psychic. There's more to tell you, but I can't stay on the phone much longer. Is it okay if I write to you instead?"

I said, "Sure. And if I hear from Temo, I'll call you."

"Thanks. Bye."

When Frances, who had been in the back room during my conversation, came out and saw the expression on my face, she asked, "What's wrong?"

I said, "That was my friend Moira. You may not remember Cuauhtémoc. We called him Temo. I knew him from the bookstore. Anyway, he disappeared a few years ago."

She said, "You mentioned him to me, a rich Mexican guy."

"Yeah. Moira thought he was dead, but I had a feeling he was alive. I couldn't say where he was, but I never stopped thinking about him." I paused for a moment. "It's impossible to describe why you're attracted to someone. Why him? He was kind of a prick, and his politics were pretty vile. But he was handsome and really perverted in a way that only boys from good Catholic families can be."

Frances smiled and said, "I think I can understand the last part."

"There's unfinished business between us. He told me he loved me, but I could never be sure if he meant it." My story trailed off, and I gazed blankly at a point on the far wall until I noticed Frances waiting for me to continue. "Moira was in love with him, too, by the way. She called to say she had spoken to Temo's mother, who's been supporting him all along. He's what they used to call a remittance man. No one knows where Temo is, but I suspect he's in Los Angeles, hiding out for reasons only he knows."

Frances drove me home, where I fell into bed and slept for a long time.

∞

I couldn't guess why Carmen wanted to meet with me, but when she appeared at my door one cool fall morning, I was happy to see her. I didn't entirely trust the woman, but I was fascinated by her ambition. She had guts and made confident, unconventional decisions, one of which was choosing Westlake, a poor neighborhood, rather than the corporate-geriatric West Side as the location for her gallery. Chinatown's art scene was already in full swing, and she had gathered as much while she lived on the East Coast. Some successful gallerists had recently moved to Hollywood or Culver City, but she preferred to strike out on her own in an attempt to make a building south of Macarthur Park into a destination for the collector class.

Carmen was dressed resplendently in clothing that looked as though it might have come from a thrift store. She wore a top constructed of two crocheted wool shawls in yellow and gray. One sleeve trailed along the floor. Under chaotic fringe, I noticed an ocher skirt that had rough, unfinished details, cinched with a plastic belt so yellowed that it could have dated from the late 1970s. She also wore high heeled boots with their big toes separated, Japanese style. They had been painted white. I said, "Once again, your clothes are remarkable."

She kissed me on the cheek and said, "I wore this for you. Brad doesn't get it at all. I knew you would."

I prepared tea while she made herself comfortable on the couch in the living room. When I emerged from the kitchen, she pointed to the painting on the wall, a portrait of Albania's dictator Enver Hoxha, and asked, "Is that an Andë Alia?"

"It is. Winston, I mean Andë, painted it as a student. He gave it to me the day after we graduated. I think this painting is his first mature work."

Carmen said, "You should consider installing an alarm system. His auction prices are reaching six figures these days."

I gasped. "Thanks for the advice. I wasn't aware he was as successful as that."

"And yet you saw it before anyone." She took a sip of her tea. "I always thought your instincts about art were spot on. You helped him and Frances, and you recommended Clarice Lispector to me at the exact moment I needed to read her. You probably weren't even aware that I have something in common with her."

I said, "No, I wasn't."

"I never told you this, but my original surname was Weiss. My family paid small fortunes for exit visas from Germany in the 1930s, and the Weisses went to whatever countries would take them. My grandparents and my father, who was a baby at the time, ended up in Chile. They changed their name to Blanco. It's like Clarice's story, a family of Jews emigrating from Europe to South America, but a generation later. I had relatives who went to Brazil, and they became Brancos." She looked down. "The rest died in concentration camps. It's a heavy history." She fell silent for a moment, then continued, "When the CIA decided to murder Salvador Allende, my father escaped yet another purge of communists and Jews and got himself to New York, with my mother and me in tow. I was only a little kid. His older brother decided to move to Los Angeles, where he invested in real estate, including the building I inherited on Eighth Street that used to be Libros Revolución. My uncle had a sentimental attachment to leftists and never cared much how (or if) the rent got paid. Obviously, it was an unsustainable situation. By the way, I wasn't aware that the eviction threw you out of work until after it was all said and done."

I said, "I didn't know you had such a personal connection to the building. But yeah, I realize that sentiment plays no part in business decisions, or shouldn't. We had a good time while it lasted." I asked, "Was your father a success in New York?"

"Not at all. He got a job in California, and we moved when I was about five. He fell in with a bunch of geeks naïve enough to think that Ayn Rand was a philosopher. Somehow they convinced my father to invest his life's savings in tech companies. My mother threatened to divorce him, because as far as she was concerned, he was a loser who'd lost his mind. A couple of decades later, he was fabulously wealthy. The 'market correction' that happened around the time we got out of grad school cramped his style a bit, but only temporarily."

"It seems you've inherited his talent for trend spotting."

She let out a hearty laugh. "It's better to play the game than to sit back and cry about lost opportunities. I can say that based on my family's experiences, trends in history are totally arbitrary. It's really a question of knowing who to hang out with." After a pause, she asked, "Have you made any art lately?"

"I'm at the beginning of a new project." I showed her the *Black Diaries* drawings and told her about Roger Casement. She seemed intrigued. I mentioned my working title for the series, "Cocksucker of the Congo." She shivered with delight and said, "That's so politically incorrect that it's guaranteed to get attention, but it might interfere with sales."

I smiled. "I figured as much."

"And you know, it's all about painting."

"I'll see what I can do."

She took a breath and said, "We had a cancellation at the gallery, and now we have no exhibition planned for the slot a few months after Frances. It's the last exhibition before the summer. Are you interested?"

I stammered, "Uh, of course."

"The opening will be some time in May, and the show will be on view for six weeks. Are you sure you can get work together by then?"

"I'm confident I can come up with something." I hadn't prepared an exhibition for a long while, but I would figure it out. I asked, "Do you mind if the work is difficult?"

She laughed. "I expect nothing less from you. If I alternate 'easy' or commercial shows with 'difficult' ones, the gallery will be fine, and it won't hurt my reputation one bit. Give me your email address and I'll send you a new floor plan of the space."

I said, "Thanks. Since I used to work in your building, I'd like to play off of that."

She said, "You old commie. I knew you'd be game."

"I've always respected you, Carmen. You don't fool around. I won't disappoint you. But I do have one question. Why me?"

She smiled. "You're totally unlike the people I'm accustomed to dealing with. You probably don't see a lot of aspiring young artists." I shook my head. "Why would you? You don't teach. You're alone with your obsessions, the way all serious artists used to be. A friend who does teach said to me recently, 'These kids have gotten so numb that they don't even know what it's like to have an interest in something.'" She finished her tea and leaned forward. "You're lucky that you've been sheltered from how professional the art business has become. It might be different in other countries, but here in the US, there's a path to follow. You get an MFA from Yale, where you learn to do exactly one clever thing very well. It becomes your brand. You make this 'characteristic work' over and over in slight variations as many times as the market will bear. Your name becomes known, and one day you can afford a house, then another house, then a whole range of luxurious amenities. You're minted. You enjoy hobnobbing with your collectors. You attend galas and charity balls. Eventually, if you're lucky, you find your name in the pages of art history textbooks. That is, if anyone will be writing and reading art history by the time you arrive at your goal. If you're caught up in all this and you're really smart and self-aware, then you realize before you die that you've become perfectly boring." She punctuated this remark by getting up to leave, with the train of her outfit dragging behind her. "I'm sure you know this already, but you, my dear, are *not* boring." At the door, she delivered her exit line, "I like having you around as a reminder of why I got interested in art in the first place."

∞

After Carmen left, I stared at Winston's painting for a long time. It had become part of the scenery in the years since I took over the apartment from Moira, and was something I mostly ignored. That neglect was stupid and habitual, but perfectly normal. The face of Enver Hoxha seemed to emerge from chaos in the painting. A few decisive gestures caused his likeness to fall into place. Few people in the Western world would have recognized a portrait of the man who held Albania hostage to his will for forty years. Perhaps this was the reason Winston felt he could part with the painting: it would get no flicker of recognition from potential collectors the way a portrait of Mao or Stalin would, and consequently might have little market value. Carmen had noted the auction prices of Andë Alia—Winston's birth name, but one that none of his friends knew until long after we met him—but she neglected to mention this particular work's visual qualities. His violent brushstrokes and swipes of a palette knife had been inchoate expressions of rage until they came together in the painting of Hoxha. It was as though he found the discipline to express all his contempt and bitterness in an instant of heightened consciousness, and had been able to exploit this ability from that point onward as a mature painter in control of his craft. Or maybe it was all a happy accident. In any case, Winston had the presence of mind to realize that he was onto something, and with my encouragement at the beginning, he had taken on the world with his particular style of painting. Others quickly saw the power of the work, and within a few years, the demand for it had become intense. This came as no surprise to me. The art market was rewarding him for making gorgeous paintings.

Inspired by Winston's work, I briefly felt less oppressed by all the taboos and restrictions my art school education had inculcated in me. I called Frances and said, "I want you to teach me to paint."

E I GHT

The scene would have struck professional artists as ludicrous: a man pushing forty learning to paint a few months before his first solo exhibition. As I saw it, I was offered an opportunity, and I'd have been an idiot not to take advantage. The worst outcome would have been an embarrassing hiccup between commercial gallery shows. I could live with that. In the best case scenario, I could make work that suggested a new way forward.

My education had been short on technical instruction, but Frances learned the fundamentals of painting in Kansas City while I was studying theory. She provided me with a large oblong canvas that she had stretched before realizing its proportions were wrong for her own exhibition. I told her that I wanted to make a painting in a very different style from hers, and I showed her several drawings based on *The Black Diaries*. She reminded me of a lesson learned in high school art class: gridding off an original to enlarge it on canvas. The resulting painting would look handmade rather than having a digital or machine-like precision. I carefully mixed colors to lay down a ground. The original pages were yellowed with a few faults and stains. I brought the book into the studio to use as a reference. I kept it as far away from Frances's paints and brushes as possible.

Frances was a good sport about teaching me to stretch canvases. It took me a long time to get the hang of it. My main physical activities—turning pages of books, walking the streets of Los Angeles, and fisting Daniel—had hardly prepared me for the work of making a sound, taut surface that held paint. She had a number of stretcher bars and pieces of canvas that were too small for her purposes. From these, I made a group of more or less identical objects, and thus I embarked on a series of paintings.

Carmen came to visit a couple of weeks later. Her main intention was to confirm that Frances's paintings could be moved to make room for last-minute renovations to the space. Having satisfied herself that the exhibition had been finished on schedule, she turned to my work. When she saw a painting in progress based on a Casement diary entry reading, "6 to Harrow, Jew X. Enormous and liked greatly," she burst out laughing. After an excruciating moment during which she closely scrutinized the other paintings, she said, "No one will have any idea what they mean, but I love them." I was so anxious about Carmen's visit, and so relieved by its outcome, that I had failed to take in what she was wearing that day.

∞

A few days later, I received an email from Moira with the subject line "family saga." It read:

Temo's mother has told me the story of her life, and I think it's appropriate that you have this information as well. I know you won't, but please don't tell anyone about the following.

Graciela is the daughter of refugees from the Spanish Civil War. She was born in Mexico City at a time when her parents lived in poverty. Her father's intransigent politics and brusque manner prevented him from securing employment appropriate to his talents. Fellow émigrés who had better luck in Mexico helped them as best they could, but lack of money plagued her childhood. Graciela worshiped her parents, and when they urged her to accept a social invitation from a respectable young man, she did so.

This man, Pedro, was the second son of a landowning family in Jalisco and came to Mexico City to seek his fortune. He had prodigious success in construction, a business that offered many opportunities in what was becoming the world's largest city. He developed expertise in bribing public officials and expressed the cynical, reactionary politics characteristic of his social class, but he was smart enough to keep his attitudes to himself when the occasion demanded. Exactly why Graciela's leftist family considered Pedro a good match for her is unclear. She describes herself as being "sold" to him.

At first, the marriage went well, but when Graciela lost their first child to a miscarriage, Pedro turned bitter. Thinking the dynasty he hoped to found might not be possible, he neglected his wife, who was recovering from a traumatic experience. He associated her physical problems with her family's politics, at times shouting "Strong beats weak!" in the heat of discussions. When their son was born, the relationship improved for a while, and Pedro even allowed Graciela to name the child Cuauhtémoc, a reference to Mexico's Pre-Columbian civilization that he would never have approved of under normal circumstances.

To Pedro's disgust, little Temo turned out to be a complete mama's boy and exhibited traditionally feminine traits from an early age. When informed by a doctor that Graciela could bear no more children, Pedro insisted on adopting a son, just in case, as he put it. Roberto grew up "normal," as Pedro never failed to say, and he placed all his hopes in him.

Pedro ignored his wife and his son Temo, but this didn't stop him from trying to exercise complete control over their lives. Graciela believes he regularly hired private detectives to keep his family under surveillance, always firing them when they failed to discover any untoward behavior.

Graciela loved Temo uncritically, even obsessively, but she couldn't deny that his behavior became erratic in adulthood. He resembled his father in this way, and as Temo grew older, the atmosphere at home became extremely volatile. Pedro threatened to have Temo locked away. He once drove his son to a bleak asylum and told him, "This is where you will end up." On the night before Pedro would finally make good on his threat, Graciela gave Temo a bag of money and begged him to leave. After that, they lost contact with each other for long periods. She was tormented by guilt for banishing him from the family home, but she saw no alternative. Pedro's reaction was "good riddance," and from then on, he treated his wife with open contempt.

Temo and Roberto never got along. In tense moments, Roberto would call Temo "faggot," and Temo would call Roberto "bastard." There were rumors that Roberto was actually Pedro's illegitimate son by one of his mistresses. Being the father's favorite did not turn out well for Roberto. He committed suicide a while ago. Graciela believes this precipitated the stroke that has made Pedro an invalid. Since then, Graciela has begun putting the family's business affairs in order. She has never given up hope that Temo will return.

I couldn't manage to compose a response to this message. I saved it as "unread" and turned off my computer. I dialed Moira's home number, and after a few rings, she picked up the phone. "I figured you'd call. It's hectic around here."

I said, "Sorry to disturb you. I have some questions."

"Of course. What do you want to know?"

I asked, "Did Pedro abuse his family physically?"

"Graciela didn't say anything about that, but it wouldn't surprise me. I think Temo's poor brother might have gotten the worst of it, considering what happened to him."

"What's wrong with that man?"

She sighed. "I'm no psychiatrist, and this is only speculation, but it sounds like his manic states manifested as anger."

"And Temo?"

Moira said, "Do you even need to ask? Mania can also be expressed in episodes of hypersexuality."

"Are you implying that I took advantage of someone who's mentally ill?"

She asked, "Did you?"

I answered, "It didn't seem that way at the time. I was doing what he asked me to do."

She inhaled calmly and said, "I don't know what went on between you and Temo, and I'm not going to pass judgment."

After a long pause I said, "Tell Graciela that I'll be looking for him."

"Just remember that he knows nothing about his brother's suicide or his father's stroke. Be kind to him." Flor started crying in the background, and Moira said, "I've got to go. Good luck."

∞

As soon as I hung up, I called Frances. Before she could say anything, I said, "Let's get drunk."

We met at our usual place, which was relatively quiet that night. In a darker corner, we saw Paul, nursing a drink that looked suspiciously non-alcoholic. He noticed us and said, "Do sit, children. I've got news." As we did so, I saw that the embalmed look that had been increasingly evident on Paul's face of late was fading. He seemed if not healthy, then farther away from death's door than at any time since the 1990s.

"Have you found religion?" I asked.

"Oh, pshaw," he said with theatrical disgust. "No, this is a career development. Between Carmen and me the hatchet has been well and truly buried. She asked if I would be her gallery director." The last words came out of his mouth in a tone of wonder normally reserved for extravagant Christmas gifts or vibrant photographs of exotic sea creatures.

Stunned, Frances said, "No disrespect intended, but what the hell was she thinking?"

"Believe me, I had the same thought myself, but it's really happening. In preparation, I'm devoting myself to healthy living, practicing my phone voice, and sprucing up my wardrobe. I'll be the picture of manly virtue by the time of your opening."

"Did Carmen tell you about the exhibition schedule?"

Paul turned to me and said, "Yes she did. I hope you're taking my advice and abandoning literature." He pronounced the last word with the failed imitation of an upper class drawl that Joan Crawford used when saying the word "embroidery" in *The Women*.

"I'm making paintings these days," I assured him. "But don't worry, there'll be a twist. I can't do anything in a straightforward way."

"I await your latest imposture with bated breath. Willing to share?" Paul raised his eyebrows halfway to his hairline.

"For now I'm mum as an oyster," I said, recalling another line from *The Women*.

He said, "Speaking of gossip and its discontents, no one told me that Carmen married *Brad*. I found out only when she met with me."

Frances asked, "How could you not know?"

"Your mother had only a physical description of the accused, no name." He flagged down his favorite waitress and said, "It seems that climbing on the sobriety wagon was a little premature. I need a real drink."

I said, "Brad looks pretty dumpy now, if that makes you feel any better."

Paul let out a loud cackle. "Child, I haven't had feelings since the 1990s." He swallowed half his gin and tonic in one gulp. "But thank you for the attempt to soften the blow. It's further proof that after graduating from art school, people really do become what they've been all along." He emptied his glass and Frances and I prepared ourselves for story time. He said, "I sucked that boy's cock more times than I can count. I even gave him product on credit. He broke what little heart I had left to break." He stared off into the distance. "We had some good times, I must say, but that boy *loved* attention. He'd do just about anything for it. And I mean anything." He laughed to himself at the thought but shared no details. He asked Frances, "Do you think he's going to *reproduce* with Carmen?"

Frances said, "I don't know. I haven't figured out what's going on. Real estate must be involved."

Paul added, "We're all pawns in that game. If it weren't for rent control, I'd be living in my car, or with some distasteful benefactor, assuming I could find one at this advanced age." He frowned.

I asked Frances, "Did you know that our friend here is a published writer?"

Paul blushed slightly, and informed me, "Darling, Frances knows all. She was a participant in some of the more unsavory episodes that ended up in the book."

Frances laughed and said, "I think you're confusing me with someone else."

Paul admitted, "Perhaps you're right." He ordered another drink. His tips, often one hundred percent of the bill, insured almost instantaneous service. When he got a fresh gin and tonic, he said, "Since you're two of my dearest friends, I'll recount for you a passage of my as-yet unpublished autobiography." He smoothed his hair and began, "You may find this hard to believe, but once I was young and pretty. In my bucolic, wretchedly Christian hometown, no one appreciated me, not for my beauty, nor for my mind. As you discerned when you read *Antics*, I had something, what laypeople call 'talent,' and it was clear to anyone who wasn't a Neanderthal that I was destined for better things. The problem came down to my family. How shall I put it? They were white trash.

"As a teenage aesthete, I took classes at the local community college, which we called 'high school with ashtrays.' This was before all those evil smoking bans. One fine day, I found out that my favorite living author would be giving a reading at this dump, and when the time came, I planted myself in the audience front row center. The program of the evening I barely remember, but that hardly mattered. Mr. Author never stopped staring; the crowd fell away and he seemed to read only to yours truly. What I had seen in perfume commercials and romantic comedies was happening to me, a mere provincial youth. After he finished, he pressed a slip of paper with his phone number into my hand and gave me a meaningful look.

"I called him as soon as decency allowed, and he asked me, 'What took you so long?' I had a lot to learn about the ways of the world and horny old men. I soon fell under the celebrated author's tutelage. For instance, I learned the meaning of the word 'rimming' in exhaustive detail. After a few arduous, long-distance forays into civilization from the wilds of Santa Barbara County, it was decided—mainly by Mr. Author, but I went along—that I would move in with him. I didn't want to be a burden, but I soon discovered that this was hardly the case. He was loaded. His family owned several blocks of downtown Santa Monica, including his charming apartment with an ocean view. Having gotten my education mainly from network television, I assumed that even middle class people had access to such real estate. How wrong I was. An accidental glance at correspondence relating to a trust fund revealed his little secret: he relied not at all on his writing to earn a living. Family money allowed him the leisure to cultivate his exquisite gifts. The question pertinent to my existence—how much of that money would I gain access to?—had yet to be answered. I resolved to play the model boyfriend in the hope that his eventual decision would be most beneficial to me.

"Despite what one might find in pages written by that literary pederast, Horatio Alger, not all older men are kind and generous. Mr. Author could be petty and mean, but in the main, I got what I wanted. The real problem was having a social life. All my friends were his friends, and I soon discovered that they did not take me seriously in the least. I was only the latest piece of ass, and despite the assurances of my new friends, their attitudes changed little even after reading my oh-so precocious poems. They merely took to hiding their condescension a little better. I later learned that some of these people were grasping for their own little morsels of Mr. Author's family fortune.

"A telling moment came when the *New Yorker* commissioned an artist's profile, understood to be of great moment in the career of a rising cultural star. The writer of this puff piece could not have been nicer. I was solicitous for a respectful interval, then busied myself with tasks around the house so the two of them could have time alone for an interview. I didn't know the full extent of what Mr. Author said in context, I only read the article in print. I was mentioned, not as a young writer, but as something akin to a domestic servant, not exactly what I would have wished in those early days when I cherished dreams of my own *New Yorker* profile. A curious detail stood out amid the banalities. My lover said, 'I don't even know how to operate a washing machine.' Why would he make such a statement? Perhaps in an attempt to impress readers with his other-worldly artistic qualities and his exclusive devotion to his art. In any case, his whole circle of friends picked up on it. Somewhat later than I would have wished, I discovered that these creatures had given me a nickname: the Laundress. I was livid. Mr. Author did what he could, telling off his hangers-on, and even writing a letter to the editor to clarify my role in his life. Back in the day when Nobel Prizes in literature meant something, Patrick White did a similar thing to scare the bejesus out of *Time* magazine after they took his boyfriend for a housekeeper. Mr. Author's letter, somewhat less intimidating—because in actual fact, he cared very deeply about what the *New Yorker* staff thought of him—remained unprinted.

"In the wake of this humiliation, I decided to make something of myself. If I succeeded on my own, there would be no reason to humiliate me. I was still a naïve thing, and I had grievously underestimated the resentments nurtured by literary folk... but that's another tale for another time. At a propitious moment, I popped the question. Not marriage, which isn't legal anyway, but a question regarding my education. I wanted to get one, and I hadn't a penny of my own. I proposed that Mr. Author do the decent thing and pay for tuition at the school of my choosing. To my delight, he consented to this arrangement. The rest, as they say, is history."

There was a long pause that I broke with the question, "What happened to your benefactor?"

"Oh, he's still around. He moved to New York. The tuition checks became more difficult of access then, but he still professed his undying love over the telephone. Being a canny operator, he knew that living on the West Coast full time had a potentially fatal effect on a career in arts and letters. He needed to suck some East Coast cock to ascend the ladder. He gathered a whole new group of friends around him, a coterie of climbers who were much better at hiding the true sources of their income than he had been, and who sometimes even published things. I found them all rather dreary and status obsessed, but he used them beautifully and learned a few tricks of the trade in the process. Eventually, he found another golden boy. No surprise, it was someone who bore an uncanny resemblance to me as a teenager. I held no grudge—how could I?—but with my source of tuition money all dried up, I was forced to adopt drastic measures to make up the deficit."

I asked, "Was that when you started dealing drugs?"

He exclaimed, "Shush, child! You *are* an indiscreet one. The walls may well have ears. But yes, I did need to peddle a few extracurricular treats to earn my keep."

Frances asked, "Is he still in New York?"

"Of course. Mr. Author has gotten quite fat and must be at least seventy years old now. I suspect he does rather well for himself on Silverdaddies.com. I derive some satisfaction from knowing that I had him when he was still relatively handsome. The peculiar thing is that his way of being in the world hasn't changed one whit since he emerged from the closet in the 1950s. He was a once golden haired twink, playing the role of wide-eyed *naïf*, and somehow or other he expects us to believe he is still that." He imitated this old man by giggling and waving limp-wristed hands just below his face, like Judy Garland attempting to mug dramatically while suffering from delirium tremens. "My sources tell me that of late his twink routine has been augmented by certain expressions from the repertoire of the maiden aunt scandalized by the decadence of it all. It strikes me as rather pathetic, but it seems to work for him at his advanced age. He's now a terribly nelly *eminence grise*."

I offered, "You've done rather well for yourself, considering."

"Oh, I get by. I discovered the main lesson to learn from such experiences. Whatever happens, you must find a way to own your life. I don't have much, but at least I know it's mine."

NINE

Bernie called me the next morning. I could barely get out of bed to answer the phone. He reminded me that we had made plans to go to the Getty Museum that day, a date I had completely forgotten. I told him about my hangover, and he said, "I'll be right over."

The shower felt like an assault, and afterward, I got back into bed. Bernie knocked on the door, and I absentmindedly reached for a remote to turn down the volume. He brought some hangover remedies and made tea and toast so I'd have something in my stomach during the marathon screening we'd be attending that afternoon.

Bernie and I arrived at the Getty in plenty of time to get seats in the auditorium. He reminded me to take off my sunglasses, a concession to decorum I made for the sake of the guest speaker, our friend Jim, whom I hadn't seen since I lost my job at Libros Revolución.

Totally unbeknownst to me when we worked together, Jim had a past as an experimental filmmaker. His magnum opus, *Anatomy of Melancholy* (1976), found no distribution in the United States, or anywhere else for that matter. I took a copy of the program notes from a pile near the door, and before the event began, I read that a Getty scholar in residence had initiated a restoration effort when he discovered that the filmmaker lived in Los Angeles. Jim had agreed to participate in an interview, and when the film ended, he would take questions from the audience, which at that point numbered five.

"I'm glad we came," I said to Bernie. "Imagine presenting your film to three strangers."

The lights dimmed and the projector started, somewhat uncertainly, as the projectionist was probably unaccustomed to 16mm equipment. I had become so used to digital sound in films that the hissing optical track (with roughly the same fidelity as an old-fashioned telephone line) came as a shock to me. I thought the poor audio quality was particularly unfortunate because the music—slow chord progressions on solo piano—sounded like nothing I had ever heard before. My hangover lent a hallucinatory effect to the film, which didn't adhere to any narrative conventions I recognized. As soon as one could grasp a coherent story, it was replaced by another episode. Various people told anecdotes suggesting autobiography, and these sequences were interrupted by animation and still photographs accompanied by a parody of traditional documentaries' "voice of god" narration. These intrusive explanations posited theories, by turns credible and nonsensical, of historical phenomena. An examination of sodomy among cloistered nuns and priests promised amusement, but the sequence ended before any satisfying conclusion. Exactly like Robert Burton's seventeenth century book *The Anatomy of Melancholy*, the film spun an elaborate web of references, many of them obscure or dubious. Antiquated looking "found footage" also made periodic appearances. While I suspect that the goal was a sense of timelessness or futurity, as in science fiction, the apparel and hairstyles of the actors and the desuetude of 1970s metropolitan London (where all location shooting had been done) gave the film a dated look, which I found charming.

At one point I began to doze off and left to take a break. I noticed Jim outside the auditorium smoking. His face brightened when he saw me, and I waved. As soon as I finished in the men's room, I went directly back to my seat, hoping that there would be time for a long conversation after the screening.

The film ended with conventional titles and credit music, which most of the spectators took as their cue to leave. No announcement had been made about a special guest—perhaps everyone involved had been stuck in traffic when the screening began—so the audience could hardly be blamed for thinking the program was over. A man I took to be the scholar responsible for the screening entered with Jim, who had an air of annoyance. They sat in Barcelona chairs placed on either side of a low table. The scholar, whose German name I didn't quite catch, made a formal introduction using a handheld microphone, then started a more informal discussion by asking about the circumstances of the film's production.

Jim took another microphone and said, "In 1974, I left the United States for a while. I landed in England with nothing much in my pocket but the address of a film collective in North London. The people there directed me to a squat where I could live. That was the beginning of a whole new chapter in my life. You can't tell from the way London looks today, but back then, there were lots of abandoned buildings that young people took over. I never paid a penny in rent when I lived in London."

The scholar asked, "Who did you meet at the squat?"

Jim put his hand over the mic and asked, "Is this being recorded?" The scholar nodded, and Jim said, "Next question."

"What was it like for you as an American to make a film in England?"

"There were good and bad aspects to it. The communal spirit in the squats was wonderful, and people were very generous with their time. A whole group of us shoplifted the film stock I used. But there were cultural misunderstandings. A bunch of Englishmen on a film set seem to come to consensus without much discussion, and their communication was a little too subtle for me. The American stereotype of the dictatorial director didn't play well there. Maybe that's why English films are so mediocre. I think my fellow collective members started to resent that I was making an ambitious film with their labor. As they saw it, this American arrived like a bull in a china shop and wanted to turn the scene into Hollywood." He laughed. "It didn't help that I'm from Los Angeles."

"How did you finish such a huge project?"

"I wasn't part of a degree program, but I was sitting in on classes at a terrible film school in Walthamstow around then. Nobody seemed to mind. Anyway, I met someone there who wanted to get into producing, though it was hard to admit to that kind of ambition at the time. On my behalf he applied for government grants to which I had no access as a foreigner. He did it for a producer's credit, because he thought the film would go somewhere. It turned out that a three hour long experimental film was impossible to sell, but in the end he did okay. He works at Channel Four now."

The scholar asked a question to which he already knew the answer, "Did you make any films after *Anatomy of Melancholy*?"

Jim took a deep breath and said, "No. I left London with a print of *Anatomy of Melancholy* under my arm. When I got back to Los Angeles, I tried to make another film, but I couldn't get any funding for it."

With an expression of surprise, the scholar asked, "What was this project?"

"I wanted to make a film about the Imperial Valley. For those of you who don't know, it's the poorest and hottest inhabited part of California, near the spot where the Colorado River evaporates. The region is intensively farmed as long as water from the Colorado irrigates it. A serf class of Mexicans works the land. The place gives the clearest view of the social relations of production that made 'the California dream' possible.

"Anyway, a man named Seymour Stern shot a documentary there at the beginning of the Great Depression. He was a leftist who wanted to make politically engaged experimental films in the Soviet manner. He had connections in the film industry and got to know Sergei Eisenstein during his stay in Hollywood. For a while everything seemed promising, but Stern soon ran into serious problems. The civic leaders of the Imperial Valley wanted nothing to do with his project. Most people in the film industry looked askance at his politics, and American communists disapproved of his 'decadent formalism.' He was probably expelled from the Party, if he ever belonged to it. Details are hard to come by. There are a few articles referring to the work in progress. I'm not actually sure if it was ever finished. Now the film is considered lost. All that remains are out-takes, which ended up in the National Film Archives of Canada. Stern later became known for writing about D. W. Griffith, but American anti-communism made him so paranoid that he emigrated, and he died in Ottawa.

"I thought I could make something interesting with the material, a critique of the political modernism fashionable in the 1970s, but no one would give me any money for it. A panelist who saw a grant application I submitted told me, 'Your project is too communist for the foundation to fund.' Maybe I should have stayed in Europe. Strange to think that the best place for a Hollywood native like me to make films was on another continent."

The scholar shifted his weight and said, "Fascinating. This opens up a whole new avenue of research. I'm so happy you shared your story." He paused and asked, "What happened to *Anatomy of Melancholy*?"

Jim answered, "I can say that I didn't feel like distributing an independent film—which was true—but it was more than that. I didn't have the hustle or the ego, and deep down I suspected that this type of filmmaking was irrelevant. I kept up with the scene for a number of years, but it took a turn that I didn't really support. Either you made animation and ended up working for the film industry in a special effects department, or you stuck with experimental filmmaking, which became more and more the domain of old hippies and trust fund babies. I guess I am an old hippy in a way, but I can't tolerate the stench of inherited money.

"I wanted to help people, as some of my comrades from the squats had done, but I wasn't sure how. I started working as a clerk in a bookstore our audience knows well." Bernie and I laughed. "I worked my way up to manager and never left, until I was forced to. Now I'm teaching classes about literature and film in prison. It feels like the right thing to do, but it's also awful. A vast amount of human potential is just going to waste. It's a system Kafka would have understood well. There are hundreds of rules, and the punishments are often arbitrary. People flaunt their power over others, but it's the tiniest power. I sometimes wonder if we're all insane." He paused and continued, "The men I teach, some of them anyway, are smarter than college students, or at least more politically astute. They intuitively understand the power dynamics of American society, they don't need to be taught about them." Jim ignored an alarmed expression on the scholar's face and continued, "Most of the convicts never had a trial. They're encouraged, if not coerced, into accepting plea deals to save the time and resources of the courts. Without these deals, the justice system would become too bogged down to function. The defendants who know they're innocent and insist on a trial are almost always found guilty if they're poor and can't afford a good defense attorney. They get harsher sentences than the ones who pleaded out. They're punished for exercising what the Constitution promises them: the right to a fair trial.

"The prison where I teach is in San Bernardino County. The state of California locates its prisons far away from major cities. The closest one is an hour's drive away from my apartment in Los Angeles. I feel like I'm visiting the colonies, and I am. Our carceral economy is a colonial enterprise relying on the work of slaves. Corporations have come to depend on convict labor. As in the days of the triangular trade, we see that capitalism can't exist without slavery."

The scholar, looking uncomfortable and sensing that the event had gotten away from him, turned to Bernie and me. "Are there any questions from the audience?"

After a pause, I said, "I think the film is very much the product of a period when experimental filmmakers distrusted narrative and wished to problematize it, to use a word popular at the time, as part of the overarching project of destroying bourgeois society's institutional system of representation. Is *Anatomy of Melancholy* an example of the 'political modernism' you wished to criticize?"

Jim laughed. "You're certainly familiar with the language used by people on the scene in London then." He paused for a moment to reflect on how best to answer the question. "At the beginning, my goals for the film were in line with the interests of my contemporaries, but then the project started to take on a life of its own. I can't say the final product impressed its original audiences as a radical critique. I was disappointed by that, but now I've had thirty years to think about these things, and I can say that the film simply belongs to a parallel narrative tradition: ancient Greek and Roman novels, picaresque novels, the narrative experiments of the Enlightenment, and more recent novels from Latin America, where postmodernism was invented. They're all loosely structured and morally suspect, at least by puritanical Anglo-American standards. They don't offer the kind of certainty and closure you get from a commercial movie, or its ancestor, the nineteenth century novel. Oddly enough, I understood this because I was a fan of Luis Buñuel's films. He completely missed the nineteenth century and all of its pieties. He grew up in what was essentially medieval Spain, then went to art school with Dalí and García Lorca, then moved to Paris, the epicenter of modernism. He didn't obey the rules of narrative cinema because he never assimilated them in the way that most film spectators did, the way film school students do now. I aspired to be a part of this other tradition, the road not taken by mainstream cinema. How successful have I been? I'm sure I can't say. Judge for yourself." The scholar was squirming with delight at the turn the discussion had taken and nodded enthusiastically.

Bernie asked, "How did you find the music?"

Jim said, "Actually, it found me. I knew Dennis Johnson from way back. He was the first American minimalist composer. When I was young, I heard a live performance of his composition *November*, which was six hours long. It was incredibly radical and transformed my sense of how time works in music. I found out later that he wrote *November* in 1958. I thought he'd become an important figure in the American avant-garde, but it didn't work out that way. He's a mathematical genius, and he got a job calculating rocket trajectories for Jet Propulsion Laboratory. It allowed him to move to a cabin in the mountains and work from home. He would go into Pasadena once a month to explain his equations. Dennis was never comfortable in social situations, so the politics of 'serious' music in America were totally beyond him. He had no desire for that kind of career. The last time I spoke to him he talked about the beauty of geometry, and it made me think that mathematics was his true love. Anyway, I had reel-to-reel tapes of one of his performances, and my younger brother Pete brought them when he came to visit me in London. I asked Dennis if I could use them, and he wrote me back to say he considered himself retired from music, but that was okay with him. I think he was amused by people's interest in his compositions." Jim looked up and saw us listening in rapt attention. He glanced at the clock and finished his speech, "I hope Dennis eventually finds his proper place in music history. He's a great guy."

The scholar said to Jim, "Thank you very much for your time. This discussion has been most enlightening." To us in the audience he said, "A transcript of the interviews I've conducted with our guest will be published in the near future. Thank you for coming." We applauded and waited at the back of the room for the two speakers to finish their goodbyes on stage, then Jim, Bernie, and I left the auditorium together.

Jim was relieved to be done. "Let's get the hell out of here. I could use a drink. Do you want to go to the Smog Cutter on Virgil?"

Bernie said, "Sure, I know where that is." Almost an hour later, we met at the bar, a step down from the Bounty, which had always been, even in its days of decline, a classy place. At the Smog Cutter, drinks were cheap, though, and when I ordered a ginger ale, I got it for free.

Once we settled at a table, I said to Jim, "You never told me you lived in London."

He said, "You never asked. I was there three years."

"So you saw the early days of punk."

"Yeah, but the underground scenes I was a part of predated all that, and they had a totally different ethos. The punks were speed freaks. They had great style, and in the end, that's what people remember."

I said, "Your brother must have taken notes when he visited you."

"Hell yes. In a few weeks he learned everything he used for his own band. I guess we could write a secret history of music, from minimalism to death rock."

Bernie said, "The '70s weren't that long ago, and they've already gotten enveloped in mythology."

I asked Jim, "What's the deal with the question you refused to answer?"

He responded, "Oh, I mentioned a friend from those days to that guy 'off the record,' and he wanted me to talk about her in front of an audience. He's German, so he's obsessed with the extra-parliamentary opposition. Do you know who Astrid Proll is?"

I said, "I've heard the name."

Bernie said, "She was a member of the Red Army Faction, also known as the Baader Meinhof Gang."

Jim shook his head. "Only reactionaries call them that." He took a long sip of his beer and said, "When I met her, I had no clue who she was, because she used an assumed name. I could see that she was serious and politically conscious, but at the same time, really innocent. She admitted that before she came to London, she had never met any working class people. Some leftist. But she participated in a lot of protests and talked to striking workers. The media made the RAF out to be a bunch of bourgeois posers who committed acts of terror out of a sense of hedonism. Astrid was anything but that. Whenever anyone said the word 'pleasure,' she'd explode and say, 'I have no room for romances.' She entered the UK with a forged passport, and if anyone identified her, she'd be extradited to Germany. It's amazing it didn't happen right away. There were wanted posters with her picture on them all over Europe. That didn't stop her from doing what she wanted. You can disappear in London. She expected to be asked for her papers all the time, but no English policeman ever asked anyone for them in those days. Anyway, I felt a little embarrassed to be making such an apolitical film, but she never criticized me. She felt it was outside her field of expertise. She helped with the production of a documentary called *Nightcleaners*, and she even helped me, though she refused to appear in the film. She said, 'We're afraid of photographs.' With good reason. She got nabbed by the cops eventually, but that was after I left England."

Bernie asked, "Were you there when the RAF members died in prison?"

"Ulrike Meinhof died around the time I was getting ready to leave. By then, I had fallen out of touch with Astrid. It must have been awful for her. She knew from experience how fucked up the German prisons were. The authorities put Astrid in a 'dead wing,' totally deserted, no human contact. They'd done the same thing to Ulrike, and it drove her crazy."

Bernie asked, "Do you believe the official story that Meinhof killed herself?"

"No, and neither did anyone else. The others, Baader, Ensslin, Raspe—they died a year later. Maybe suicide in their cases, I don't know. They weren't as serious, I think, and they persecuted Ulrike for her 'deviation' from the RAF line. It was childish, but what can you expect? Treat people inhumanely and you get inhumanity."

I interrupted, "But they killed so many people with those bombs."

"Yeah, fucking stupidity if you ask me. Astrid wasn't like that. I got the impression she didn't approve. There was something very upright and Protestant about her radicalism." He paused. "I sometimes wonder if their 'actions' as they called them were really expressions of religious fervor."

Bernie asked, "Wasn't Meinhof the daughter of a Lutheran minister?"

Jim shrugged. "I never knew her. That would make sense."

I asked, "Were you in love with Astrid?"

He guffawed, "Not at all. In those days, she preferred the company of women. Still does, I reckon." He took a gulp of his beer and said, "Our friend Moira reminds me a bit of Astrid. She's like a Catholic version, a little less severe. I guess that's why I hired her at the bookstore."

Bernie said, "The RAF isn't a good topic for a public talk. You never know who's listening."

I added, "Before I moved to California, Moira referred to the Getty as 'the CIA of art history.'"

Jim laughed. "She's not wrong. The Getty reminds me of a description I once heard of Hitler's taste in architecture: a combination of grandeur and pettiness. I'm grateful that they supported the restoration of my film, but I don't want to get too friendly."

After a long pause, Bernie said, "A few years ago, I visited the International Center of Photography, where I used to teach, before it moved to midtown. My friend Stephen Barker taught a lighting class I sat in on. There was a tallish and very slim older German woman in it. I thought she was gorgeous. Stephen did a slide lecture in the class using Gerhard Richter's RAF paintings, which are owned by the Museum of Modern Art now. He was speaking about the lighting in them—news photos transposed to painting. In the midst of this lecture the German woman began sobbing uncontrollably, telling us that these were her friends and that she was involved with one of them. It was a very intense moment. I don't think she was registered under the name Astrid Proll. She said she was publishing a book of photos from that time, which I assume is what came out not long after that."

I said, "I bought a copy of that at a used book store. When I opened it, I saw John Waters's autograph. Someone told me that he gave copies of Astrid's book away as Christmas gifts to people who worked on his film *Cecil B. Demented*."

Jim smirked and said, "And here we have a convenient summary of the last fifty years: collective political action degenerates into individual consumerism. We all end up in retail."

TEN

Jim called me unexpectedly after I saw him at the Getty. He said, "I don't know if anyone told you, but I'm moving."

I asked, "Where?"

"I found a house in Pomona. I'll live with Pete, and it's a lot closer to work."

"A big change from Angeleno Heights."

"Not really, it's an old Victorian, like the one where I'm living now, but I'm buying it."

I said, "Wow, you'll be a homeowner."

"Real estate is a lot cheaper out there. I never thought this would happen. Thank the California Department of Corrections. Anyway, I've got way too many books to move, and I thought I should get rid of some of them. Interested?"

Within ten minutes, I was on the Temple Street bus to Jim's place. His apartment, which I had never seen before, was almost exactly what I expected it to be. There were piles of books everywhere, and the place smelled like decaying paper. The kitchen cabinets contained no food or dishes, only books.

As he pointed to an especially precarious pile balancing on what had once been a dining room table, he said, "I've been trying to separate out the doubles from my collection. You can have as many of them as you want. I'll try to find a box or two somewhere." Most of the books he no longer wanted were in poor condition due to extensive markings. He explained, "There was no way I could sell them in the store," but he didn't mention how they came into his possession in the first place.

The pile contained three copies of *Ten Classics of Marxism*, published in 1948. It was a collection of short books and pamphlets by Marx, Engels, Lenin, and Stalin, and it had little resale value even in pristine condition. One copy had underlining in light pencil; another had two generations of underlining, in black pen and orange colored pencil; a third had passages marked with a fluorescent blue highlighter. I put the books in a box that Jim had found. I looked at a lot of others, some from Progress Publishers in Moscow, some from Foreign Languages Press in Beijing, and most from International Publishers in New York. As I did so, an idea occurred to me: I could make paintings based on the marked and annotated passages, which were simultaneously texts and images. This would be a way of making a more painterly object than the simple black on white of the Roger Casement paintings, and it would satisfy one of my requirements for the show by referring to the former use of the Blanco Projects building as a communist bookstore. I asked, "Do you have a lot of books with underlining or highlighting?"

"I suppose I do. Is that what interests you most?"

"Yeah."

"Okay, I'll box those up and take them over to your place. I was considering just throwing them out."

"I think I've got a use for them. You're helping me a lot, thanks."

About a week later, Jim dropped off ten boxes of books that he would otherwise have discarded. We hugged for the second time in the course of our friendship, and he said, "I'll see you around." It was an expression he always used, but in this case, it seemed unlikely that I would see him, except on special occasions, because he would be living an hour's drive away. The last time I had been to Pomona was when I found a ride to see his brother Pete's band perform at the Glass House. The venue occupied almost a whole city block in Pomona's midcentury-style downtown, a pedestrianized zone full of small stores and restaurants that attempted to defy the dominance of car culture and sprawl. The area was accessible by commuter train. I had a recurrent fantasy of renting a spacious studio in the area and taking Metrolink into Los Angeles for visits, but I never made any steps toward realizing it.

∞

Shortly before the opening of her exhibition, Frances called me and said, "I think I'm going to stay in LA. Carmen says she can help me find a cheap studio. I like it here, even if I'm not getting laid."

I asked, "Are you looking for an apartment, too?"

She answered, "Yes. Do you have any leads?"

"I can check with the manager of my building. The tenants in the other units usually don't last long. That is, if you don't mind being my neighbor."

"It would be fun."

I said, "I'll try to behave myself. I think the downstairs neighbors were disturbed by the noise my friend Daniel makes when I fist him. Or at least I hope so."

She said, "I won't mind, as long as you don't complain about *my* sex noises. By the way, has Gregorio emailed you?"

"I don't think so, why?"

She said, "He'll be in town for my opening."

"Fantastic."

"He wants to stay with you."

I laughed. "Okay."

She asked, "Can you come by the studio tomorrow? We need to move everything out so the show can get installed. Oh, and I need a place to stay, too."

I smiled and said, "The more the merrier."

After I got off the phone with Frances, I turned on my computer, and I saw a one line email from Gregorio: "I'm coming to see Frances's show. Can I stay with you?"

I responded, "Yes, of course, but I warn you, my place will be a mess."

The next day, Frances and I loaded most of our things into her van and brought them to my apartment. We left the finished paintings behind. Some went into storage and a dozen of them were hung on the walls of the gallery. My apartment became an interim storage space, with works in progress and art supplies strewn all over the living room. I caught the building manager as he was going out and introduced him to Frances. He told her that a unit had just opened up and needed to be cleaned before she could move in. He would try to do that as quickly as possible.

∞

On the day of Frances's opening, Gregorio's flight arrived late, and after renting a car, he didn't make it to my apartment until early evening. In the dying twilight, I saw the new Gregorio, much thinner and sporting a black goatee and a closely cropped military-style haircut. He wore a track suit and sneakers that made him look like a European thug. We hugged and I felt excited to be near to him. I wondered if we would have sex. He interrupted my fantasy by saying, "I thought a non-stop flight from Berlin would be easy, but LAX is a nightmare."

"As always. It's great to see you, finally."

"It's been years, and you never visited."

I looked down. "Sorry."

He said, "There's lots to talk about, but I don't want to miss Frances's opening. I have to take a shower and change my clothes." Fresh from the shower, Gregorio still looked exhausted, so I offered to drive his rental car to the gallery. I found a place to park a couple of blocks away from it. As we approached on foot, we saw valet parking attendants in front of the building. A throng of rich people dressed in expensive yet casual styles filled the space. Gregorio gasped. "What has Carmen done?"

I said, "It's a surprise even to me."

Inside the heat was oppressive, and we couldn't see any of the paintings properly. Somehow Paul spotted us in the crowd and shouted, "Look what the cat dragged in!" He approached and kissed Gregorio on both cheeks. "Child, you look good enough to eat. You must tell me your secret diet."

Over the din, Gregorio said, "It's simple. I don't eat as much as I used to. I don't really care for German food."

An elderly white woman turned to Gregorio and handed him an empty plastic cup. Her face, freshly paralyzed by Botox, shocked me, even though I had seen many people that night with similarly immobile faces. She asked, "Can you tell me where the rest room is?"

Paul pointed and said, "Back there at the end of the hall."

Gregorio frowned. "I bet the only Latinos she knows are the help. Welcome to Los Angeles."

Paul took the cup and said, "These people look so excited to discover a new neighborhood." He put his hand on Gregorio's shoulder and said, "You must visit during gallery hours and tell me all." Immediately afterward, he waved to a person across the room and shouted, "Darling!" He turned to us and said, "I must go. So much flesh to press."

I asked, "Where's Frances?" but before Paul could answer, he was gone. I said to Gregorio, "Let's try to find her in this madness." I took him by the hand and headed toward the sound of her laugh.

We heard a shriek. Frances shouted, "My love, you've brought my favorite portrait subject." We saw her in a dashing brown pinstripe suit, with hair somewhat less wild than usual, face flushed either from the heat or the champagne she had been drinking. "I haven't seen you since the turn of the century." She kissed Gregorio on the mouth.

"Congratulations."

Paul grabbed her by the elbow and nodded in the direction of someone nearby. With an apologetic look she said, "Thanks. Let's hang out soon."

We made our way to the front desk and managed to get two plastic cups of champagne. Carmen abruptly came up and handed us both small slips of paper with an address. She whispered, "For the dinner. Lovely to see you." I was about to explain that Gregorio was fading and we were unlikely to attend, but she took her leave as suddenly as she had appeared. We headed for the door.

Outside we sat on the window ledge, and Gregorio started to fall asleep as his jet lag caught up with him. Bernie and Jim ambled over to us. I said, "I didn't expect to see you two here."

Jim frowned and said, "Someone convinced me."

"I wanted to walk in and say, 'I love what you've done to the place,' but it was too crowded." Bernie had a tone of sadness in his voice.

I took the directions to the dinner out of my pocket and gave them to Bernie, saying, "In case you want a nice dinner."

He responded, "Some free meals are too expensive, but thank you."

I said, "I have to get this guy home. It's about 6:30 in the morning in Berlin."

I roused Gregorio. He made an indistinct greeting to my friends and said to Bernie, "Let's catch up soon." We walked the two blocks to the rental car, and I drove it to my street, where there was little parking available. We had to walk another block to the apartment, and I held Gregorio up, since most of the time his eyes were nearly closed. He sprawled on my bed fully clothed. I took his shoes off and arranged the covers as best I could. I got into bed with him and fell asleep.

∞

The next morning I heard Gregorio stirring very early. Because Frances was asleep on the couch and I'd forgotten to give him an extra key to the apartment, he had nowhere to go. When I woke up, he was lying on his side reading in the pale morning light.

I slipped into the kitchen to make some tea for Gregorio and me. I handed him a mug and he said, "Sorry, I've been up since four AM, which was lunchtime in Berlin. I'm starving."

"We can go out to eat as soon as I get dressed." The two of us got ready as best we could, trying not to disturb Frances. Just as we were about to leave, she woke up.

"It was a great dinner. We went to some place called the Pacific Dining Car," she said as she rubbed her eyes.

Gregorio said, "I'm really sorry we missed it. The jet lag was awful."

I said, "We're about to go out for breakfast. Do you want us to bring anything back for you?"

Frances said, "I think I'll make something here."

"Um, good luck. There really isn't any food in the kitchen."

"The bachelor has house guests. Maybe you should take him shopping, Gregorio."

He laughed and said, "Definitely. Get some more sleep, and we'll see you in a while."

As we walked down the hill to Don Felix, the closest restaurant, Gregorio said, "I miss the heat and light of California. I'm even nostalgic for August in Santa Clarita. This time of year it's overcast every day at home."

Over our breakfast, I asked, "How is Berlin?"

"I love some things about it—the museums, the music, the trains, and all those crazy bars."

"How's Winston?"

"He's conquering Europe as Andë Alia, art star. He misses you a lot. So do I."

I protested, "If I had any money, I'd come visit."

"Maybe Winston will give you a Christmas present. He's got plenty of money."

I shrugged. "I wouldn't say no. My job as a porn producer isn't very lucrative, and I'm too lazy to look for other work."

He said, "There are lots of art supplies around the apartment. Does that mean you've been making paintings?"

I smiled. "Most of that stuff is Frances's. She's waiting for her apartment to be cleaned, so we'll be three for a little while. I forgot to tell you. But yeah, I've started to paint. Carmen is giving me a show at Blanco Projects in a few months. I have lots to do before then."

He said, "Winston would be amused."

I asked, "Do you think you can stay until my exhibition opens?"

"When is that?"

"Some time in May."

He shook his head. "I can't be away that long. Besides, I don't want to impose on you or deal with my parents for months."

"How long can you stay in New Mexico without going nuts?"

"Well, I lived there for twenty years, but that was before I moved away and got a life. I've changed."

I said, "You look great, never better."

"Thanks."

I asked, "Are *you* making any art?"

"I am now. I didn't at first. It doesn't get shown, but I don't really care. I do what I enjoy. We have so much space that I've started making installations. I photograph them, then take them down. When I see the pressure Winston is under to make art for the market, I feel free."

"Our teachers would be proud. Of all of us, you turned out to be the most radical."

After we finished our breakfast, he drove us to a supermarket and bought groceries. We returned to find Frances fully dressed. He made some eggs, toast, and coffee for her, and we relaxed in the living room. Gregorio apologized, "I wish I'd been able to stay awake for the whole party. Congratulations again."

"Carmen really pulled something off." Frances reached for her digital camera. She found a picture that made her laugh and showed it to us: Paul in a wig, passed out on a toilet in a bar. "We did karaoke at one in the morning. Paul sang 'Total Eclipse of the Heart' and projectile vomited all over Brad."

Gregorio, who wasn't aware of the latest developments, asked, "You mean the Brad we know from school?"

I said, "Yes, he's back here after living in New York. He's in real estate now. And he married Carmen."

The expression on Gregorio's face looked like a combination of nausea and perverse glee. He asked, "How is that even possible?"

Frances rolled her eyes and said, "True love triumphs over all. I'm getting a solo show out of it, so I'm not complaining."

"Does Paul have to work today?" I asked. Frances nodded. "We should visit him. Besides, nobody was able to get a good look at your show last night."

We took the rental car back to Blanco Projects and found Paul at the front desk looking pale and sweaty. His eyes had the appearance of fried eggs swimming in a pool of blood. Frances brought him a bottle of mineral water and some crackers, in case he needed to put something bland in his stomach. He said, "Thank you. Your mother is feeling a bit unwell, so please refrain from making any loud noises or...." He couldn't continue and placed his face in his hands.

We walked around the gallery silently and gazed at the paintings. They seemed to shimmer in the sun coming through the front windows. Their color schemes were lurid, yet there was something austere about them in their directness. The titles were image captions recognizable to anyone familiar with recent news stories. My favorite painting, the portrait of the man at Abu Ghraib, hung alone on the wall behind Paul's desk. I stood in front of it for a long time, while Frances and Gregorio whispered about a painting depicting the aftermath of a car bomb. The phone rang, and Paul roused himself to answer pertly, "Blanco Projects." After a brief conversation, he came over to me and said, "We have a meeting with a collector in ten minutes."

I said, "I suppose you'd like me to escort the artist from the premises so she doesn't queer the deal."

Paul took a sip of mineral water from a plastic cup and said, "Exactly."

As we walked away from the building, we ran into Carmen, who looked as though nothing had happened the night before. She said to me, "You were missed."

"I apologize. Gregorio was passing out."

"It's wonderful that he came to the opening. And believe me, the end of the night wasn't pretty." She looked at her watch and said, "I must go, important client to see."

ELEVEN

One day when Gregorio and I were alone, I grabbed him and kissed him passionately. He didn't resist. We started to undress and made our way to the bed. We continued making out. I was very pleased to see Gregorio's naked, toned body, and I felt lucky that the interest was mutual. The only problem was that my penis wouldn't cooperate. It had always seemed to have a mind of its own, and the barely noticeable swelling Gregorio inspired was a dire embarrassment. I asked myself, Will he think he's to blame? Do I believe deep down that I'm about to commit incest? Am I intimidated by the many sexual experiences Gregorio must be having with the men of Berlin? Or am I just getting old? These questions running through my mind only made the situation worse. We stopped kissing, flopped on the bed next to each other, and I emitted a heavy sigh. I turned to Gregorio and said, "I'm sorry."

He said, "It happens to everyone sometimes." Then, in a tentative whisper, he said, "You know, fisting is way more normal in Berlin than it is here."

I perked up immediately and asked, "Have you been fisted?"

He propped himself up in bed and said, "I've done a lot of things I never did when we were in school."

All I could think to say in response was "good to know," but still embarrassed by my inability to perform, I hesitated to take Gregorio up on his implied offer.

He took the matter in hand and said, "We should go to Circus of Books." We got dressed and drove there. He bought a shower shot, an attachment that diverted water from the shower head with the flick of a switch and sent it down a tube that went up an ass in need of cleaning out. It wasn't cheap—my chief reason for never having bought one—and I was grateful that Gregorio was paying, possibly with Winston's money. He also bought good powdered lube, a new blender bottle, and strong European poppers.

When we returned home, I mixed up a batch of lube while Gregorio occupied himself in the shower. I put all but one bottle of poppers in the freezer and filed my nails quickly. Once he was done in the bathroom, he came into the bedroom wearing nothing but a towel. We started kissing, and I stripped as quickly as possible. He lay down on his back, and I grabbed the lube. He lifted his legs. I massaged my cock and stuffed it into his ass to try to fuck him, but that didn't work at all. Rather than using a bogus line like, "This has never happened before," or attempting some clumsy explanation that would have destroyed the mood, I said, "Flip over."

"Okay," he said, and immediately did so. I spread lube on my right hand and started to work my fingers into his ass. In a few minutes I had four fingers and a thumb inside him. He tapped the bed, a signal I took to mean "stop." He said, "I'm not used to such a big hand," and inhaled from the bottle of poppers. I decided to try my non-dominant hand, which was slightly smaller, though not as coordinated. I covered it with lube, and as the poppers kicked in, I worked four fingers and the thumb of my left hand somewhat deeper into his ass. I felt his rectum expand and noticed that there would be a place for my fingers to go, but the widest part of my hand still wouldn't pass through his outer sphincter. I bent my fingers while inside him, and he groaned. I nearly made a fist, clenching and unclenching it very slightly. His eyes rolled up in his head and he let out a louder groan. My hand hadn't gone far, but that didn't matter. He was having a wonderful time. I pulled my hand out in one slow, smooth motion. The next moment he began shaking. A full-body orgasm came in waves. After the last wave, he said, "I think I'm done. Hold me." We lay together on the bed in silence for a while.

I got up to go to the bathroom, and when I returned, I asked, "Did you enjoy yourself?"

He laughed and responded, "You're silly. Of course I did. You're so good with your hands that I completely forgot about cock while you were playing with my ass."

"That's a relief." I sat on the bed next to him. "I have a skill to fall back on when I can't get it up."

He said, "You think too much about performance anyway. Working in the porn industry has fucked you up. All those guys in videos take ED meds, and some of them inject stuff into their cocks."

I asked, "Have you seen that?"

"I've seen a lot of things in Berlin, and tried most of them." He looked me in the eye and said, "There's a lot of posing. It's all play acting. None of it matters. What matters is intimacy, and you don't need a hard cock for that."

I paused and said, "I don't believe in gods or karma or anything like that, but I wonder if this is a lesson for me. I spent decades playing the 'selfish top,' and no one ever complained. I was a jerk to some of my partners. Maybe now I'm making up for things I didn't do in the past."

"Hey, if this is a *mea culpa*, I'm okay with that. Whatever you need to think, as long as you keep giving me those orgasms."

I asked, "Am I becoming a lesbian?"

He said, "I don't know. When you were doing whatever the hell you did inside me, I thought to myself, This is the end of phallocentric sex."

We both laughed. I couldn't think of a response to that, so we held each other quietly and fell sound asleep.

The next morning, I woke up alone. Once again, Gregorio had gotten up early. He was talking to his parents on the phone when I came into the living room. After hanging up, Gregorio said that he could stay with me until he left to visit his family for Thanksgiving. He would spend a few days in Truth or Consequences, return his rental car, then drive back to Los Angeles in the old Toyota truck that his parents had been storing in their garage.

∞

I had never lived with anyone since college, and I felt as though we were experimenting with what that would be like. It was generally quite pleasant for me, and Gregorio enjoyed it, too. He prepared a lot of Mexican food, which he had been missing for years. Berlin was hopeless, because it was impossible to get the ingredients available in Mexico or the American Southwest, and New Mexico wasn't much better, because outside the big cities, the standard of cuisine was poor. He found everything he needed within a few blocks of my apartment, buying fresh meats and vegetables, a *comal* for heating up tortillas and a *molcajete* for grinding the ingredients of *moles*. He even went to a Oaxacan neighborhood to the south and west to find the aromatic ingredients of *mole negro*, one of the most delicious meals we shared, and probably the most labor intensive. When he cooked in Berlin, he usually made Middle Eastern food, and occasionally Albanian recipes that Winston requested. I had never been able to make anything more than simple dishes, and I tried to learn from him, but it was clear that he was the one who had real talent as a cook. I always did the dishes. Our days often consisted of planning meals, cooking, and eating them. Sometimes we invited Frances, who had cooked for us often when we were students. Predictably, Gregorio started to gain weight. This annoyed him—I didn't really care one way or the other—but he was happy enough with me that he rarely complained. Occasionally, he fasted, which had the added benefit of making fisting easier. He told me one day that he was getting addicted to the feeling of my hands inside him. I was surprised by how quickly I was becoming domesticated.

∞

Frances came to visit me one day while Gregorio was out shopping. She said, "I've finally got a decent mattress in my new place. Now I can sleep through the night."

I asked, "Will you send for the stuff you have in storage in Brooklyn?"

"I don't know. That depends on a lot of things, like how my show sells and what happens with job applications back east."

"Well, it's nice to have you here for now. It's tough meeting people outside of school. Even working at the video store was better in that way."

"I guess I'm lucky. I'm pretty social, and when I was living in New York, I did the gallery rounds every Saturday. Here it's almost inevitable that you live in isolation. It helps for getting work done, but there's more to life than that." She asked, "How are things going between you and Gregorio?"

I said, "It's been fun."

"Details, please."

I blushed and said, "Um, he likes ass play, which came as a surprise. When he leaves, it'll be lonely."

"He really loves you."

"I know, and I love him." I said sheepishly, "That's what makes it so difficult, you know, sexually. I can't get an erection with him. Somehow all that emotion gets in the way of me pounding his ass. My hand makes up for what my cock can't do, though."

She said, "He hasn't complained to me. You must have skills."

"I admit that I've been distracted a bit by Temo. Until I know what's going on with him, I can't commit to anything with Gregorio."

She frowned and asked, "What's that guy ever done for you?"

I said, "I don't think I can ever explain what I saw in him, I mean, what I see in him." I paused. "The guy has no limits. He's a toy I can do anything I want with, including smashing it against the wall. Intellectually, I know that this isn't exactly compatible with a loving relationship, but I can't resist. The guy's a mess, and even on his good days, he's a prick. Maybe if I talk to him again, I'll understand why he's no good for me."

Frances looked at me intently and asked, "What is it about you gay guys, always pining after men who are just trying to hurt you?" Realizing she'd get no answer to her question, she said, "Be good to Gregorio. Things are not great with Winston right now. He's considering moving back to California."

I was surprised. "He hasn't said anything like that to me."

"Well, he wouldn't, would he? Try to behave yourself. Gregorio's a treasure."

∞

Over the weeks we spent together, Gregorio talked to me about his relationship. From the beginning, Winston had occupied himself almost exclusively with painting and rarely thought about domestic matters. When he arrived in Berlin, he took over a building near Ostkreuz, a neighborhood in the East that I had never heard of. He did little to fix the place. It was up to Gregorio to plan and execute renovations, to decorate and furnish the interiors, and to cook and clean. He didn't especially resent this role, but it left little time for making his own art at first. Winston seemed indifferent to creature comforts—Gregorio thought he would have made a good monk—and never questioned any improvements made to the building unless they had a direct effect on his studio. He painted in a large attic space on the fourth floor, which had the best light. Winston hadn't even bothered to figure out how to heat his studio properly, and when Gregorio arrived in Berlin during the winter, he saw his lover's breath in the cold as he painted. It was a difficult transition, but little by little, the two of them had made the building (and their relationship) livable. After the beauty of rural New Mexico and the desert sprawl of Southern California, the cold gray austerity of Berlin came as a shock. Gregorio initially hated the city, but over the years had gotten used to the particular kind of alienation its residents endured. He told me that he had few interactions with Germans outside of official contexts or chance encounters in the street. His good friends were mostly expatriates. In order to stay in the country legally, he needed to learn German, but among their circle of acquaintances, he and Winston usually spoke English.

Through Winston, Gregorio had seen what was necessary to maintain a career in the international art industry, and realized that he had little appetite or aptitude for maneuvering in the field. Curators, gallerists, collectors, and miscellaneous others visited Winston's studio. They rarely acknowledged Gregorio's existence. With very few exceptions, he found them to be rude and arrogant. If this is what Europe's cultural elite is like, he thought, their politicians must be real monsters. While art industry operators tended to socialize only among themselves, Winston and Gregorio preferred to befriend non-artists. This gave them a wider view of the world and kept them from becoming petty and parochial. When it came to painting, though, Winston could be monomaniacal. Gregorio said, "Sometimes he reminds me of that awful guy who visited our studios at school. What was his name?"

"Jack Goldstein?"

"Yes. Winston isn't as bitter, but he can get very angry, and his ambitions are about as big as Jack's were." He asked, "Whatever happened to him?"

I looked down and said, "He killed himself a couple of years ago. Apparently, there were a lot of suicide attempts, always with pills, so he could be taken to the hospital and revived. The last time, he hanged himself."

"Terrible. He was so smart, but he was his own worst enemy. I mean, who could love someone so unpleasant?"

I asked, "Winston doesn't get that way, does he?"

"No, but there's an intensity that's hard to be around sometimes. I'm used to it, but superficial people avoid him."

"That's a shame. Or maybe not. He's found a way to repel anyone who isn't serious."

He said, "Well, I have a decent social life. You need one in a place where the winters are so long. But Winston suffers. He curses your decision to stay in Los Angeles."

"That's odd. I never hear from him."

"He's too busy painting, and he's insecure about his English." Gregorio went on to talk about the social scene in Berlin, which he described as an island of lost souls, populated by young people more interested in the line at Berghain than the problems of their art. They often nursed drug habits and lived off unseen resources. In a city where the unemployment rate hovered at thirty percent, people did what they could to earn money, unless they didn't have to. The background noise of all their fake crises was difficult to tune out, but Winston had an unerring instinct in determining who was real and who was a fraud, who was useful to him and who was a time waster.

I asked what he did for a living and how he handled immigration. He gave me vague, dissembling answers, and I chose not to pry. If Gregorio didn't entirely live off his lover, then at least their relationship made everything easier. In the recent past, Gregorio began protesting that he was being exploited in a situation that amounted to domestic servitude. To placate him, Winston found a housekeeper who would clean and occasionally help with the shopping and cooking.

Winston employed several assistants, and over the years, Gregorio had noticed a pattern in the workers he chose to hire. In the office, he tended to prefer hyper-competent, if slightly neurotic, German women. Until the most recent one, they never lasted long, because they inevitably had ambitions beyond being studio managers. As assistants, he preferred young proletarian men from Southern Europe. Some of them were remarkably attractive, looking as innocent as young deer once they dropped the macho posturing that was expected of them in daily life. Occasionally they modeled for Winston. Gregorio imagined that his lover also had sex with them, but he didn't ask any questions, especially since he had cultivated his own outside interests. The gym where he worked out was very cruisy, and after he dropped the extra weight that he had carried around since adolescence, he was popular there. He tended to hook up with German men who often took him for a Muslim, because he was dark-skinned and circumcised. If and when he spoke, they found out he was American. Sometimes that worked out well, and sometimes not. He rarely approached Turkish men at the gym, because they kept to themselves, but he was fascinated by them. Many had no privacy at home and needed a post-workout wank to release their tension. He told me that some wore brief black bathing suits in the shower, even when they masturbated in the hot steamy water. After he had seen this happen a few times, he worked up the courage to ask one of the Turks why they never took off their Speedos and why these swimsuits were always black. The youth responded, "This way, Allah cannot see what we are doing."

∞

Shortly before he left to visit his parents, Gregorio confided that he and Winston were in a period of transition. The equilibrium of their relationship had been disturbed by a man named Elend. He hadn't become a third partner in their relationship yet, but that was an unspoken possibility, and he spent most of his free hours with them. He was born in the Kurdish region of Iraq and had come to Germany as a refugee when he was young. His parents had both died of cancer within a few years of their arrival, the delayed result of chemical weapons attacks. Elend was all alone in the world, and there was a profound sadness in him. Like Gregorio, he preferred white guys, but his attempts at dating them went nowhere. Elend spoke Kurdish and Arabic as a child, and learned to speak his third language, German, perfectly. He quickly discovered that in German his name meant "misery." In Berlin everyone called him El.

El was trained as a scientist and collaborated on research with a team of psychologists in Vienna. Their work concerned the sense of smell. Gregorio found what little he understood of it interesting. He looked through the pictures in his digital camera. I caught glimpses of nudes that were possibly of El, but Gregorio didn't acknowledge this and apologized for having no portrait of him. I said, "It looks like you're having fun."

"He's great." Gregorio put down the camera and said, "You know, I want to apologize for being such a jealous little bitch to you when we were in school. I didn't ever have a boyfriend before Winston, and I thought you wanted to steal him from me. I was really insecure. Since I lost all that weight, I get more attention from guys, and it's boosted my confidence. And being with El and Winston at the same time has helped me get beyond the jealousy thing. I can't put it into words very well, but I feel like we're building a new kind of life for ourselves. It's taken a long time to see beyond the traditional ideas about family and marriage and monogamy that I grew up with. I think they killed my grandpa, and they don't seem to be doing my father any good, either. Anyway, El has been a great influence on me, on us. He's so unselfish and sweet. Even Winston is charmed by him, and he's no pushover."

"I suppose I'll meet him if I come to Berlin."

"*When* you come to Berlin. You're always welcome." He looked as though he might cry and said, "We miss you a lot."

TWELVE

During a visit to the gallery, I thought I saw Temo out of the corner of my eye, stopping momentarily to peek inside. The man was his height, but heavier and somewhat disheveled. I interrupted talking to Paul at the front desk to bolt out and see if it really was Temo. He disappeared before I could catch another glimpse of him.

After I came back in, Paul asked, "Darling, is it true love?"

I tried to conjure up exactly the right version of Temo's story to tell Paul, but all I could do was mutter, "I know that guy from before."

"Before what, his lobotomy?"

I said, "That's not funny."

"It wasn't meant to be. If you want your mother's advice, I'd stay away from that creature. She's a right nutter."

I asked, "Do you actually know her, I mean, him?"

"Not in the biblical sense, but he was a client of mine in the recent past." I was surprised to hear such a thing, if indeed it was true. I asked Paul to join me at HMS Bounty after work so I could hear more, but he made an excuse and I didn't insist.

As soon as I got back home, I left a message for Moira: "I saw Temo, at least I think it was him, at the gallery today. Paul knows him, how well I can't say. I'd never seen the two of them together, so I didn't think to ask about Temo earlier. I'll call you when I find out more." I took a breath, and the answering machine cut off.

Moira called the next afternoon, the day I expected Gregorio to return from visiting his parents. I told her what little I had gathered about Temo. She asked, "Is he as handsome as he was?"

"I didn't see his face well. I recognized him right away, but he looks a bit bloated."

"That's a shame."

"I'm hoping Paul will divulge what he knows once I get him to sit down with me outside the gallery. At work, he's all business." I asked, "How is family life?"

Moira sighed. "Better now. Being a stay-at-home dad didn't suit Miguel, and everyone he knew made fun of him for letting his wife support the family. His mother helped for a while, but we really needed someone to look after Flor full time. We found a local woman, Berta." She paused and continued, "She has a tragic story. Berta and her husband José left for the big city, Guadalajara, where he had family. Things turned out terribly. The only work either of them could find was very shady. José's relatives made their money from the drug trade. He started working in a factory handling chemicals. He was paid well, but he started feeling ill within a month. The place was a giant factory manufacturing methamphetamine."

"There's a lot of that in Mexico, isn't there?"

She said, "Has been for a long time, but this is something new. Amateurs making meth from ephedrine is a thing of the past. This chemical stuff can be produced on an industrial scale. It's toxic and very cheap." She exhaled and continued, "José died of liver failure. His family didn't seem to care. Maybe they were sampling too much of the product. They left Berta to fend for herself, and she had no choice but to come back to Chiapas."

"That's brutal."

"Yeah." She took a moment to collect her thoughts. "The old cartels don't have a lot to do with this new wave. It's each man for himself, independent producers and distributors in competition with each other, struggling to make a profit—the capitalist way. In San Cristóbal, we're so remote that most trends pass us by, but even here, we can tell there's a change happening. God have mercy on us. And you, too. I'm sure shipments of cheap meth are heading straight for Los Angeles."

I heard a key in the front door. Gregorio was returning from his Thanksgiving in Truth or Consequences. I put the phone down, kissed him, and asked if he wanted to talk to Moira. He raised his voice and said, "Hello," then excused himself to go to the bathroom.

I said, "I'd better say goodbye. I'll call when I get to the bottom of the Temo story, but I bet it's a bottomless pit."

She laughed and said, "Take care of yourself and Gregorio."

He came out of the bathroom and asked, "What were you and Moira talking about?"

Without thinking, I said, "Temo. Remember him?"

"*That* guy," he said with a tone of disgust indicating that he wanted to hear no more about the man.

Not taking the hint, I said, "He's still alive and in Los Angeles."

With contempt and anger in his eyes, Gregorio said, "If you want me to stay here any longer, don't say another word." He walked out the door to unload his truck.

I called after him, "Do you want any help?"

"Just leave me alone, okay?"

Once a decent interval of time had passed, I asked, "How is your family?"

He said, "My mom is the same as ever. My sister is moving to Washington, DC. Santa Fe wasn't big enough for her." He laughed to himself. "I think my dad is in love with his best friend. Mom has noticed."

"I guess we know where you got it from, then."

He shook his head. "No, my mother's father was the gay one. After he left grandma, he moved to LA. No one talks about what he did there. He didn't live very long. No family to take care of him. I'm not even sure where he's buried."

I said, "I'm sorry I brought it up."

As tears welled up in his eyes, he said, "You don't realize how important being part of a family is, even if they totally suffocate you."

At that point, it occurred to me that I had forgotten to call my mother on Thanksgiving, or to celebrate the holiday myself. I said, "I've been living alone so long that I don't think much about things like that anymore."

"Maybe you should." Gregorio said this with a dejected look in his eye. I went over to him and embraced him tightly. As tears streamed down his cheeks, he said, "I missed you in New Mexico. I wish you'd come with me."

"I would have liked that. We could have kept your parents awake while I fisted you." I let out an evil laugh.

"On second thought, it's better you didn't. They have enough trouble understanding my Albanian partner."

Gregorio stayed with me for three more weeks, and I felt as close to him as I had when we were in school, the days of listening to music and taking road trips to Ventura for thrift store shopping. I asked him, "Do you still collect records?"

"Not the way I used to. I play a lot of music, but it's usually from mp3s." I looked at him with astonishment. "I know, I know, but I don't want to screw up my vintage vinyl or my turntable with the mess I make in the studio. And I've expanded my horizons. Winston and El love Romantic music, and it's rubbed off on me. We saw *The Pearl Fishers* by Bizet at the opera, and I was hooked."

"That's great. There's no reason to be stuck in early 1980s Manchester. It's not like The Smiths are releasing any new records."

Gregorio asked, "Do you think you can visit us?"

"I want to. I'll see what I can arrange."

"I've got to get back for Christmas. Winston is a Muslim, or was, but he's got this sentimental attachment to Christian holidays. I have to say, the Germans do Christmas well. No tamales, but lots of decorations to compensate for endless cloudy skies and sunset at three in the afternoon."

I smiled. "It sounds like you've made a whole new life there."

"Yeah, who would have thought?"

∞

Practically the moment he finished teaching at USC, Bernie left town, and I didn't hear from him for a while. I assumed that he had made his way to New York and found a place to live there. I had almost resigned myself to hearing no more from him when I received an email:

> The car died in St. Paul, so I'm stuck at the home of my half sister for the foreseeable future. I don't know if I ever told you about her. She went unmentioned by the rest of my ultra-Catholic family, because my father had her with another woman, out of wedlock. I only found her because of a hint dropped by my aunt Lucille. There's no telling what demons torment this old lady, but finally she saw fit to reveal something about a "secret" sister in Minnesota. And now here I am. It's been good to connect with her, even if we don't have much in common. Her husband took an instant dislike to me and complains about the multiple boxes I'm storing in the garage. My sister pointed out that I don't have a permanent address to forward them to, and he grumbled. I take a little enjoyment (one of the few pleasures here) in annoying him.

I wrote back and told him that for what it was worth, I sympathized with his plight. I had been carless for many years, and I could only leave Southern California if I flew away. I mentioned that Gregorio promised to leave me the truck he had used in grad school when he returned to Berlin. Later that day Bernie responded, "Outside of cities on the East Coast or Chicago or maybe Los Angeles, getting around without driving yourself becomes difficult. This should be an adventure." He had little to say about his current surroundings, aside from this: "Minneapolis-St. Paul is Midwestern Deluxe, but its economy isn't grotted out like Indiana, Michigan, and Ohio—the economic base has been agriculture and transportation—it's kind of dark and staid, but it doesn't have the apocalyptic charms of a place like Detroit."

∞

Gregorio stayed with me until a few days before Christmas. His reaction to the news about Temo discouraged me from investigating further until I was alone. I wanted to have a conversation with Paul, but the opportunity for it didn't arise. I limited myself to sending Temo another email, which probably remained unread. Gregorio gave me the key to his old truck, but I didn't have a chance to use it. It disappeared from my street almost immediately after his departure for Berlin. I later learned that Toyota trucks, a favorite of the small businesses that do yard work in fancy neighborhoods, were the most commonly stolen vehicles in Los Angeles.

THIRTEEN

During the season of exhibitions that followed Frances's, Blanco Projects became phenomenally successful. Carmen established her profile as a young gallerist showing highly collectible art. She reached this goal so quickly by specializing in what I called "dollhouse art." The works she sold looked to me like decorations in Malibu Barbie's house: paintings complementing a plastic décor, not fussy or overly concerned with technique, but colorful, bold, and graspable in an instant, as though originals the size of a postage stamp had been greatly enlarged. These works would fit perfectly in the living room of a West Side McMansion, and if critical or curatorial consensus elevated them to a level above interior design, they could hold their own on the wall of almost any museum. They presented nothing potentially disturbing or idiosyncratic that would hinder their circulation in the market. Seen as a group, the paintings in any given exhibition were virtually uniform, like the interchangeable parts used on an assembly line. This type of painting required the artist to be less a painter than a designer, delegating the execution of details to assistants. The mode of work left artists free to socialize with cultural gatekeepers who could help their careers and collectors belonging to the class they wished to join. Dollhouse art was therefore the product not only of a specific management style, but of certain social aspirations. The wealth of collectors grew and grew, but somehow they still felt a lack. They never saw the sweatshops where workers made their consumer goods, and they needed to be reminded of the material world, albeit gently. In the art they collected, no reminders of poor people and their unsightly dwellings or the global south and its problems or an environmental catastrophe in the making threatened their peace of mind. Pretty colors and shapes provided a kind of palliative care as their consciences died.

Not every artist working with Blanco Projects fit this eminently marketable profile. Frances had banished herself from the ranks of dollhouse artists by making paintings that referred to carnage on the other side of the world, though rehabilitation in the future remained a possibility. I was disqualified from being a dollhouse artist, because many of the texts that inspired my latest series came from a communist bookstore. Collectors might either dismiss them as irrelevant or interpret them as insults. Andy Warhol, the god of the contemporary art market, often did what commercial artists called "kidding the product"—letting spectators in on a joke and making them feel intelligent—but he never came close to advocating the overthrow of the capitalist system. I had no illusions about my work as a radical critique; instead I saw myself in the role of irritant.

Carmen pursued the goal of becoming the most important gallerist of her generation in Los Angeles, and improbably, had taken Brad along for the ride. I came to think of Carmen and Brad as a two-headed monster with complementary agendas, art and real estate, working in concert. Their business affairs had already outgrown the former Libros Revolución space, which the best potential clients were reluctant to visit, as the two of them learned. The neighborhood was too full of immigrants, too run down and druggy, and it wasn't near a freeway or other shopping opportunities.

Carmen planned to move the gallery after my exhibition closed. She decided to locate it near where major collectors lived. She had also become tired of downtown and wished to live as close as possible to Maxfield's, the boutique where she bought new Margiela garments to expand her impressive (and in her profession, indispensable) wardrobe. West Hollywood might also provide convenient outlets for any sexual desires that Brad still harbored under all his preppy, buttoned-down flab.

The cost of renting the Libros Revolución/Blanco Projects building on Eighth Street would have been too much for me to afford—Carmen had been supportive, but she didn't believe in charity—and since I was unable to take the place as a studio, it would languish unused. Owning a vacant building must have been useful as a tax write-off for Carmen and Brad. Other artists in her stable preferred to maintain studios in Vernon, the small independent city southeast of downtown that smelled like slaughterhouses and rendering plants. I felt an intense sadness at the thought of a place where I spent much of my young adulthood being abandoned. It had been Libros Revolución for decades, and an art gallery for about a year. Soon it would be nothing.

∞

Paul made the most startling transformation among my friends. He became so skilled at playing the professional gallerina that this had become the main part of his personality. The raconteur, the embittered writer, the alcoholic, the slut—these roles had been carefully tucked away, and if they emerged, it was no longer in my presence. He was unfailingly polite and competent, but occasionally, he would show a hint of his wicked former self, especially when Brad was the topic of conversation. Immediately after such a slip, he would return to directing the quotidian affairs of the gallery.

Frances was also reckoning with changes. She acquitted herself well in job interviews, with the result that in the next academic year, she would be an assistant professor of painting at Rutgers University. She found an apartment in Washington Heights, which was more convenient for her commute to New Jersey than Brooklyn. She loaded up her van, moved back to the East Coast, and in short order became the New Yorker she had formerly been. From then on, I would probably see her once a year, if that.

I stayed in my rent-controlled apartment while the city of Los Angeles changed around me. Waves of young people arrived, tried their luck, then moved on, either to fancier parts of town, to suburbs with "better schools" (shorthand concealing racist sentiments), or in the least desirable outcome, back to their parents' basements. I sometimes heard rumors about the attractions of other cities like Portland or Austin, either of which would have been a plausible staging ground for giving up the last of my artistic ambitions in a dignified manner, but the only bohemia I troubled myself to think about was the one in Los Angeles, even though the sort of person I cared to know seemed rarer all the time there. Fancier makes of cars with out-of-state license plates appeared on my street, and the length of stay in my neighborhood (still without a homeowners' association to give it a name) became briefer. The new arrivals either discovered that their hopes and dreams would come true or traded them for more realistic plans. The most deluded ended up destroying themselves, but these people, unaware that my neighborhood even existed, tended to congregate in Hollywood. The sidewalks of Echo Park and Silverlake became crowded with flocks of strollers containing blue-eyed IVF babies, pushed by their nannies, who invariably had no genetic defects preventing their eyes from producing melanin. Stores selling simple, practical goods with low profit margins were replaced by shops offering things like children's athletic shoes, designer eyewear, and artisanal cupcakes. I sometimes had the feeling that my days in the city were numbered, but I held my ground nonetheless. Los Angeles had lost the ability to scare rich white people away, the one quality that had been essential to sustaining an artistic bohemia. During the early 1990s, no self-respecting bourgeois would have dared to raise a child on my side of town, but after a lull in the waves of destructive earthquakes and riots, a feature article in *Vogue* declaring Silverlake the finest neighborhood in the United States, and an influx of thinly disguised apartheid schools, the game was over. Most neighborhoods I passed through were now places only the rich could afford, except Westlake, perennially the domain of immigrants and the urban poor.

∞

My job as a gay porn producer continued to provide income, but not stimulation, either of an intellectual or a sexual variety. After a year of producing compilations, it became clear that I would soon run out of source videos. The HIS library contained approximately one hundred fifty titles, and I used the material at a rate of sixteen hours per month. I was told I could re-use scenes for new comps, so I recycled the same material in different combinations until VCA reached a decision about what to do next. Their lawyers were in the process of verifying that the company had access to the videos of Planet Group, a consortium of independent producers who sold the VHS distribution rights of their videos to VCA. If the company had the DVD rights as well, the number of potential sources for compilations would increase to more than seven hundred fifty.

After VCA's rights to Planet Group titles were confirmed, I had a look at this expanded library of gay porn. The vast majority of the videos were shot in the early 1990s. The chief interest of the Planet Group titles was not aesthetic but historical or sociological: for the first time, VCA was distributing a large number of videos featuring men of color. Around the same time that identity politics was becoming prominent in the upper reaches of American culture, the porn industry was cashing in on the trend.

The Planet Group producers made porn on an extreme economy of means. It was common to see a video that had been shot entirely inside one apartment in the San Fernando Valley or on a single studio set. As I watched dozens of these videos, I began to recognize the same cottage cheese ceilings and vertical blinds or the same artificial flowers and Patrick Nagel prints over and over.

VCA was a large company with substantial assets and costly overhead. Even while it was profitable, it suffered periodic minor crises that affected its ability to adapt to new conditions in the market. It was ripe for a take-over, and eventually it was bought out. The new boss was a celebrity in his own right: Larry Flynt. Soon after Larry Flynt Publications acquired VCA, the lay offs began. Eventually, almost all of the people I knew personally at the company found work elsewhere. For some reason, perhaps because no one else at the company wanted to handle gay material, I was allowed to continue working in the same way for the same rate of pay. I received paychecks in the mail; the only difference was the Hustler logo with a silhouette of a naked woman that appeared on the envelopes. I never went to the prominent building Flynt owned on Wilshire Boulevard in Beverly Hills, and I never met the man who signed the checks.

The takeover created opportunities in production, at least for the people lucky enough to stick around. Hustler continued to be the main brand of the company, but there were plans to make new gay videos under a revived HIS imprint. I was asked to present a proposal for a gay porn movie that I could direct, and I went to work writing a scenario.

∞

On a gay-themed website, I found a page called "Mansfield, Ohio Tearoom Busts." The video file uploaded there was a degraded copy of something called *Camera Surveillance*. Produced by the Mansfield Police and intended as an instructional film, *Camera Surveillance* demonstrated how the department had set up a sting operation in a men's rest room under the central square of the city. The voice-over narration, as illiterate and hateful a text as I had ever heard committed to film, provided abundant evidence of law enforcement's unenlightened attitudes. While I knew that these attitudes existed, in *Camera Surveillance* I saw them not only acknowledged as official policy, but held up as a standard for other police forces to imitate.

Over the course of three weeks during the summer of 1962, Mansfield Police officers hid in a closet and from behind a two-way mirror filmed men as they used a public rest room for having sex. The film, entered as evidence in court, led to the conviction of dozens of men on charges of sodomy, which at that time carried a mandatory minimum sentence of one year in the state penitentiary.

I decided to make a fictional adaptation of the Mansfield cases. I envisioned two policemen behind a mirror watching other men having sex. After a while, the sight of all this tearoom action would be too much for the officers hiding in the closet, and the cameraman would plead with his partner to give him a blow job. One thing would lead to another, and soon the two would forget themselves and start having loud, hot sex. Patrons of the men's room would hear the commotion from behind the two-way mirror and break into the policemen's hiding place. They would question the officers about what was going on, and in a rage, would teach them a lesson by gang raping them. More horny men would arrive on the scene, and the city's public facilities would be transformed into an orgy room. I wrote this story with enthusiasm, and decided to call the video *Fuck the Police*.

I discussed my scenario with Malachi Ecks, a director who was my last acquaintance still working for Flynt. He helped me plan a budget and offered to present my proposal to the managers at the company. As I worked on the budget, it became obvious that the production of *Fuck the Police* would be complex, involving the building of sets, the blocking and filming of complicated action and the coordination of a large cast for the orgy scene. The budget that Hustler Video was willing to devote to a gay production was paltry, around $5000. I later found out that a typical budget for one of Hustler's straight productions was $25,000. I took this as an indication that the company no longer had any real commitment to producing new all-male videos. Under such budgetary constraints, a video that required more than a weekend of shooting was out of the question. The pay for crew members would be minimal, and certainly not adequate for the long days necessary to finish the scenes as written. I didn't want to exploit the friends and acquaintances I could convince to work on the project. There simply wasn't enough time or money to realize *Fuck the Police* as I wished, and I abandoned the project. My career as a porn director was over before it began.

FOURTEEN

After the fiasco of *Fuck the Police*, I concentrated on looking through the books that Jim had given me and choosing which sections of text seemed most promising. Jim's collection, while mostly devoted to Marxism, contained non-fiction books on other topics as well as some fiction. There were delightful finds, including a yellowed copy of Thomas Mann's *Death in Venice* with a single word underlined in pen: "fatuously." I found a copy of *Animal Farm* full of pink highlighting and decorated with animals drawn in blue ballpoint pen, but I found no text that stood on its own out of context. I also found compelling excerpts of text with only subtle markings that would have had little impact when enlarged. I was obstinately literal-minded, and I didn't fake the highlighting as I pleased. I wanted to use the material as found. I called the series "Amended by Hand," and I set to work transforming my choices into paintings. Each text would be isolated on a plain background the color of the page from which it came, without any of the surrounding details—no title, author, or page number.

Occasionally I would call Frances for advice, but I worked most days completely alone, with only the books for company. When I had several finished paintings, Carmen came over for a studio visit. She nodded at the work appreciatively but made few comments. One painting in particular caught her eye: "Man was born free, but he is everywhere in chains" highlighted in acid green.

"I see you can't resist dragging Karl Marx into it," she said.

I laughed. "Actually, that's from the beginning of *The Social Contract* by Jean-Jacques Rousseau. It's one of the fundamental philosophical texts of American democracy. Even your more conservative collectors can agree with Rousseau's politics."

Carmen brought one hand to her cheek and sighed. "I knew you'd be a cagey one."

We sat down on the couch and I asked, "What do you think?"

She said, "This show might be easier to sell than I expected. Minimal compositions and fluorescent color palettes are becoming fashionable."

"I can hardly believe it."

"The work is a bit denser than people are accustomed to seeing, but if I present it in the right way, this could be an advantage. Rousseau isn't exactly a household name, but with a little work, I think I can place a painting like that."

Somewhat against my better judgment, I asked, "Any suggestions?"

She shifted her weight and looked me directly in the eye. "I'm a novice at this, too, but my hunch is that these paintings will work. Just make more of them. The gallery isn't small." At that point, the kettle started whistling, and I went into the kitchen. I came back with a pot of tea and a pair of mugs on a tray. In my absence, Carmen looked at her phone. She tore herself away from the texts, and took a sip of tea. She summed up the situation: "Going forward, I believe the point will be to make a name for yourself, because there's no overestimating the fetish of the proper name. I've discovered that some collectors will buy third-rate work by a famous artist long before they'll buy the best works of a less well-known one. It makes breaking into the art world pretty difficult. I sometimes wonder if these collectors actually have eyes, but then they're able to read the invoices well enough." I looked at her with a sense of awe. Just as she had done when she was an artist, she sized up opportunities with brilliant precision. I had a grudging respect for this kind of calculation, and I was happy that Carmen was on my side. She continued, "Your work has the advantage of being impersonal enough that some tasks can be delegated to assistants. That's important if your career takes off and you need to step up production. I think the size of them is fine at the moment, because we don't know yet if your market will support larger paintings. The only reservation I have is that an Enlightenment *philosophe* and a bunch of Marxists aren't very sexy, especially not in this town."

"Well, it's a tribute to the former use of the gallery space."

She said, "Oh, I appreciate that, but remember that if you have any degree of success, these paintings will circulate in places where no one will know about Libros Revolución." She added, "These days, art has to grab people's attention by looking good in a booth at an art fair. If the reference is immediately recognizable, all the better. If you really want to up your game, think of celebrities or artists more famous than you to involve in your project. Isn't there a Marxist pop star out there? Quoting dead white men isn't exactly an expanding field. I know you're sincere in your wish to make a critique, but you'd be better off doing some logrolling and covering yourself with virtue, which will rub off on whoever buys the work. Or that's the hope."

I was left speechless by the pragmatism and cynicism of what I heard. In response, I could only mumble, "Um... well... I..."

After glancing at her phone, Carmen rose abruptly and said, "I must run. You wanted the truth, my dear, and that's what you got. Don't say I never did anything for you." She hugged me tightly and whispered in my ear, "I know you won't ever take my advice. That's why you're my favorite artist."

∞

On an early evening walk through Westlake one Sunday, I passed a storefront church near the gallery. It was much like others in the neighborhood, a no-frills space serving an immigrant community. Music followed an emphatic sermon in Spanish, with no more than two dozen people participating. I saw them through a large window that must have invited customers into the retail establishment once occupying the building. Now it invited potential converts. Just as the evening service was ending, I looked inside, and among the worshipers I saw Temo. I was stunned. Perhaps he had been there all along, only a couple of blocks away while I was working at Libros Revolución, and then at the studio that became the gallery. I never noticed him because he belonged to another world.

I waited for Temo as he helped break down the sound system and returned folding chairs to the place they were stored. As he left the church, I called out to him. For a second he hesitated, as though he didn't recognize me, or perhaps was unwilling to acknowledge me, then asked, "*Flaco*, what are you doing here?" We hugged for a moment, and he said, "I have to catch the bus on Sixth Street."

I wanted to ask questions about what had happened to him, but I couldn't speak. We walked together up the long blocks to Sixth in silence, and I looked at him. He had grown a head of long, unkempt hair and a full beard since I last saw him. A few subtle wrinkles had formed on his forehead, but otherwise, his face was the same as I remembered. He had gained weight, and his whole body seemed bigger, as though he had been blown up with air like a balloon. I tried to get a good look at his eyes. It appeared that something was missing from them—a sexual hunger, a hint of malice, or a spark of life. He caught me staring, and I said, "I'm sorry I didn't answer your emails. I saw them only recently."

"I thought you didn't love me anymore." His tone was flat, as though the question no longer mattered to him.

Instead of trying to explain, I asked, "How have you been?"

He stared at the sidewalk. "I'm okay." No more was forthcoming.

We reached the bus stop on Sixth, and I said, "How far are you taking the bus?"

"I live in the Hotel Normandie now."

I asked, "What have you been doing?"

He responded, "What have *you* been doing?"

"I've been painting. The bookstore is now a gallery that'll be showing my work in the spring. You should come to the opening."

"Libros Revolución is an art gallery? Weird."

I saw a bus approaching, and I made a last-ditch effort to engage him. "May I have your phone number?"

"Okay." I took out my phone and entered the digits. He said, "I need to catch this. Not many buses at night. It was nice to see you." He kissed me on the cheek, then turned and boarded the bus. As it moved away, I sent a text to the number he gave me: "I'm happy I found you." Hours later, he sent a text back: "I was never lost."

I slept fitfully that night, unable to stop thinking about every brief utterance he made to me and what it meant. I was in love with this man at one time, I thought, and maybe I still am in love with him; how could he treat me so indifferently? I needed to call Paul, the only person who had any information that might help me answer that question.

∞

I knew that Monday was Paul's day off, so I called him the next morning. We arranged a meeting for dinner and drinks at the HMS Bounty. As I slid into the booth that evening, he looked up from his BlackBerry and said, "You're radiant, my dear. The adult video business has done wonders for your complexion."

Passing up an opportunity for a punch line about "facials," I asked, "Is Carmen keeping you busy?"

"You've no idea, darling. She has the ambition, if not the equestrian skills, of Genghis Khan."

"I'm happy to hear it. The more she sells, the farther away I am from the poor house."

He leaned in and said, "Between us girls, your current price point is a bit too low for her purposes. You should make more colorful work if you want a prominent spot in her booth at Art Basel, and I don't mean that pile of cocaine and collagen in Miami Beach."

"In Switzerland?"

"Exactly. You only get one of those booths when some old art geezer kicks the bucket. Our friend Carmen has become a world-class operator." He looked around briefly, then said under his breath, "If you don't do anything silly like growing a conscience, you might even be able to purchase a house in this real estate market." My eyes opened wide in amazement. He smiled and said, "But surely you didn't call me all in a tizzy to discuss the market value of Neutra's architectural works. What *are* you interested in discussing with your dear, careworn mother?"

I said, "I saw Temo recently."

He furrowed his brows. "When you say 'saw,' is this a euphemism for 'rimmed and fucked'?"

"I wish. There's plenty of unfinished business between us, but none of it got done while waiting for his bus home. I ran into him outside a church. I guess he's found religion."

He gave me a look of disbelief. "Now I've heard everything." He folded his arms and sighed. "I suppose you want me to explain how he reached his current state of decrepitude."

I said, "Temo and I were pretty seriously involved a few years ago, but then he disappeared. He walked out one morning and never came back. My friend Moira thought he'd been murdered. I had some indications that he was alive, and I suspected he was in Los Angeles. Then I saw him that day outside the gallery, and again last night."

He took a gulp of his gin and tonic, and signaled for the waitress to bring another. "I must fortify myself for this story. It's a humdinger."

I asked, "How do you know him?"

He took a deep breath. "As you're abundantly aware, before my opportunity to join the ranks of the international art industry, I was a petty dealer in unauthorized medicaments. Temo was one of my customers. Sometimes he'd get high and hang out at my place. It was amusing. He'd do pretty much anything with anyone. It's a wonder the boy didn't end up rotting away from tertiary syphilis." I shuddered, and he raised his eyebrows. "And now comes the *truly* distasteful part of my sad tale." He spoke more softly. "In the not too distant past, my connection started offering me the cheapest meth I'd ever seen. It was one tenth the price of the stuff I used to sell. How could I resist? But..." His voice trailed off for a moment. "It was terrible, full of impurities. I found out that it was made from things like lye, benzene, and sulfuric acid. How I yearned for the days when one merely cooked up a batch of decongestants in a trailer in the desert. After some months of peddling these wares, I noticed that most of my customers were simply unable to fold their napkins. I started to meet them in the lobby of the Bryson Building, because I didn't want a big mess to clean up in my gracious drawing room. Temo was one of the first to use the new meth, and it transformed him posthaste into a slobbering idiot. At first, he twitched and saw people who weren't there—garden variety amphetamine psychosis, nothing I hadn't witnessed before—but eventually, he reached a truly frightening degree of madness. He barely acknowledged that I was there. He forgot how to speak English. He collected shiny things like bicycle parts and tried to trade them for drugs. I nearly vomited from the stench emanating from his person. This poor little rich kid suddenly had no permanent address. Had he stopped cashing those checks from home? It was a spectacular decline, and it well and truly gave me pause. Even I, hardened sociopath that I am, was moved to quit dealing."

I asked, "Do you know what happened to him after that?"

"I haven't the slightest idea. If I had to guess, I'd say that once he felt the hard surface of rock bottom, an extended period of recovery followed. I understand the damage can be massive." He became pensive for a moment. "I'm happy I got out of the racket when I did."

"Horrible."

"You said it, child. Opiates might fuck you up, but if you manage them well, you can live forever and a day as a junky. On the new meth, you're homeless within a year, and if you keep using, your brain will end up a puddle of mush. That is, if you survive that long."

I said, "I wonder what I can do to help Temo."

"Precious little, Florence Nightingale. I suggest keeping your distance, especially since he found old-timey religion. Whether this is the result of a fucked up childhood or various twelve-step groups, I can't venture a guess, but if you ask your mother, all that primitive superstition is as bad for you as any illegal substance."

I said, "*His* mother hasn't heard from him in a long time. She's awfully worried."

Paul sat up straight and said, "If I were you, my darling, I'd stay far, far away from that family drama. Temo told me that his mother is a monster, every bit as evil as his criminal of a father. Those people are as corrupt as the Cloaca Maxima, and there's not a whole lot you can do to help your erstwhile lover extricate himself from the muck."

"You may be right."

"Don't say I never did anything for you." He finished his drink, and as the liquor hit him, he asked, "Is it true that you once put a traffic cone up Temo's ass while a group of neighborhood ruffians looked on?"

"No. Where did you hear that?"

"Carmen told me there was a greasy one hidden in the back room of Libros Revolución. Workers threw it out during renovations, after having a good laugh at the expense of passive sodomites like yours truly." He thought for a moment. "Jumping Jehoshaphat, maybe it was your friend Bernie's. It does my heart good to think that under his catatonic demeanor lay the pulsing heart of a tremendous pervert."

I laughed. "That would be amazing. I'll be sure to ask him about it the next time we talk. By the way, I'm happy the old Paul is back, if only for a night."

He got a resigned look on his face. "It's no fun being professional Patty every day. I implore you to understand, dear, that a chance to escape the turpitude of my former life was too good to pass up. I could very well have ended up in prison if I kept going. But believe me, respectability leaves a lot to be desired. The only compensation I get is in teasing that swine Brad. He's an outrageous fraud, all fake chumminess, so I launch a few zingers that go right over his head. Carmen is entertained. It's probably why she hired me."

I smiled and said, "You're incorrigible."

He smoothed his hair and responded, "I bet you say that to all the girls."

"By the way, can you tell me why the two of them are married?"

He put his hand to his mouth to mime a bashful expression. "Please don't say you've heard any of this from me, but I believe I have penetrated the mystery of their *mésalliance*." I leaned forward and he continued, "Dear Carmen is a fin dom." I gave him a perplexed look, and he explained, "Stands for 'financial domination.' Not like she needs the money. She's soaking him for his inheritance just for the fun of it, and throwing in humiliation to boot. The insight came to me the night of Frances's opening, after I unleashed a torrent of vomit over Brad's tasteful outfit. Carmen looked as happy as a pig in shit. She also made Brad pick up the tab for our karaoke excesses. The worse she treats him, the better he likes it, apparently. A little bird told me that blackmail is involved as well. As long as Carmen never breathes a word about his penchant for penis, he'll be hers."

I blinked in disbelief and asked, "What do they do for sex?"

He laughed and said, "Oh, it's truly touching. Forced feminization. She pegs him in the ass with a giant strap-on dildo while he's wearing a girl's school uniform. In return for her loving attention, he has bought her a cunning cottage about a block east of Doheny. That woman is a remarkable operator, I must say. She'll go far!"

At that moment, Jerry walked through the front door, with an entourage in tow. I didn't recognize most of them, but I waved, and they came our way.

Paul whispered, "Remember, silence on the subject of Carmen," then raised his voice to address Jerry, "Hail the conquering hero!"

I said, "I take it Eon McKai is a success."

Jerry laughed and said, "Yeah, I've been directing porn videos one after another since last year. I started a new series called *Kill Girl Kill*. It's selling even better than *Art School Sluts*."

"Congratulations."

"Thanks." His companions began to wander off, and he said, "I better get back to these kids," before turning away and joining them.

Paul said, "Well, he looked as high as a kite."

"How can you tell?"

"My dear, you are totally unaware of the ways of the world, aren't you?" I shrugged, and he continued, "No street drugs for him. Strictly pharmaceutical grade speed, a marvelous party while it lasts, but once you crash, it's all the same." He sighed.

The liquor had begun to take its toll, and when he got up to smoke a cigarette, he almost careened into a nearby table. I said, "I think it's time to go home."

He said, "Perhaps you're right." I steadied him as we went out the door, and since he seemed unable to walk unassisted, I accompanied him all the way to the Bryson Building. He fell into a corner of the elevator, and I pressed the button for his floor. After a struggle to gain access to his apartment, I let him in and placed the keys in his hand. He slurred, "That'll be all. I'm afraid I don't have a gratuity at the moment," then collapsed on something I couldn't make out in the darkness, either a broken down sofa or a large pile of dirty laundry.

FIFTEEN

Bernie emailed me to say he'd be missing my opening, entirely unsurprising considering his lack of transportation and precarious finances. He assured me that he would try to catch the exhibition before it closed, but I didn't see how that would be possible. His efforts to get to New York consumed all his resources and energy. As arduous as the trip was, he looked forward to visiting places from his past as he made his way east from the Twin Cities without a car. After a brief stay in Chicago, he found a ride to the city where he grew up with a man named Jeff, the little brother of his former babysitter:

> When my parents separated my mother made the decision to move to Muskegon from the suburbs of Detroit, to put geographical distance between her and my father. If that weren't jarring enough, my mother got a day job and a high school student named Sally was hired as my babysitter. Sally was nice, but I was semi-fostered out with her and her family—she lived down the street and was the second oldest of fourteen children (good fertile Catholics). I would go there for meals and spent way too much time with them. It was

a few years of hell. I haven't seen Jeff since I was fifteen. He "hung out" at our apartment sometimes while I was in high school, which I didn't understand, but he seemed to get along with my mother.

During the three-plus hour drive we spent together, Jeff had me as a captive audience. He started unspooling years of sexual abuse at the hands of a coach who was friends with the family. I vaguely recall the coach—people being friends with coaches seems implausible now, but most of the boys were athletic— and I recall hearing that the coach left town suddenly. As per what I heard, the coach had been molesting Jeff and three of his brothers over a period of four years. He disappeared after Jeff threatened to go to the police. The coach had expressed interest in two other younger brothers he hadn't molested yet. Then Jeff's parents got divorced. The father worked at the Brunswick Bowling Ball factory and was physically abusive to the mother. The mother ended up in a secret home for battered women at one point, until tempers dimmed and the father remarried (so simple a solution somehow). And then according to Jeff, his mother started having an affair with a priest, who is still here, who I knew. Jeff started talking about the priest giving his mother an STD, which probably led to her death from cervical cancer. He asked me whether my mother, if she had known about his situation, could have helped. I didn't know how to respond to such a thing.

The whole way, all I could think was, Why didn't you kill yourself? My life feels like an MGM musical by comparison. Given that over thirty years have passed, I'm skeptical of some if it, but some of it was very recognizable. I think there's a Catholic trait of presenting your life as horribly as possible when speaking about yourself, so that's unreliable, too.

The priest is an interesting character. He was very political and involved with local civil rights and always getting into fights with the diocese, which was extremely conservative. I actually have a copy of translations of Baudelaire, Verlaine, and Rimbaud that he "loaned" me when I was fourteen. He had a scruffy beard, read poetry, he was a fly fisherman, smoked cigars and drank fine whiskeys, and I swear all the women who attended his masses were swooning over him as they were mostly married to alcoholic brutes and had scads of children. They cleaned his house, they gave him food, they spent Sundays in the parish hall with him. Years later I read a Zola story describing a priest giving a sermon thinking about an expensive dinner later at the house of his patroness, while she in turn is on the verge of orgasms while he prays and the incense burns and heaven is invoked. The scene in Muskegon was way more lumpen and depressing but the parallels were striking.

Around the time I left for Ann Arbor there was a gay bar in Muskegon called the Eagle's Nest which drew a clientele from an eight county area. The Eagle's Nest was so popular that it was necessary to make reservations to go on weekends, usually two weeks in advance. The exciting part was that it was owned by a dwarf who had been one of the flying monkeys in *The Wizard of Oz*—there was a shrine to Judy Garland in the bar, but otherwise it was decorated in late 1970s shiny disco style. I went there only once and by that time I was a bit of a sullen punk and unappreciative of it.

The two gay bars in Ann Arbor weren't much more interesting than the one in Muskegon. There was a tavern, The Flame, and a disco, The Rubaiyat. It had some variety. I would go on Sundays for the punk night. The DJ was a psychotic woman named Laurie who used *Interview* magazine as a style guide. In the pre-barcode days of retail, she worked out what she called "negative shopping." She would go to J. L. Hudson's, the local department store in Detroit, with about seven hundred dollars, change the price tags, buy clothes at a fraction of their actual prices, then return most, with the original tags, and get refunds for full price, keeping what she wanted. She had a mania for two of everything, so every outfit she had was duplicated, every album was doubled. She also had two Alfa-Romeos, and God only knows how she conned that.

The stories in Bernie's emails were as vivid as the ones he told in person, and I was grateful for the diversion from all the painting I had been doing.

∞

I finished the works for my exhibition just in time for installation. Because they were oil paintings, some of them were hung while still wet. The gallery had three walls available for displaying art, one short and two long ones. I arranged the paintings in a line reading like a story from left to right. Along the wall to the left of the gallery entrance, I placed a passage from an introduction to Nietzsche's *The Birth of Tragedy*: "impossible child of a homosexual union between Apollo and Dionysus" highlighted in fluorescent yellow; from James Fogle's novel *Drugstore Cowboy*: "We want to do with our bodies what we ought to be entitled to" underlined in blue pen; from Hélène Cixous's introduction to Clarice Lispector's *Água Viva*: "Pleasure is lost in the act of love" with black pen underlining and an anonymous annotation, "absolutely false"; from a biography of Rosa Luxemburg: "She refused to narrow herself" underlined in pencil; and from Herman Melville's "Bartleby, the Scrivener": "I would prefer not to" underlined in blue pen. Along the short wall facing the door, I placed a phrase from J. G. Ballard's *The Atrocity Exhibition*: "imaginary diseases of the genitalia" underlined in pencil; from Marx's *The German Ideology*: "Here we ascend from earth to heaven" highlighted in fluorescent pink; and Thomas Mann's "fatuously"—this was the very first painting sold at the private view. Along the right wall, I placed Rousseau's "Man was born free, and he is everywhere in chains"; then a line of dialogue from Thomas Pynchon's *The Crying of Lot 49*: "You're so right-wing you're left-wing" underlined in pencil; then a blue-highlighted phrase from *The Communist Manifesto*: "No other nexus between man and man than naked self-interest"—a gay couple expressed a wish to buy this work until they were informed that the passage was written by Marx and Engels; and last of all, just to the left of Paul's desk, a question from the text of a Christian marriage guide, highlighted in fluorescent yellow: "Is this person submissive to constituted authority?" I was quite surprised to find this last item in Jim's book collection, and I was pleased that it added to the show's running theme of sexual innuendos. Carmen mentioned that such things would appeal to critics, and was so amused that she convinced Brad to buy the "submissive" painting even before it was installed.

I hoped that Jim would come to the opening, and I was not disappointed. He brought Pete, scowling as always, and a few other friends. He seemed well pleased that his old books had found a new use. "Radical chic may be dead," he said, "but you've found a way to mix things up that doesn't totally destroy the texts." He shouted in my ear over the voices of the throng in the gallery.

I was shocked at how many people had come to my opening, but I shouldn't have been. Blanco Projects was the "hot new gallery" of the moment, and Carmen said to me, "We're giving the Lower East Side a run for its money."

There was another dinner at Pacific Dining Car after the last spectator had left the gallery, and as I declined to engage in a marathon karaoke session, there was no vomit to finish off the night. Paul put me in a taxi, a rare luxury for me, and rather tipsy,

I made my way to bed by midnight. I saw no reason to get very drunk, since all my closest friends were out of town. I took a few digital pictures at the beginning of the evening before the space got crowded so I could send them to Bernie, Frances, and Gregorio. I imagined that Winston would take a dim view of my attempts at painting and would feel sufficiently indignant to email me.

∞

Temo was nowhere to be seen that night. Perhaps he had been at a worship service. As the weeks passed, my curiosity about his whereabouts only became more intense. Every time I visited the gallery during the run of my exhibition, I would walk by the storefront church where I found him, but I never saw him there again.

He mentioned the Hotel Normandie in our conversation, so one day I took the Sixth Street bus there. Built in the 1920s, the hotel had survived the Long Beach earthquake, unlike most of the other brick buildings in the area. Once a prestige property, the building had fallen into disrepair. I entered the lobby with its checkered floor and wooden ceiling beams and saw several people arguing over a television program. The smell of the place, a combination of cheap food cooked on hot plates, body odor, and urine, made me wish to discharge my business as quickly as possible. I went to the front desk, a beautiful construction of dark wood that looked like a piece of ecclesiastical furniture from a Spanish church, and rang the bell. An ancient, stooped man wearing a tattered polyester shirt and an even more tattered toupee emerged from a back room. I inquired about Cuauhtémoc. He looked at me as though I had asked if I could shit in his mouth. He yelled, "I never want to see that son of a bitch again! The room was a shambles when he left it. We had to chuck a dumpster worth of garbage, resurface the floors, and repaint. He was a pig."

I asked, "Did he leave a forwarding address?"

"No, and I'm not sure I'd tell you if he did."

I stared at a spot on the wall beyond this man's ear and made up a lie: "You see, he owes me money. It's a real hardship, because it was rather a lot of money." I hoped this would make it clear to the desk clerk that I wasn't good for a bribe. I gave him my most pathetic look.

My deception worked, and he said, "It was almost a month ago, and I'm sorry, there's no forwarding information. The outstanding amount he was billed for repairs got paid by a bank transfer from Mexico. It was enough to cover the work, but what a pain in the ass."

I asked, "Other than the mess he left, what was he like as a tenant?"

The man grimaced and said, "That was the oddest thing. He seemed civilized. We didn't talk very much. He was always off to church. At least that's what he said. It just goes to show, you never can tell about people."

"No, you can't." I changed the subject. "You know, Malcolm Lowry wrote part of his novel *Under the Volcano* here. He left Los Angeles in such a hurry that he forgot to pack the manuscript."

There was no sign of recognition from the man. He said, "Must have been before my time. We haven't had a writer as a guest in years and years."

I nodded. "I see. Too bad there isn't a historical plaque or something."

"What did you say his name was?"

"Lowry."

"Nope, I can't say I remember. Good luck getting your money."

I said, "Thanks for your time."

I turned to go, and as I crossed the lobby, an elderly man wearing an eye patch called out to me from a wheelchair, "Hey, mister. Who you looking for?"

I went over to him and said, "A Mexican guy named Cuauhtémoc. I called him Temo."

With a piercing gaze, he asked, "Are you sure he owed you money? He seemed pretty well fixed to me."

"I was just telling a story. Did you know him?"

"I did. Handsome guy."

I cleared my throat and asked, "Um, was he okay?

He perked up. "More than okay. He gave great blow jobs and didn't want paid."

I blushed and said, "I mean, did he seem like he was doing drugs?"

The man laughed and said, "Of course he was doing drugs, and he didn't mind sharing, either. We had some good times. His dealer was down the hall. That's probably why he lived here."

I asked, "Do you know where he went?"

"Damned if I know. To be honest, nothing he said made a lick of sense. All this religious stuff. I'm not a holy roller, but I could tell he was cracked. I didn't really care. He made an old man very happy. He'd slam some meth and we'd do things I hadn't done since before my last heart attack." He stared lewdly and asked, "How about going upstairs with me now?"

"Sorry, I have somewhere to be in a little while. Got to catch the bus."

Deflated, he said, "No harm in asking. You sure are curious. Was that guy your boyfriend or something?"

"Or something. Did he say where he was going?"

The man took a while to think and said, "Palm Springs, I'm pretty sure. If he likes meth and old men, that's the place to go. Better than Koreatown."

I nodded and said, "Thanks. If I find him, I'll tell him you say hello."

∞

Bernie's arrival in Detroit triggered a flood of memories from his childhood, as well as from previous visits and explorations of the city in decline. Many of them had some relation to a religious upbringing tied to reactionary politics. He never mentioned these things in conversation, but writing emails to me a couple thousand miles away had somehow freed him to deal with them.

My family belonged to Charles Coughlin's parish church, the Shrine of the Little Flower, in Royal Oak, Michigan. Does anyone talk about him anymore? He was a right-winger who had a hugely successful radio ministry. He came from Canada, but he adopted an indescribable accent, a sort of Irish brogue intended to appeal to his audience, which was all disgruntled and pious working class whites. Supposedly he started his radio show in response to a Ku Klux Klan cross burning. (Which might never have happened, but it was a great publicity coup.) He'd broadcast from the outrageously phallic bell tower of the church. During the Depression, Father Coughlin supported the New Deal at first, but I think the presence of so many Jews in Roosevelt's administration was more than he could tolerate. He started extolling the virtues of Hitler and Mussolini—whose economic policies weren't really all that different from FDR's at that point—and published a newspaper called *Social Justice*. (Leftists, take note of *that*.) The government tried to force him off the air, but he was too popular to touch until the United States entered World War II, when his sermons supporting the Axis powers were considered seditious.

Coughlin was at my baptism—he didn't retire until 1966. In my mother's effects after her death I found a letter he wrote to me on the occasion of my baptism, waxing poetic about a future when I would be there in church again, with my own son at his baptism! I have no memories of him and didn't know anything about him until I was an adult. The party line for my family and their friends (all of them New Deal Democrats and good Catholics) was, "People say bad things about him, but he did a lot for the parish."

The decorations of the Shrine of the Little Flower, finished in 1936, are really fascinating. It has never been in any architecture books—my guess is it's too eccentric and kitsch. It was built with millions raised over the radio and is kind of a hybrid of Romanesque and Zigzag Moderne. There are a lot of WPA-esque murals but they're a bit more Hollywood. When I took out-of-town friends there, they commented that all the female saints look like Rita Hayworth. There are numerous small altars, including a marble statue of St. Sebastian flanked by murals of football players and soldiers praying to the crucifixion, which is fairly over the top. I grew up around all this without much reflection. One of the comments that piqued my interest a few years ago was hearing someone refer to the Shrine as the "Church of the Burning Jew," which is a lot darker than what I was told back in the day.

On previous visits, I stayed in Royal Oak a few times with a friend of my family's, Kathleen, who was in her seventies, a "spinster" who went to mass at the Shrine of the Little Flower twice a day, and lived in the house once owned by her father (who she lived with until he died). She was a block away from my grandparents and three blocks from where I spent my early childhood. Although Royal Oak is an old town with a business district, this area was purely suburban—no market, no anything close by. By that time, Kathleen was legally blind from macular degeneration but she still drove to mass (two miles away) and to get groceries—she lived on instant coffee and Milano cookies. When I stayed with her she would insist on taking me to International House of Pancakes (next to the Shrine) which involved being driven by her—that was always a bit of a panic. Kathleen's Catholicism was complex. Regarding most things she could be downright Marxist, although she would not acknowledge it, but her positions about women's rights, birth control and abortion were anything but that. She belonged to an evangelical Catholic group, and the members I met on occasion were among the most bizarre people I can recall. Bizarre in a banal, to-be-avoided kind of way.

Transportation was a perpetual challenge for Bernie. I began to suspect that he enjoyed the rigors of his demanding and impractical journeys, or at least that he saw redeeming aspects to the physical discomfort they caused.

The distances and lack of basic amenities are intense. Public transportation in the metro Detroit area is a perpetual episode of *The Twilight Zone*. Even years ago it was a challenge and it's just gotten worse. A typical modern improvement, the "People Mover," was built as an attraction in the early 1980s and goes almost nowhere, although it's a good way to view the buildings downtown. One time when I went there, I didn't want to spend money for a taxi to Kathleen's from the airport—which is about a twenty-minute drive but costs something like sixty dollars—so I decided to take a suburban bus. The bus connecting to the airport goes through the downriver suburbs. That's when I saw the most of Westland and the areas around it. It took three and a half hours to get from the airport to the foot of Woodward Avenue on the river, where I could get another suburban bus out Woodward to 12 Mile Road (where the Shrine is), and from there I had to walk two miles to Kathleen's. And the flight from New York took something like ninety minutes. Mike Kelley is from Westland (or Wayne, next to it), which is one of the several suburbs spawned by the presence of the River Rouge Plant and industries around Ford in Dearborn. I'm from the northern suburbs, some of which are wealthy— Royal Oak was redneck when I was a child (as opposed to now being termed "The Soho of Detroit"), but Royal Oak looks like a garden city compared to downriver. Is this splitting hairs? At any rate, I don't think Westland has any threat of becoming "The Soho of Detroit" even now. (This refers to the post-industrial loft-living artists' Soho, not the current hectic retail hub—Midwesterners are always years, if not decades, behind in acknowledging developments in urban reality.) So much of Mike Kelley's work reminds me of Michigan. He did murals for the 2001 Detroit Tercentennial (founded in 1701) that include a lot of great Detroit culture, although right now I'm remembering only Soupy Sales.

Bernie described the stark contrast of city and suburbs in a way that emphasized that the decline of Detroit was by no means a natural phenomenon, but rather a triumph of social engineering and cruelty.

I want to point out a seemingly unintentional barrier: Jefferson Avenue, which is parallel with the river. Going northeast to the Grosse Pointes, the border between Detroit and Grosse Pointe is a cross street called Alter Road, where Jefferson becomes Lakeshore Drive. On the city side of Alter Road, Jefferson is filthy and unkempt, with poor, irregular lighting (one of the effects of the past decades is the large number of broken street lights). Crossing Alter, Lakeshore Drive is clean, well ordered, with decorative trees, flowers, etc.

In contrast with the Pollyanna sentiments of "Minnesota Nice," there's a lot of normalized black humor in Detroit. A friend likes to go on night rides, and he often takes me along. He knows I do a lot of walking in the city's destroyed neighborhoods, and he advised me to write his name and phone number on my stomach with a permanent marker in case I got in trouble. He said, "You can't be all jiggly on the street—those mofos are going to see that right away and go after you. Even though I'm forty-five minutes away, I'll be faster than 9-1-1." His company is not for the faint of heart, but I enjoy his unofficial tours. On one of them, he pointed out other cars on the street where we could see people inside lighting crystal meth pipes—the way genteel Minnesotans count Volkswagens.

∞

My favorite aspect of Bernie's emails was that they described an extreme version of what I saw during my own childhood. His stories reminded me of my hometown, and in a way, they saved me from having to go there. I had grown up in a much smaller city a few years later, and the decline I had witnessed was not so spectacular. The collapse of the economy that once thrived in Detroit and other places like it caused a political, economic, and cultural crisis that never went away. On the West Coast, no one discussed this or was even more than dimly aware of it. If this complacency was due to Californians thinking the forces that destroyed Detroit couldn't affect them, they would be wrong. As I saw it, there was always another crash coming, no matter how many people said the good times of prosperity would last forever.

I imagined that I was the only person who received such long messages from Bernie. He never mentioned whatever feelings he had for me, but I think I understood him in a way that others didn't. That wasn't the same as an intimate relationship, but it was something.

SIXTEEN

One afternoon as I contemplated what I would do with my evening, I received two texts from Temo. The first read, "Help me." The second was an abbreviated address: 475 main no 2 el centro. I turned on my computer and searched for the location. I texted back and asked, "What's wrong?" The answer was "dying."

I texted Jim, and within a few minutes, he called me. I explained the texts, and he asked, "Do you think he's crying wolf?"

"He's never said anything like that to me before, so no."

There was a long pause. Jim said, "Take the train to Pomona Station on the Riverside line. I can pick you up. We'll go in Pete's car." After I hung up, I looked up the schedule and saw a 4:50 train. I packed a few things in a small bag and walked quickly to the subway. I made it to Union Station just in time. I texted Jim from the train. He arrived at the station and took me to a ramshackle Queen Anne-style house. As he pulled into the driveway, he said, "Home, sweet home." He let me in and told me to prepare for a long trip. Within a half hour, his brother Pete arrived. We left in his car, a hearse with a vanity plate that read, "MRCUCUY" (for Mexican children, the Bogey Man).

We headed down I-10 toward San Bernardino in heavy traffic, which dispersed once we passed the city limits. By the time we hit Redlands, we were going a little over the speed limit. "We'll be there in less than three hours." These were the first words I heard Pete say that day. We stopped for gas in Banning. The sun had set, but the air was still as hot as a furnace. Pete turned to me at the pump and said, "We're driving into hell. It doesn't even cool down at night there." We continued past Palm Springs and all the other desert communities where Temo had probably scored drugs and gotten involved in sex scenes with rich retirees. Once we passed Indio, there was a noticeable drop in elevation and rise in temperature. I sent a text to Temo: "We'll be there soon."

"So what have you gotten us into?" asked Jim as we descended into the Imperial Valley.

I said, "I have no idea, to be honest."

Jim nodded over to Pete and said, "He knows how to handle himself in dodgy situations, but obviously it'll be better if whoever's involved isn't armed." He turned to me in the back seat and said pointedly, "I must say, you sure can pick 'em."

I said, "Temo doesn't have many friends as far as I can tell, not real ones anyway. Only drug buddies and tricks."

"I hope he's still alive when we get there."

We arrived in El Centro under a pall of inky darkness. We passed the police station and courthouse on the way to the address, and I wondered why Temo hadn't called 9-1-1. When we reached his apartment, we found the door open a crack. Jim flipped the light switch, and as a multitude of cockroaches scuttled away, we took in a scene of disorder and filth the likes of which I had never seen before. The stench was overpowering. Papers, plastic bags, fast food wrappers, and bottles that had once contained water but looked as though they now contained urine were everywhere. On a shabby upholstered chair sat a man who was either dead or unconscious. He had a hypodermic needle stuck in his arm. Beyond him on a couch was Temo. He looked like another piece of furniture, a surface for someone to sit on. He wore only a t-shirt and a pair of motorcycle boots. His ass and balls were exposed for anyone to violate or torture. His legs were in the air, his knees practically in his face, and he was gagged and blindfolded. I couldn't determine how he was holding that pose until I noticed that his legs were bound with a rope that was tied in a slipknot around his neck. If he tried to make any sudden movements, he would be strangled. His left hand was free, but his right was handcuffed to an O-ring screwed into the wall behind the couch.

He groaned to let us know he was alive. With the skill of someone who had experience dealing with this sort of thing, Pete set Temo free from his restraints. Temo unfolded himself on the couch. I brought him a glass of tap water from the kitchen. He drank it greedily. I returned to get more water, and I took a good look around. On an island separating the kitchen from the living room, there was an array of drug paraphernalia: syringes, pipes, empty foil packets, a couple of glassine envelopes, charred spoons, and cotton balls. There was also a Spanish language New Testament that appeared to be from the 1970s, *Lo mas importante es el amor*. The pages had yellowed considerably and the spine was broken in many places. I slipped this into the bag that hung from my shoulder. In close proximity to the syringes I saw a King James Version of the Bible opened to a book of the Old Testament. This I did not touch, as it had been spattered with blood, stained with yellowish dried semen, and smeared with dark brown daubs of excrement. I didn't investigate more, but filled the glass again at the sink, which was full of dirty dishes and covered in black slime.

Jim had taken responsibility for dealing with the other person in the room. I heard slaps and looked over to see him locating a pulse on the man's neck. He said, "He's alive, barely."

In a deadpan tone, Pete said to Temo, "I don't think you're going to get your security deposit back."

Temo stared blankly at the man Jim was attempting to revive. I said, "Let's get you dressed." I picked up various items of clothing strewn across the floor, and I handed him the ones that appeared least soiled. He struggled to put on a long sleeve shirt to hide the wounds and abrasions on his arms. The best I could find for his naked bottom half was a relatively clean pair of sweatpants. I asked, "Is there anything of value you need to take with you?" He nodded in the direction of a backpack at the corner of the room.

After checking on Jim, Pete came over and said, "Find a comb. He needs to appear as normal as possible for the trip back to Pomona. There's a Border Patrol checkpoint on the way. If he looks dirty or poor, we're fucked."

I went into the bathroom and started gagging. Not only had the toilet never been cleaned, it seemed as though it hadn't been flushed in a long time. I grabbed a hair brush from the medicine cabinet, which contained another stash of drugs, in this case, prescription medications. I saw Temo's name on some of the bottles, so I placed them in his backpack. Then I attended to his hair.

Jim said, "We've got to get out of here before this guy dies." The man was sprawled out on the chair at an odd angle, almost fully reclining and face up.

Temo responded with the only words he said that night: "Fuck him."

Pete knew what to do. He grabbed a half-full bag of ice from the freezer and dumped the contents all over the stranger's naked chest. He said, "Let's go *now*." We left the door to the apartment ajar, went downstairs and piled into the hearse. Pete drove us to a fast food restaurant near the Imperial County Airport. We all used the much cleaner toilet there, and I led Temo to a mirror so he could get himself together. We bought some soft drinks to go, then headed north on Route 86 through the towns of Imperial and Brawley, then turned left at Westmorland. We were able to catch brief glimpses of the region's main tourist attraction, the Salton Sea, an accidental body of water created about a hundred years before, when an irrigation project flooded and for many months, the entire contents of the Colorado River emptied into a depression below sea level. The smell of the water, as rank as it was, came as a relief after Temo's disgusting apartment and the odor of chemical fertilizer that pervaded the outlying areas of the county. We passed through the border check without a problem. The officer on duty merely laughed at Pete's license plate and waved us through.

We spent the night at Jim's house. After disinfecting Temo's wounds and wrapping his arms in gauze, I put him to bed on the couch. I joined Jim and Pete on the back porch for a drink. I said, "Thank you for everything. I think someone might have died if we hadn't gone out there tonight."

Jim took a sip of whiskey and said, "When he texted for help he wasn't kidding."

Pete asked, "Is that guy your boyfriend?"

"Was," I emphasized. "I haven't seen much of him for the last few years. He was never like that when we were together."

"Not that you knew," Jim said. "He came into Libros Revolución looking pretty rough sometimes. I suspected something funny was going on."

I looked down at my drink and said, "I guess I was totally naïve."

Pete lifted his glass and said, "You and every other guy who falls in love."

∞

Late the next morning, Pete drove us back to my place, and since it was Saturday, Jim stayed home. As he dropped us off, Pete said under his breath, "Good luck with that guy. You'll need it." I practically had to carry Temo up the stairs to my apartment. He immediately collapsed on the couch and fell into a deep sleep.

I washed Temo's clothes, and I managed to get him into the shower a few hours later, but the bad smells emanating from his feet and his mouth didn't go away. During one of his naps, I threw his boots in the garbage then looked through his filthy backpack. Although he could have been mistaken for indigent, Temo still had responsibilities and income. I found a driver's license, a health insurance card, and a green card. I inspected the bottles of medicine I had taken from the apartment: one for erectile dysfunction (almost full), one for HIV (nearly empty), and an empty bottle of lithium.

I went to the strip mall at Vermont and Santa Monica to fill his prescriptions, or at least to attempt to do so. The complications and expense drove me away from the pharmacy, but I did manage to buy a toothbrush and a spray to kill the fungus growing between his toes. I bought new sneakers and socks for him at the shoe store in the same mall. Then I visited the dental clinic across the street and made an appointment for a couple of days later. From a small corner store nearby, I bought t-shirts and a package of boxer shorts. His size was close enough to mine that he'd be able to wear a pair of baggy jeans too large for me. I was relieved to find my guest still on the couch when I returned to the apartment.

∞

On the third day of his stay I convinced Temo to prepare to go out. I told him that a walk would be a good idea and suggested we head toward Los Angeles City College, about a half mile away. Once we reached that neighborhood, I led him beyond the school and the subway station to the dental clinic. He put up little resistance. X-rays showed that his neglected cavities weren't very serious, and all of them could be fixed at the next appointment. I paid for the office visit with my credit card. As we left the building, Temo made his first complete utterance since arriving at my place. In a sheepish tone he asked, "Can I have a new backpack?" I bought him a bag emblazoned with the LACC logo at the campus bookstore.

He seemed a bit livelier on the way back to my apartment. We stopped at a market and bought food for dinner. I could barely cook, but I would have to improvise something for us. I used the *comal* that Gregorio had bought during his stay to make *quesadillas*. Temo was grateful to be fed after days of eating nothing. Immediately after dinner, he carefully transferred items from his old backpack to the new one, then he wrapped himself in a sheet and went to sleep again.

The next day, I decided to brave the subway with Temo. He seemed to resent the trip but he said nothing. We took the Red Line to Hollywood and Highland, and the sight of the tasteless tourist attractions in the area cheered him up. We walked to the Gay and Lesbian Center, where I had a word with someone on the staff. I was given a stack of papers to fill out. We sat in a corner of the waiting room, and I asked Temo for answers to the questions on the forms. He mumbled responses. I transcribed information from his insurance card, took a guess at his yearly income when he refused to tell me how much money he received from his mother, and made a note of his medications. I listed myself as his emergency contact. On the pretext of helping him walk, I went with him when his name was called. The nurse told me that all doctor visits and test results were confidential and that I wasn't allowed to sit with him during the appointment. The doctor arrived just then, and I took her aside to explain the situation as best I could. I said that Temo had gone missing, was homeless for a while, and had been staying with me for the last few days. I also mentioned his regular medications. She nodded and entered the room, closing the door behind her. Temo submitted to STD tests, which involved an anal swab, a throat swab, a urine sample, and a blood draw. After about an hour, he emerged from the offices with two pieces of paper: the results of his rapid HIV test (positive), and a referral to a psychiatrist who could authorize a refill of his prescription for lithium. The former came as no surprise to me. The latter would require more phone calls and an appointment on a future date, but one not too far away, I hoped. We filled the prescription for Temo's HIV medicine at the Center. As we waited, I wondered how he would be able to keep track of all the appointments necessary to maintain his physical and mental health. He needed someone to take care of him, and at the moment, that person happened to be me.

We ate a late lunch at an Indian restaurant down the block, then went back to my place on the subway. Right away, I made a call to the psychiatrist's office, and I successfully impressed the seriousness of Temo's case upon the receptionist, who gave me an appointment for the next afternoon, as well as the address of the office, a medical building in West Hollywood, close to the gay bars on Santa Monica Boulevard. Temo grumbled about me discussing him in the third person while he was in the room, and I sensed that the person I once knew was returning.

∞

The next day was not pleasant. Temo put up resistance to getting out of bed or taking a shower. He ate only a few bites of breakfast. I got him out of the apartment in barely enough time to catch a bus to his appointment with the psychiatrist. I brought the empty bottle of lithium with me, because I suspected that Temo would lie when asked about his medical history. He filled out the forms himself, but I wasn't convinced he was answering with the whole truth. He asked for a key to the rest room, and while he was inside, I passed the bottle to the receptionist, in case he had neglected to mention his previous doctor and medication. Temo emerged from the toilet and returned to the lobby, sitting restlessly until his name was called. I occupied myself with looking at old magazines during his visit with the psychiatrist.

When Temo came out, he said he wanted to go home right away. I told him that we'd need to fill the prescription he had in his hand, and he looked angry. We went to a pharmacy near the office to get a new medicine called by a name I didn't recognize. With the little cash I had, I bought Temo some candy. I wondered what bribe I would have to offer to convince him to return to the dentist. He was relieved to make the bus trip to my neighborhood. The psychiatrist's appointment, filling the prescription, and travel back and forth to West Hollywood had taken up the better part of a day.

∞

After Temo's teeth got fixed, at somewhat greater expense than I had expected, his situation reached something like normality. He started to take an interest in the books around the apartment and suggested we see a movie one evening. During the whole time he stayed with me, he never attended the storefront church, or even so much as mentioned it. We went shopping for clothes nearby, and he complained that the choices available were terrible. He said, "I don't want to look like an immigrant."

"You are one," I said.

"But I'm not some peasant selling fruit on the street."

"That's true enough." I was secretly happy that Temo's cynical personality, which I recognized from before, was showing itself again. I wondered if his libido would also return. He had gained weight and looked defeated by his circumstances, but I still found him attractive. I decided to wait for him to initiate things, or to signal his interest. Thus far, I'd received no such indication.

SEVENTEEN

I realized that caring for Temo would be a full time job, and one for which I was ill-prepared. I remembered Moira telling me that when she first had dinner with his parents, he let his mother cut his food for him. I didn't envy the woman. I resolved to contact her as soon as I could without sending Temo into a panic. I wrote an email to Moira, telling her what had happened in the last few weeks. Within a couple of days, Graciela called the land line in my apartment. When Temo heard her voice leaving a message, he rushed to pick up the phone. There followed an hour-long conversation entirely in Spanish, with many tears and a few moments of shouting. I retreated to the bedroom with a book so as not to eavesdrop. I read the same page over and over until Temo came into the room. He said, "The old bitch knows where I am now. Did you tell her?"

I said, "No. She has the phone number from when Moira lived here. And don't call your mother a bitch."

"You don't know her. She'll dominate you totally if you give her a chance."

I asked, "How long has it been since you last spoke to her?"

He shrugged. "Six months? Two years?"

"You certainly know how to break a mother's heart."

He snarled, "If *you* start nagging me, I'll walk out the door and no one will ever see me again."

"Don't be so dramatic. Come over here and lie on the bed." He flopped down next to me. I held him in my arms for the first time in years.

He said, "She's making arrangements to visit. I told her she can't stay here."

"I don't know where we'd put her if she did."

"On the couch. I can sleep with you."

I looked at him and said, "Maybe that's a good idea even if she doesn't stay here."

He looked confused. "I thought you didn't like me in that way anymore."

I said, "I didn't want to rush you into anything or take advantage. You were a mess when we found you."

"I was. Thank you for not trying to fuck me. No one else has been so kind." There was a long pause, and looking out the window, he began to tell me about his recent experience. "Thirty days of rehab is never enough to recover completely. I left that church where you saw me because I wanted to do drugs again. I was sober for a while, but you know, that got boring. I watched a lot of television. I thought every program was communicating with me personally, telling me to leave town. I wasn't myself back then." He paused. "In my mind, I know that God isn't speaking to me, and I know that TV programs are for millions of people, but I *felt* some divine presence controlling me. I felt I had to go to Palm Springs, but I missed the exit and drove all the way to the Imperial Valley. I thought this was a sign from God. In the middle of the night, I arrived in El Centro. My car broke down. It wasn't built for the heat. I wasn't able to buy myself a new one. I mean, I knew my mother had the money, but I couldn't ask her. I had an idea that she was in league with Satan." He laughed bitterly.

"I found a place to live in downtown El Centro. Main Street has covered sidewalks to protect people from the heat. There are a lot of pedestrians, farm workers too poor to afford cars. They wear hats to keep their brains from baking. My brain was already baked, I guess, but I wore a hat, too. My window had a view of Main Street. For a few days, all I did was look out at the men—there were never any women—walking back and forth. On the other side of the street, there was a porno shop. They called it an 'adult bookstore.'" He laughed again. "These men were cruising for sex every day, every night. They had nowhere else to go, and they were horny. It made me horny to look at them. I masturbated a lot."

He started to get up, but I motioned for him to stay in bed. I poured him a glass of water in the kitchen. He drank, and when he was done said, "I don't know why, but my mouth is very dry." He took one more sip and continued, "Suddenly I asked myself, Have I come to this place to sit on my ass and jerk my cock all day? Why am I here? That night I went to bed very late. I had a dream that told me what I should do. I thought it was another sign from God. The next day I bought a Bible at the religious bookstore down the street. I was their only customer. I took the Bible home and read it every day. Sometimes I fell asleep. Most of the time, I got distracted by the men cruising below me. Some of them were very handsome. I think they were all married, with wives in Mexico. I started going out on Main Street and picking them up. I didn't look like a typical El Centro man. My clothes were too nice, my skin was too pale, and I was taller than everyone I met. I let the men do anything they wanted to me. I thought that God told me to act this way. Anybody could come in at any time and ask me for a blowjob or fuck me in the ass. My reputation got around, and soon I didn't even have to go on the street. I left my door unlocked. Sometimes men would bring me food. I would spend whole days naked. Why get dressed if I'm a thing men can use for their pleasure?

"One guy was different than the others. He reminded me of someone, but I couldn't remember who. We became friends. Maybe he thought he was my pimp. I never saw any money, but he would go out whenever I had a visitor, unless he felt like watching. He whispered to the visitors. It made me paranoid. I thought they were criticizing my body or my ability to have sex. When I think about it now, they were probably talking about prices. This man had the biggest cock of anyone in El Centro. He didn't fuck me with it. He only wanted blowjobs. I didn't suck. I would lie on my back and he would fuck my mouth. It hurt me at first, but then I got used to it. He fucked me very hard one day. It was a rape. I gagged and coughed, but he didn't care. He always took a long time to come. This time it was like torture. Then I understood. I knew this man. He was my father's best friend." He gestured for more water. I quickly got it for him, bringing a whole pitcher with me. He poured a full glass and drank most of it in a single breath.

I asked, "Was he really your father's friend?"

"No, I knew he wasn't, but at the same time I felt it was him. I can't explain any more than that. I knew I had been in this situation before when I was young." He paused and looked intently at me. He continued, "My father had a friend who was a priest. He was famous in Mexico. He would come to dinner. After we finished eating, he would visit my room for what he called 'religious instruction.' My parents were honored that this busy man very high up in the Church took an interest in their son. They never interrupted us. Did they know he was raping my face every night? I think my father knew what was going on, but he didn't stop it because he hated me. He saw something in me, something I didn't understand about myself. I was only eight or nine years old, but he saw a little faggot, worse than a street whore or a beggar. I was useless for his purposes—that's why he adopted my brother—but I could be useful to *someone*. Maybe he sold me to this man. It's strange, I don't even remember his name, but that day in El Centro, I remembered his cock, or my throat did. I had a strong reaction. I threw my friend out and locked the door. No one came to see me for days. I fasted and read my Bible. When I thought I was going to starve, I went to a market and bought some food. I felt everyone looking at me. I knew they were asking, 'What is the town *puto* doing outside?'

"I slept very deeply that night, and as I was waking up, I had a vision. It wasn't a vision exactly, but some knowledge came to me from outside my mind. I remembered the words that the priest said to me as a child, *Él que come mi carne y bebe mi sangre, en mí permanece, y yo en él.*" He thought for a moment and translated, "'Whoever eats my flesh and drinks my blood remains in me, and I in him.' Then I remembered the lessons. They were about *eucaristía del semen humano.*" I gave him a puzzled look, and he translated, "Human semen Eucharist. This priest taught me that when Jesus told his disciples to eat and drink him, he didn't mean it symbolically. He wanted them to suck him off. The Last Supper was an orgy. I don't know how Jesus could come twelve times in one night and still shoot enough for his disciples to drink. Maybe that was a miracle. The fucker convinced me that what he was doing to me was a holy ritual, and the cum he shot down my throat was like communion wine. I never read the Bible when I was young, so I didn't know he was full of shit. His religious lessons came back to me when that guy raped my face in El Centro. I hated it, but at the same time, I loved it. I got so confused and upset that I lost it and tore up the apartment in a rage.

"My friend came back later with some meth for me. I don't think he was on meth, he was shooting something else. Then he overdosed while I was tied up like a fuck chair, and there wasn't anything I could do. One hand came loose and I reached for my cell phone. That's when I texted you." After this, he stared blankly into space. After a few moments that seemed to last an hour, he said, "Thank you for helping me and listening to me."

"It wasn't so much trouble."

He said, "You saved my life," then rolled over and dozed off.

∞

I awoke early the next morning. Temo was still asleep when my phone started to vibrate, and I saw a number I didn't recognize appear on its tiny display. I answered. It was Bernie. He asked, "How are you?"

I left the room and whispered, "I'm okay, considering. I can't talk any louder, because Temo is here sleeping." I explained my recent interactions with him as best I could. There was silence on the other end of the line.

Bernie finally asked, "What are you going to do?"

"I told Moira and she told his mother. He hates her, or so he says, but she needs to know he's alive and..." I paused because I couldn't bring myself to say "well."

"Do you think it was a good idea to let him back into your apartment?"

I said, "He has no one else."

Bernie abruptly changed the subject. "I'm calling from my new cell phone. I'm still in Detroit."

I asked, "Are you planning to live there?"

He laughed out loud. "Not on your life. I just bought a one-way ticket to New York. I was waiting to see who can put me up. I'll be staying in Harlem at first, but I want to find an apartment in Brooklyn."

"At last."

∞

As his stay in Detroit came to an end, Bernie sent me an email about one of his closest friends in Ann Arbor.

I first met Julie, who I knew as "Chloe Rasputin," just before she was taken out of school by her mother and admitted to the Cleveland Clinic for one of her stints there. (I know of eight times or so that she was institutionalized.) We met again months later, when she had returned and re-enrolled at University of Michigan. She lived in an "all woman" house, and most of them were dykes. It wasn't a separatist house, although there were a few such houses among their friends. Most were connected to the Women's Studies program within the Residential College, the program I was in, which had been set up in 1967 after riots on campus.

Chloe and I met up one Saturday morning for breakfast at a diner in downtown Ann Arbor. The conversation began as a word association game and never faltered. We had breakfast, went to junk shops, walked in the Arboretum, and in the evening we went to the Cinema Guild—there were three film groups with double features every night—for a program of Winsor McKay cartoons and *A Night at the Opera*. The word game lasted something like fifteen hours.

Considering how aggressive Chloe could be, she was also reclusive. People did not notice her until she became very manic and acted out, much later. She didn't do drugs because of all her medications, except pot, which she smoked constantly. She and the others in the house grew their own.

Over a year later when Julie/Chloe was going deep into her manic phase (no eating or sleeping, nonstop talking which left her with a raspy voice), there was an incident at the Residential College TV lounge one afternoon. Chloe could be black at times, or maybe she always was and we didn't know.

She went to the lounge to watch *Soul Train* but was voted down by the oafish boys who were always there watching sports. Chloe screamed at them and left. The lounge was ground level and had windows on a courtyard. No one saw who did it, but minutes later a brick was thrown through one of the windows with the words "white motherfuckers" painted on it. We all assumed Julie/Chloe had done this, but she never would admit it or even react when we tried praising the culprit. The college did not pursue any investigation and the boys just went back to their sports programs. That was an early public moment of Chloe's manias.

Chloe took up with a forty-four year old black man named John Cochran from Ann Arbor's two-block skid row and she brought him to campus for a few weeks before going to the Cleveland Clinic for "manic depressive psychosis." She told everyone he was her husband and the yin to her yang. I would phone her at the hospital where the orderlies knew her as "Julie Cochran." Names had some gravity. I sometimes suspected that John was a father figure, or reminded her of her father. I now wonder if he might have actually been her biological father, making the marriage idea especially perverse, or as psychiatrists would say, inappropriate.

She also had some delusions of omniscience: the big separation between us began when she got very angry that I didn't obey her telepathic commands. She (or her unconscious) must have chosen the name "Rasputin" to suggest invincibility; you couldn't kill her spirit. And maybe there was a Slavic aspect; her mother was of Lithuanian descent. There could have been a sexual dimension to this, too—the real Rasputin was reputed to have a massive penis—but she never tried anything with me. She called me and other friends "you whore" a lot.

I miss Chloe. She was an unforgettable friend, and exciting (if tiring) to be around. She reported in a moment of great lucidity that one psychiatrist who was especially sympathetic defined mental illness as "thinking differently," without any kind of moral judgment. She approved of that, and so do I.

One more thing: you mentioned something to me about Temo not saying anything about his "missing years." It's possible he doesn't remember them, because the antipsychotic meds they dispense at hospitals can have drastic side effects. A long time after the fact, I asked one of our mutual friends if he knew what had happened to Chloe, and he said, "They gave her a huge dose of Haldol to calm her down, and it turned her into a vegetable. The next thing she knew, it was eight years later."

Bernie must have sent this message to me as a way of being helpful. I wondered how much of what he wrote applied to Temo. I couldn't quite believe that he had lost whole years of his life. He had been to hell and back, possibly several times, and I wasn't sure I had the stamina to endure accompanying him on these trips. I didn't want to abandon him, but I had come to the conclusion that Graciela was the best person to care for him.

EIGHTEEN

Once I told Moira about Temo's return, it took only a couple of weeks for Graciela to come to town. She discovered that the tenants were moving out of one of the other apartments—the turnover rate in the building was extraordinary—and rented it sight unseen. One night she knocked when both Temo and I were home. I let her in, and she completely ignored me. Her eyes were on her son. They embraced, and Graciela began to sob. After she calmed down and dried her tears, she finally looked over at me and asked, *¿Es este él que te infectó?* She spoke quickly, and my Spanish comprehension was far from perfect, so there was a slight delay in me figuring out what she said. I smiled at her, then a moment later understood that she had asked, "Is this the one who infected you?"

The question disgusted Temo, and he was embarrassed that his mother would talk that way. He must have come to the hasty conclusion that I had shared the news of his HIV diagnosis indiscriminately, because he shot me a contemptuous glance and said, "I'll talk to you later" in English. I hadn't said a word about his HIV status, but his mother had assumed (correctly) that he'd seroconverted, and blamed the first male homosexual she saw. It wasn't a promising introduction.

There followed a heated discussion from which I decided to absent myself. As I retreated to the bedroom, I passed the closet where I still kept the bag that Graciela had given Temo years before, when he escaped from the family home in Mexico City. I spent the money it contained when I thought Temo might be dead. I remembered the note he had written, saying that I was welcome to whatever he left behind. I rummaged through an overflowing drawer until I found the outfit he was wearing the last time we saw each other before his disappearance. I was disappointed to find out that the smell of Temo on the clothing had faded away. Not only had his personal appearance changed in the intervening years, but his scent had changed, too. Whether that was due to the drugs he took or to a medical problem, or was simply the result of growing older, I couldn't say. I pondered the possibility of giving the bag back to Graciela, but I quickly came to the conclusion that nothing good would come of such a gesture. She would probably ask questions about the money, even though her son had never brought it up. The only object remaining in the bag was a small handgun. In the past I had had opportunities to dispose of it, and yet I never did. Now I wasn't about to hand it over to its original owner. There was no telling what she or Temo would do with it. As they shouted at each other in the next room, I took a frayed pillowcase from the bedroom closet and filled it with Temo's old clothes, which wouldn't fit him because of his weight gain. After the two of them left for Graciela's apartment downstairs, I placed the pillowcase in the old vinyl flight bag and discreetly threw everything in the trash.

About an hour later, a door slammed and suddenly there was silence. Later I heard random words of whatever argument the two of them continued to have, but in general, the atmosphere was peaceful. I assumed that Temo would be staying with his mother, so I gathered his possessions and placed them in a neat pile on the kitchen table. I thought about all the traces that a roommate or lover would leave in random places. None of these particularly annoyed me, and I found some of them endearing. The electric shaver Temo used to trim his beard every day was where he always left it, on top of the toilet. I thought it would be the first thing he'd ask for when retrieving his possessions.

∞

A week passed, and I wondered if Temo would ever visit me. He came to my door late one night and said, "She's asleep in front of the television. Can I come in?"

I said, "Yes, please."

Temo smiled. He seemed healthy, and he was dressed in new clothes. Life with mother agreed with him, or so it appeared. On impulse I grabbed him and kissed him. He whispered in my ear, "I really need to suck a dick."

"Come right this way," I said.

"I don't have much time."

I took off all my clothes and lay on my bed. He remained dressed and started to work on my cock. It swelled immediately. He swallowed it whole. I came very quickly. I relaxed and said, "Lie with me."

He said nothing to that, but unzipped his fly and brought out his beautiful brown cock. As he stood at the foot of my bed, he worked the foreskin quickly up and down over its head and started breathing heavily. Within a couple of minutes, he ejaculated all over my bedspread. He grunted, put his cock back in his pants, and said, "I needed that."

I rose and approached him, accidentally putting my knee in a puddle of cum. I grasped his arm and said, "Please, stay a while."

He shook his head. "No, I have to get back there before she wakes up. She'll wonder where I was." I was disappointed. I didn't want to torment him, but I needed to have at least a short conversation.

"Your things are on the kitchen table. Do you want to take them?"

"No, keep them."

"I suppose your mother will buy you all new stuff." I said, "You're looking well."

He gazed in my eyes with a desperate look. "I can't see you anymore, unless she doesn't know I'm gone. I'm sorry." I let out a gasp, because it was the first time that Temo had ever apologized to me. "Maybe if we find another place to stay and I get a car, I can arrange to meet you."

"Ah, so I'm not invited to dinner with the mother-in-law."

He frowned. "We're not married."

"I'm well aware of that. But there was a time I would have done anything to be with you."

He looked down and shook his head again. "Why didn't it work out?" There was a single tear at the corner of his eye.

"We can think of a lot of reasons."

With a sour expression he said, "Don't bother to make a list." He turned to go. I followed him to the door. Before he left he said, "You don't want a crazy husband anyway. I can tell." He kissed me lightly on the cheek, and as he stood in the doorway, he said, "My memory is getting better. I remember everything that happened between us. It makes me feel ashamed sometimes. And horny, too." I reached down to grab his crotch, and he swatted my hand away. Then he reached in his pocket and brought out a phone. Temo had convinced his mother to buy him the latest electronic gadget. He asked, "What's your number?" I gave it to him, and he sent me a text. I heard my old flip phone buzzing across the room.

I said, "I suppose you'll let me know when you can step out for a few minutes."

He nodded. "It's all that's possible now."

I laughed and said, "I'll fist you yet, my dear."

He put his hand over my mouth and said, "Be quiet. I have to go." He walked away and started to descend the stairs. I stood at the door frame completely naked and watched him. As he reached the landing, I caught a glimpse of him looking back, or perhaps it was only shadows playing tricks on me.

A short time later, I heard another argument between mother and son. The only word I could make out was *basura*, which I hoped referred to taking out the trash, his excuse for leaving the apartment, and not to the upstairs neighbor he had just fellated. I knew I was better off without Temo, but at the same time, I was sure that such a sensible thought would vanish from my mind the moment he texted me.

I looked through the possessions that Temo had left behind. I decided to keep the electric razor in the bathroom, in case I ever grew a beard, or (somewhat less likely) Temo ever spent the night. I placed it in the medicine cabinet, next to his toothbrush, which I couldn't bring myself to throw away. I grabbed his backpack and dumped its contents onto the living room table. There was a foul smell coming from it. I saw no driver's license, but I found his green card, which had expired. I put on some clothes and slipped it under the door downstairs. I went back up and continued searching his bag. At the very bottom of one pocket, I found a Polaroid picture of me. I didn't remember having given it to Temo. The photo came from my art school studio, and I concluded that Temo had stolen it on one of the few occasions he visited. Unlike everything else I found, it was clean. I looked at the image of a younger and skinnier me dressed in thrift store clothes, and I felt a slight stabbing pain in my chest. For a brief moment, I was seized by the belief that I had wasted my life, or at least ten years of it. I set the photo aside, then took the backpack down to the trash. I washed my hands thoroughly, took off my clothes, and got into bed. The covers reeked of Temo's semen. I decided to wait until morning to wash them. I masturbated until I fell asleep.

∞

I went down to the basement the next morning, and I heard noises coming from the laundry room. Inside I saw Daniel fucking Temo on top of a dryer. I decided not to make a scene, but instead of slipping away silently, I placed my sheets in the washer and started the cycle. I didn't make eye contact, and nobody said anything. Back in my apartment, I collapsed on the couch and pondered what I'd just witnessed. I doubted that Daniel had fucked Bernie and Paul to provoke me; it was probably only a coincidence. This time, it was no coincidence.

After about fifteen minutes, there was a knock at my door. I opened it to Daniel, who had a gleeful expression on his face, and Temo, who looked as though he was about to get a spanking. I asked, "Did you boys have fun?"

Daniel laughed and Temo said, "Let us in, will you?"

The two of them entered and sat on the couch. I played host and went to the kitchen to prepare some tea. Daniel called to me, "Hey, we didn't come over for breakfast."

I walked up to them and asked, "What do you want, a three-way?"

Temo looked down and said, "I didn't know you two knew each other."

"Something tells me Daniel was aware."

He smiled. "When this guy gave me his address, I couldn't believe it. I thought, maybe I can have sex with everyone in the building. Never done that before."

Temo gave him an appalled look and said, "I live with my mother."

I introduced the two of them: "Daniel, this is Temo; Temo, this is Daniel... in case you two aren't on a first name basis yet." Daniel waved and smiled, then an instant later, he figured out who he had just fucked. He peered at Temo and said, "Damn, you're the guy who broke his heart."

Temo scoffed, "He broke *my* heart."

At that moment, the kettle started whistling and I went to the kitchen. I turned off the burner but didn't prepare tea. I returned to the living room and said to Temo, "You know, I was avoiding you because I thought maybe you associate sex with meth, and I didn't want to trigger a relapse. But then you get rammed by my main fist buddy." He looked mortified that I had brought up his drug problem. I shook my head and said, "You're such an incredible slut. Do you even remember the first time you got fucked?"

Temo's face fell and he said, "I'm not here to talk about my father. Mind your business." He turned to Daniel and asked, "Does he speak to you that way?"

Daniel said, "All the time, but I don't care, because I like being humiliated."

Temo got up to leave and said, "None for me, thanks. I have to get back to my apartment."

I asked, "What are you going to tell your mother?"

Temo responded, "She's out shopping. She'll be home any minute."

Daniel groaned and said, "Somebody has a case of *mamitis*." Temo shook his head and left.

Within minutes, we heard more yelling from the apartment below. I said, "It's a miracle the old girl hasn't had a stroke." Daniel laughed uproariously. "Let me put my load in the dryer. I'll try to avoid the loads you two splattered all over it."

After I returned from the laundry room, Daniel said, "Let's get out of here. We can talk over lunch. My treat." I rode in his giant truck to the sushi restaurant on Hyperion next to Videoactive.

Daniel ordered an absurd amount of food, most of which he consumed as sloppily as ever. When he took a break from gorging himself, I asked, "Did you pull this little stunt on purpose to piss me off?"

"No, of course not." He took a big bite of his tempura roll, and with his mouth full, said, "I was thinking with my cock again." He paused and asked, "That's the guy who disappeared, right?"

I nodded and said, "Yeah, at last you're putting it together. The poor guy went through some bad times."

"Not that bad, I'm sure. He's a rich kid, I can tell."

I frowned. "I get the impression everyone in his family is some kind of monster, including him."

Daniel guffawed. "Mexicans are all thieves."

"So are Americans. We just have more expensive lawyers."

He attacked another roll with gusto and said, "Temo's *nalgas* are wide enough to drive a bus up there. But he probably can't take you up to the elbow the way I can."

"No, unless he's been playing with lots of other men."

Daniel said, "He probably has. I normally don't like other Hispanic guys, but he's hot."

"He used to be thinner and really gorgeous. I think the medications have distorted his body a bit."

"He's still handsome, and not bald like me. Lucky bastard." He asked, "What meds does he take?"

I said, "Lithium, or something like it, and Truvada. I found Viagra in his backpack, but I don't know why he had it. He's a total bottom."

"I bet he's into old white men like I am. Sometimes they need a little help, and they're too proud to get a script."

"It's not just old men who need help."

"You never had any problems with me."

"No, but I can't play the stud the way I used to." I paused. "I tried some of his Viagra recently and jerked off, but I didn't like it. I got a terrible headache."

"You just need blowjobs from someone who knows what he's doing. I can make you rock hard."

I changed the subject and asked, "Do you think he was serious about his father fucking him?"

Daniel said, "Who knows? He's the star of his own *telenovela*. How did you meet him?"

I said, "He worked at Libros Revolución with my oldest friend."

"He's a communist? Now that's a fucking joke. Has he ever worked a real job?"

"I doubt it."

Daniel frowned. "I wouldn't trust that guy."

"Yeah, I know what you mean, but it's too late now."

"You do like the drama, don't you?"

I said, "Not really. Drama finds me."

"If we were both free, I'd say we should be together. But we're not."

I said, "*I'm* free."

He gave me a skeptical look. "That's what you think." After lunch, we went to Videoactive, and Daniel rented some fetish videos. I rented *The Mother and the Whore* by Jean Eustache. He laughed at the title and asked, "Is that about your friend and his mom?"

I rolled my eyes. "It's a three and a half hour black and white French film about... I'm not sure if I can explain what it's about."

"And it's on VHS. You sure can pick a winner."

"Who are you to talk? You're renting *The Cheesiest Uncut Cowboy in West Texas*, for heaven's sake."

He grinned. "I'm a pervert and I'm proud." We drove back to my place. Daniel kissed me and said, "I love you." I started to answer him, and he put his hand over my mouth. "Don't say anything, because I know you're in love with the *cerote* downstairs. Just remember, when he disappears again, I'll still be here."

NINETEEN

I received an email from an account I didn't recognize, and since it had no suspicious attachments, I opened it. The message was from Winston:

> Congratulations. Gregorio showed me digital images from your exhibition at Carmen's gallery. I laughed when I saw some of the photos. You are truly an artist. Since you are an artist, I will challenge you. The work leaves me with questions. What is the future of this project? Is it the basis of an artistic practice or is it a joke? Your indifference to craft is the result of your education. As you know, I did not adopt that way of working. My goal is a well-made painting. You have many ideas. Perhaps this is your weakness. You sit on the divan and think instead of making objects. Your paintings look more like ideas than images. I hope you do not run out of ideas. I remember when we were in school, Michael Asher talked about reification, and it was necessary for me to consult a dictionary. The definition of the word is "treating an idea as a concrete entity," a logical error. The map is not the territory.

Are your paintings examples of reification? For what purpose? The only answer I can give you is that the market demands it. The artist in academia has the luxury of ignoring the market, but you did not pursue that career. Do you make a good living from pornography? Perhaps this question is aggressive. I have no problem with aggression, but some people consider it impolite. At some point I would like to discuss these matters with you in person. I apologize for my terrible English. I miss you every day.

After reading this, I turned off my computer and lay on the couch for the rest of the afternoon.

∞

In the days since I had seen him having sex with Daniel, Temo didn't speak to me. Then he unexpectedly came to my door and said, "My father died yesterday." There was no emotion in his voice.

I said, "I'm sorry."

"Thank you. He never recovered from his stroke. Now that he's gone, my mother will return to Mexico. She wants me to go with her, but I can't because my green card expired, and I won't be able to enter the US again if I leave. My absence from his funeral will be a scandal. Another one. I missed my brother's funeral, too. I don't care about rituals. And I hated both of them."

I asked, "Do you want to come in and sit down?"

"Not tonight." He stared blankly. "My mother will be out of town for a few days. Are you going to fist your friend Daniel again soon?"

I said, "I don't know. I'm keeping my distance from him." I stared at Temo in the doorway. I began to wonder who this person standing before me really was. He seemed to feel nothing for his family. They had done violence to him, and he had banished them from his mind. Perhaps his attempts to make sense of his experiences crowded out any emotions. In Temo's life, there was no room for anyone but Temo. I imagined that if I had been the one who died, I would have inspired more or less the same non-reaction.

He said, "I need to get fucked soon. The gym is the only place I can go without my mother. All I can do there is work out and suck cock."

I said, "I'll see what I can do."

∞

One evening I went to the market. Shopping without a car in Los Angeles was always a chore, and even with a wheeled cart, the climb up the hill to my apartment exhausted me. When I entered the building, I noticed that the door to Temo's apartment was ajar. I approached and heard loud noises coming from inside. I walked though the door and heard Temo scream. I headed toward the back of the apartment. I knew that I shouldn't have done this, since he was obviously having sex, but I couldn't resist. I told myself that he had left his front door open intentionally. I peered through the doorway to the bedroom.

Temo was on all fours and showing a rosebud. Medical professionals would have called this a prolapse and expressed concern about the health consequences of a man's asshole falling out of his asshole, but for some, this bright red sleeve of flesh was a status symbol. I heard a voice say, "Man, I'm jealous." It was Daniel. The next moment, he got behind Temo and buried his face in his ass. After nearly suffocating, he drew back a little and kissed the rosebud. Then he peeled off his jockstrap and started jerking his cock. He plunged it into Temo's hole and started to pump away. The hole made a sound, not exactly a fart, but something like a squeak.

Daniel's thighs started to slap against Temo's ass. He was about to reach orgasm and said, "I'm gonna shoot."

Temo responded, "Don't pull out, fucker." After Daniel came, I heard a muffled voice say, "Fuck my face." Daniel pulled out his messy cock and inserted it in Temo's mouth. Temo gagged and nearly vomited, and Daniel paused. With an angry look, Temo said, "More." Daniel raped his face violently. When Daniel had had enough, he sat back for a moment. Temo barked at him, "Lie on your back," then he got up and squatted over Daniel's face. With a long, slow farting sound, he lowered his hole onto Daniel's mouth, and released whatever his rectum contained. Daniel greedily slurped it up. He rose to kiss Temo. The two of them made out for a while. When they pulled away from each other, both their faces were covered in viscous pale fluids that dripped down onto their chests. The look in Temo's eyes made me think that he was using meth again. My first impulse was to say something, but I stood where I was and remained silent.

Temo's asshole was far more open than I'd ever seen it. Daniel's meaty hand, larger than mine, slipped inside easily. His ass swallowed most of Daniel's forearm, then slowly, the arm went deeper, until the elbow disappeared as well. I had never seen anyone take an arm so deep, and I couldn't turn away. A half hour later, Daniel's brawny arm was buried up to the armpit inside Temo, who had a completely vacant expression on his face. I realized that this was Temo's desired state: a piece of flesh beyond the realm of normal sensations with a mind bereft of anything aside from the hunger to be violated. I suspected that all his protestations of love and friendship were only strategies to achieve a goal, which was the complete obliteration of his person.

Daniel slowly pulled his arm out while Temo moaned as though he was giving birth. His breathing became erratic and his skin glistened with sweat. Daniel's arm emerged covered in patches of blood and mucus. Temo shuddered at intervals on the bed. He looked as though he was about to go into shock. As Temo gradually recovered from the intense sensations that had taken hold of him, Daniel turned to me with a smile and asked, "Did you enjoy the show?"

Without saying anything, I turned away and left the apartment. Leaving my cart full of groceries at the door, I flung myself on the couch and lay still for a while, thinking about what I had just seen. Daniel couldn't deny that he had planned this spectacle to mess with my mind, but I doubted that this was his main motivation. He had a compulsion to get as much sex as possible, without paying heed to the possible consequences. If drama unfolded as a result, that would simply provide some extra entertainment value. Or perhaps Temo had planned the scene, to show what he really wanted from me, or from any sex partner. I looked down at my arms, longer and thinner than Daniel's, and imagined them inside Temo's colon. I wondered if Temo had been this voracious for as long as I'd known him, or if his desires had become more extreme over the years. Daniel and Temo as sex partners made sense, because they had their remorseless pursuit of pleasure in common. I couldn't raise a moral objection to hedonism in and of itself—that would have been hypocritical—but I couldn't imagine making it my life's goal. In sex, I enjoyed friendship and intimacy, and they seemed to have no use for either.

I began to understand that Daniel and Temo weren't pursuing pleasure so much as enacting a bleak compulsion. Both of them at one time or another had said, "I love you," but, as I realized to my cost, people will say just about anything to get what they want. The two of them had revealed their true selves to me, if indeed either of them had what conventional people would call a self. I was glad that they had found each other.

∞

The next day, I called my friend Raúl. Originally from Peru, he had moved all around Latin America and ended up in Los Angeles, where his father was a Protestant minister. Raúl was the man who had taught me how to fist, and before he moved away to attend the University of Chicago, he introduced me to Daniel. He had known Temo in Chicago, though the two of them had parted on bad terms. He was involved in a serious relationship with a man named Sean who taught in southern Illinois. I hadn't heard from him in a long time, but I figured he would be curious about what was happening with his former fuckbuddies. He answered my call right away and said, "I'm in Phoenix now."

I asked, "What brought this on?"

"Sean got a new job in Tempe. It's been a whole adjustment for him. He comes from New England. Mostly he's trying to avoid heatstroke."

"What's Phoenix like?"

"It's a lot more conservative than the places I'm used to. Sean sort of likes that, because he's pretty conservative himself."

I remembered his conflicts with Temo, whose politics were practically fascist, and asked, "How do you two get along?"

"Sean is an American who hasn't seen much of the world. He's patriotic in a way I had never seen before, but he's getting a different point of view from me." He paused. "You don't know him. He's a genuinely kind person, and he really listens to people when they talk to him. That's why I love him."

I asked, "Does he fist you?"

"He's still getting used to the idea. I'm allowed to play with other guys, but in this city, that's a whole project."

"Not many fisters?"

Raúl laughed and said, "Oh, there are guys who do it, but a lot of them are snowbirds. These old white guys from the Midwest retire and go wild in Arizona. There's a lot of verbal abuse and race play to deal with, and I hate that."

"Have you been to any sex parties?"

"Yeah, but the fisting groups here are really cliquish. It's like high school, and I'm not part of the 'in crowd.' It's depressing."

I asked, "Do you miss Los Angeles?"

"Actually, I just got a job working for the Lutheran bishop of Southern California, so I'll be coming into town regularly. No plans to move, because Sean's got a tenure track position, and he hates Los Angeles."

"I'll be happy to see you. What will you be doing for the Lutherans?"

"It's complicated. The Lutheran Church owns a lot of real estate in the area that's just sitting vacant. The bishop wants to sell it off and use the money to fund social programs like affordable housing, food pantries, community clinics. I'm advising them on how to do that, because social work is the main reason I've been involved with Christian churches. And the Lutherans paid for my education. The denomination is Northern European, and in the US, it's big in Minnesota and the Dakotas. I belong to the whitest Protestant denomination that isn't explicitly racist."

I said, "And now they have a big Peruvian fist pig in the church hierarchy."

He laughed. "Yeah, I'm really conspicuous. They need me because I'm in touch with what's going on outside the church doors. My colleagues mean well, but they don't have a clue sometimes. Anyway, I'll let you know when I'm in Los Angeles... actually Glendale; that's where the church offices are." He apologized. "I'm sure you didn't call to hear about church politics."

"Well, no." I summarized the story of Daniel and Temo for Raúl as best I could, and I told him that I didn't particularly want to see them anymore. I asked, "Do you think I'm judging them too harshly?"

He answered, "I don't know. Both of them are trouble. I saw that right away. Maybe you did too, but you found out that trouble can be fun."

"Oh, it was, but now I think I never really knew either of them."

"You take your chances with these fist pigs, you know? Some are great guys, and others will make your life miserable if you let them."

I said, "I let Temo do exactly that." I told Raúl the story of my lover's reappearance, and ended by saying, "I did what I could for him."

"Some people are beyond help until they decide they truly need it."

I asked, "Did you suspect Temo was mentally ill, or that he was doing drugs?"

"He seemed unstable, but that just added to the thrill of the sex while it lasted. The new meth wasn't in Chicago yet, but I bet he was using ketamine. Maybe he was in a k-hole when he took Daniel up to the shoulder. I'm sorry I can't say more. Our relationship wasn't very pleasant, and I stopped paying attention."

I said, "I believed that I was going to be connected forever to the men I fisted. It turns out you're the only one I'm still in touch with. I was enough of a crackpot to think I was building a community. In this age of consumerist zombies, I thought fisting was a way of finding the last interesting homosexuals in America—the malcontents who aren't satisfied with the crumbs we're thrown, like niche marketing and 'representation in the media,' whatever the fuck that means."

Raúl laughed. "You're not a crackpot, you're a utopian, my friend. I wish you could have met my uncle in Lima. He would have agreed with you."

I asked, "What happened to him?"

"Don't you remember me telling you? He died of AIDS in the late 1980s."

"Oh yeah, I'm sorry."

"He lived in a place and time that was really oppressive for anyone who didn't conform to the model of heterosexual coupling, but he figured out a way to live his life surrounded by men who loved him. Well, that's how I imagine it. When I'm trying to find fist buddies in Phoenix, I sometimes think of him and his buddies trying to build a community. The objective circumstances of their situation were much tougher. I think that made their bonds stronger and their relationships more authentic."

I said, "It sounds almost like you want more oppression."

"No, believe me, there's enough shit to deal with in Arizona. It's easy to meet men online, in theory, but I can't ask for what I really want, a circle of good friends I just happen to fist fuck. I'm still searching."

∞

Temo knocked on my door the night before his mother's return from Mexico. I let him in, and he sat on the sofa and sighed. The conversation started uncomfortably. He said, "Since that night with Daniel, I decided I need to live on my own again. I should have this kind of experience whenever I want without anyone restraining me."

"Do you think that's a good idea?"

"Probably not, but I don't want my mother controlling my life."

I asked, "What does Daniel mean to you?"

He laughed. "He's a piece of meat, better than a sex toy, but not exactly the man of my dreams. For now, he's convenient. There are lots more like him out there. I know from experience."

I said, "The last time you lived alone, it didn't turn out well."

"Don't remind me. I'm embarrassed by a lot of things in the past. You don't know what it's like, seeing people in the street and asking yourself, 'Did I have sex with that guy?' or 'Did I say something awful to him?' I don't think I can live here anymore."

"Not without a green card, no."

He heaved a loud sigh. "Yeah, that too. I'll only be able to come to Los Angeles for short visits, if I come at all. My mother wants me to return to Mexico City. I don't know if there's a choice. I have no money of my own."

I said, "Speaking of money, I've been meaning to ask you about the cash you left with me when you disappeared."

His face brightened. "Do you still have it?"

I looked at him with an incredulous expression. "What do you think? I used it to pay off my student loans."

"Ah, of course. You were smart."

I asked, "Do you want me to pay it back?"

"Nice of you to ask, but it's a trivial amount."

"Not to me it isn't. It was almost $30,000."

He said, "Then you should have it. Really, it doesn't mean that much." He shifted his weight and said, "I'll tell you something. Three days after my father's death, my mother started to renovate his sick room. A little tasteless, but that's my mother. She hated him. The workers tore down a wall and discovered money hidden behind the plaster. They found a few million US, big bundles of hundred dollar bills wrapped in plastic."

"That's incredible."

"Not in my family. They do everything they can to hide money and launder it, with help from the good people at HSBC. My family would buy art, but they don't care about Jasper Johns or whoever, and there's always the risk of buying a forgery. They prefer to buy and develop real estate. My father made his first fortune in construction. He worked his way up in the business and knew how it was done." Suddenly he looked at me with the expression of someone with a brilliant idea. He asked, "Do you want me to buy this building?"

I was startled. "What?"

"It can't be very expensive. That way, I'll have a reason to visit, and you won't have to worry about getting evicted. Don't you want a secure place to live?"

I paused for a moment. My first thought was of my arm buried in Temo's ass up to the shoulder. I felt a tingle in my crotch, but I decided to give him an answer he might not have expected. I said, "I don't think I'd feel comfortable being dependent on you in that way."

"What difference does it make? There's cash we didn't know existed. Look at yourself, and look at this place. Face it: you're poor. You have to sell yourself to someone. Why not me? You should do it before you're bald, toothless, and impotent."

"Well, thank you." I pointed out, "That money in the wall is your mother's. Your plan depends on the good will of a woman who hates me."

"You have to admit it's not a bad idea."

I said, "From a certain point of view, yes, but my intuition tells me it'll end in tears."

"Like our relationship, like all relationships."

"Now you're just being cynical." Realizing I would have to choose my words carefully, I took a breath. "We had some good times, but I think they were at the expense of your mental health."

He said, "My only regret is that I didn't try harder to be a real boyfriend to you."

"It's a bit late to say that, don't you think? You're on the verge of leaving town."

He smiled and said, "If you don't want me to buy the building, come with me. You would love Mexico City."

"I can't. I need my independence, and you need to work on making a life for yourself. Besides, how would I get along with your mother?"

He snarled, "You always bring her up."

"You brought her into this conversation, if I remember correctly."

"Logic won't get you anywhere." He rested his face in his hands and began to cry. "You're the closest I ever came to having a boyfriend." I pulled him closer to me and let him cry on my shoulder for a while.

I said, "You should figure out what you really want."

Neither of us could think of anything to say. Temo pulled himself together and got up to leave. He said, "Take care of yourself."

"You too," I said, without mentioning the obvious, that taking care of himself was something he was barely capable of doing.

As I shut the door, I wondered what words Temo could have used to convince me to live with him. I began to suspect that they didn't exist. He could spin a web of intrigue and seduce a man, but ultimately, his ability to take an interest in another human being was extremely limited. Any serious relationship I could imagine having with him would be punishing. Perhaps one day he'd find the perfect lover who cared for him as a person, not just as a sexual object, who had a similar emotional makeup to his mother, but who just happened to have male genitalia.

TWENTY

Since I was nowhere near running out of material, I continued to work on DVD compilations for Larry Flynt, watching hundreds of hours of monotonous nullity. I made only the most schematic notes and spent most of the time with my thumb on the remote's fast forward button. I listened to music during the viewing sessions, and I found that my favorite accompaniment to the material was Led Zeppelin. The songs about love and lust and the rituals of pagan religions set to the tune of modern blues pastiches complemented the porn perfectly. I associated the band with pot smoking lumpen proles in heat, lunging at Robert Plant in his fringed outfits and long hair, worshiping the guitar pyrotechnics of Jimmy Page, and rubbing one out later in the privacy of teenage bedrooms. That was a concise description of my high school milieu. What had become of subsequent generations? Perhaps they moved to Los Angeles, got into speed, and performed in porn so that pot smoking introverts all over the world could rub one out in the privacy of adult bedrooms. I thought about the people with whom I went to high school, the ones who had never left town. I had no notion of what they experienced in the bleak landscape where I grew up. Perhaps they were having orgies to the sound of *Houses of the Holy* or *Physical Graffiti*, but I doubted it. From a certain point of view, I was exacting a revenge on my former classmates as the glamorous producer of adult videos. If only they knew that the real Hudson Wilcox was a homebody earning a pittance and barely scraping by in a city getting more expensive with every passing year. I was lost in such self-indulgent fantasies when Jerry called me. He asked, "What are you doing?"

I answered, "Listening to 'When the Levee Breaks' and masturbating." He laughed, and I said, "I wish I were being entirely facetious. Doing this work is drying up my soul."

"You're still working for Flynt? Good for you. I thought maybe they discontinued their line of DVDs, since video-on-demand is where things are going." He paused and said, "Working in porn, I'm going to hell for sure, but before that, I'm going to Berlin."

I said, "Sounds fun."

"It's a free trip. The Pornofilmfestival invited me to talk on a panel."

"Congratulations. When are you leaving?"

He said, "In a few weeks. Here's the thing, they want a gay dude to speak, because the organizers and the audience are mostly gay. I'm working for Vivid Video now. The place is about as straight as VCA was, and there's no one who'd be a knowledgeable speaker. Do you want to come along?"

"Maybe." I asked, "What do I have to talk about?"

"Vintage gay porn, your specialty."

"Yeah, I'm up for a trip. Put me in touch with the festival people."

"Great. You won't regret it."

I asked, "How is Eon McKai doing?"

"Man, it's weird being famous. So many people dragging you on message boards. I spend too much time putting out fires."

I asked, "Are you making money?"

"Oh sure, but to be totally honest, the drugs are sort of catching up with me."

"Damn, what are you doing?'

He exhaled audibly. "Speed. It's really helped. On television they show all these people with caved in faces and rotten teeth. That's only the alarmist side of the story. Doctors prescribe speed to kids with ADHD to help them concentrate. I'm more like that. I can focus my mind better on the task at hand. What's the difference between a boy failing math class because he can't sit still and a pornographer like me? A few years, that's all."

"Well, be careful."

He said, "Hey, I'm in this for the long haul. I'm not going to mess up."

"You don't want to get strung out like Tony Passolini did. He could have had a brilliant career."

"I guess so. I found out a while back that he actually went to USC, so the porn industry is about the right destination for him."

I laughed. "I suppose if he had a degree from Harvard, he'd be writing for *The Simpsons* or *Futurama*. Or he'd be a lawyer for adult video producers."

He said, "With my education, I'm lucky to be working."

"Aren't we all? I'm really proud of you. You're innovating in the shittiest, most exploitative business in America."

"You say that now, but wait until the tech industry takes over the planet." He paused as though he was glancing at an email. "Hey, I have to go, but I'll see you in Berlin if not before. Don't forget to bring warm clothes. I've been warned."

"Thanks for thinking of me." I hung up the phone and was tempted to tell someone the good news right away. I quickly realized that I had no local friends I'd want to bother at that hour, and it was way too late to call Berlin. I emailed Gregorio, and he responded the next day. He said he'd be happy to see me, and Winston (who was working in the studio preparing for an exhibition) felt the same way. I was welcome to stay with them, as they had plenty of room. He'd let me know about ground transportation once my flight was arranged. Their building was not in the sort of neighborhood where tourists ever ventured.

As it turned out, Air Berlin offered non-stop flights from LAX to Tegel Airport. This came as a pleasant surprise, because the last time I had made such a trip, German airlines were barred from flying directly from the United States to West Berlin. (It was only then that I realized it had been more than fifteen years since German unification, and I suddenly felt rather old.) I told the festival staff that I could stay with friends and didn't need a hotel room, and they booked a ticket for me leaving mid-October, with a return flight I could change without penalty.

∞

I landed at Tegel on a cool sunny day. Gregorio was there to meet me as soon as I cleared customs and immigration. He said, "Welcome to Berlin," and kissed me. I had had only a couple of hours of sleep on the plane, and I was feeling rather punchy. We got in a taxi and headed for his neighborhood. The route involved travel on a highway at the periphery, so I saw the center of the city only from a distance. The sun coming through the car window warmed me up. Gregorio held my hand.

We arrived at a somewhat isolated freestanding building near disused train tracks. It had formerly housed offices of the East German state railroad system, and to the left of the front door, a plaque with its old logo, the letters DR in a circle of text reading "Deutsche Reichsbahn," was still in place. At the right side of the door was another medallion with the hammer and compass no longer seen on any German flag. Bars on the windows and a dirty gray exterior gave a forbidding impression. From the looks of the place, it seemed as though I would be stepping into the 1950s when I crossed the threshold. At the center of the door was a sign: Studio Andë Alia. *Bitte klingeln.* The entry opened onto a large staircase that was in a less than perfect state of repair. I heard footsteps. It was Winston coming down to meet me. Even from a distance I noticed that he had gained a considerable amount of weight during the eight years I hadn't seen him. He now looked like a bear in designer clothing. The suit, perfectly tailored for his frame, was dark gray wool with pinstripes that didn't reach all the way to the end of the fabric. There were paint stains all over it. Winston was as pale as ever, and had lost most of the hair on the top of his head. He had grown a bushy black beard to compensate. From what I could see, there wasn't a single gray hair in it. He took a long time making his entrance so that I might have a good look at him. He exuded the nonchalant yet intimidating air of a man with plenty of money.

I looked over at Gregorio, whose attire I hadn't noticed up to that point because it was so nondescript. He wore jeans and a hoodie, with the only sign of affluence being an expensive pair of athletic shoes. I thought for a moment about the transformation of skinny Winston and chubby Gregorio into the figures they now cut. Just as Winston reached me, I thought to myself, I wonder if they still sleep together.

Winston opened his arms and said, "My friend, you have finally graced us with your presence." He had the same accent I remembered from school, a unique combination of Albanian and German, and he seemed to have lost none of his proficiency in spoken English.

As we hugged, I said, "I'm happy to see you. It's been too long."

"Indeed." Winston looked intently at me and pronounced his judgment: "You are looking well, but somewhat underfed. We will fix that." We walked into the kitchen to the right of the staircase. It was much warmer and brighter than the lugubrious central hall, which must have cost a fortune to heat. To my surprise, there was another person there, standing at the sink. Winston announced, "This is El. He does not live here, not yet."

El put down a cup of coffee and stretched out his hand to shake mine. He was tall, about my height, and wore a dark blue wool suit (as impressive as Winston's, but without the paint stains and ironic stripes), a white shirt, a silk tie with a subtle check design in blue and black, and a slightly preposterous lilac colored vest. He had the aspect of a dandy, with every detail immaculate. There was something old fashioned about his look, and I wouldn't have been surprised to see him reach for a bowler hat. His full head of hair was dark brown, and his beard, dense and uniform with a slight reddish cast, was so precisely trimmed that he made Winston look like an unkempt bohemian by comparison. His eyes were a vivid green and his gaze had an intensity that almost dared me to look away. He cleared his throat, and I snapped out of my reverie. I had no idea how much time had elapsed while I looked at him. In perfect English with a German accent, he said, "You boys from America are never dressed warmly enough. You don't want to catch cold. Perhaps I can lend you something." He turned and left the room.

Gregorio said, "Before I forget, here are our numbers." He placed a sheet of paper in front of me, and I searched my pocket for the cell phone I had turned off during the flight. He asked, "Does your phone work?"

"I bought a SIM card for Europe. I think I'm technically calling from Estonia while I'm here." I started entering the information, and I noticed that Winston had no number. I looked up and asked, "What's +43?"

"The country code for Austria, which has cheaper cell phone service than Germany." Gregorio said, "That reminds me, do you have a number for the festival people? I should call to tell them you've arrived." I fumbled for a paper and handed it to him, and he promptly called the office. Somewhat to my surprise, he had a whole conversation in German. When he was done, he said, "You have the day off, no need to show up at their office until tomorrow. Your panel is on Thursday."

Winston said, "I must paint now. El has a meeting at Charité Hospital later today, but before that, he can keep you company. Museum Island is on the way."

"All I want to do is sleep."

Gregorio said, "A bad idea. You have to get over your jet lag. Drink some coffee. Maybe you'll wake up." He poured me a cup that I nearly spat out. Seeing the look on my face, he laughed and said, "El made the coffee. Don't worry, I'm making dinner." He showed me to my room, on the other side of the staircase from the kitchen, and I quickly unpacked a few items, brushed my teeth, washed my face, then went back to the kitchen.

El came in with a houndstooth overcoat, which he held for me to put on. "Here," he said, "Borrow this so you won't freeze." I noticed that he was no longer wearing the vest that had drawn my stare. We went out the back door to a parking lot. I half expected to see a fleet of Trabants, the East German model of automobile, but El drove a small Opel, nothing fancy. There were no other cars. As he turned on the ignition, I noticed that the nail of his right index finger had been painted copper. I didn't ask why. He announced, "First stop, Kreuzberg. I need a haircut. Perhaps you do as well."

"I hadn't thought of getting one." I looked at him. "Your hair looks fine to me."

"It grows so quickly that I need a trim every two weeks. It will be fun, you'll see."

He parked in front of a nondescript building. Remembering that we had passed from the old East to the old West, I said, "I didn't see any trace of the Wall on the drive here."

"Little of it remains. We can pass by Checkpoint Charlie if you like. It's a tourist attraction now." We entered a barber shop, and since it was mid-day on Monday, there were no other customers. El hugged and kissed the barber on both cheeks. They spoke a language I didn't understand and couldn't recall ever having heard. The barber, who looked older than El and wore a traditional head scarf, nodded a greeting. El turned to me and said, "He speaks no English, but he says you are welcome to sit. He can bring you tea."

I said, "No thanks, I just had some of your coffee."

El responded, "I make it quite strong. I'm sorry." The barber laughed as though he understood what his customer had said, then started to work. He used a pair of scissors and an electric trimmer to clean up stray hairs, of which there were very few. The ritual was less for grooming than for socializing. I noticed that the barber also had a single copper fingernail. I guessed that it was like the green carnation in Oscar Wilde's England, a sign used to identify those men who preferred the company of other men. The barber looked my way a number of times. The two of them had a brief conversation, once again glancing over at me, and El abruptly rose and took off his jacket and shirt. He was extremely hairy, front and back, and I noticed a crucifix around his neck. The barber went to a special dispenser and came back with a hand full of hot shaving cream. El asked, "Should he shave my back?"

"Certainly not."

He smiled. "Ah, you're not one of those Americans who is repulsed by body hair. Good." After a few more words exchanged and another glance in my direction, the barber spread the foam only on El's neck. He shaved it delicately with a straight razor. He took a small amount of leftover shaving cream and spread it on El's cheeks, then shaved them even more gently. The whole process of the haircut, beard trim, and shave looked so sensual that I felt myself getting an erection, and I was glad that El had lent me an overcoat that hid it. After checking his appearance in a hand-held mirror, he got up from the chair and dressed. The barber looked at me, and I rose from my chair. The overcoat fell open, revealing a sizable bulge in my pants. He said something, and the two of them laughed. El said to me, "If you grow a beard, you must go to Goran. He will be happy to trim it for you." Euros changed hands, and we were soon out on the street.

I asked, "Did Winston tell you that this is my first time in Berlin after the Wall came down?"

"No, that's amazing. We should drive through Mitte."

"Yes, please."

Mitte, the center of Berlin, had experienced one of the most radical peacetime transformations of any city in modern history. I saw little that I recognized. From my last visit, I remembered sooty stone buildings riddled with bullet holes from the war and shops displaying goods decades out of date by Western standards. We passed giant buildings and new construction. I looked around and began to get dizzy. I felt like a visitor from another planet.

As we approached Museum Island, I saw the Palast der Republik partially shrouded in scaffolding. El said, "They have now started to demolish that monstrosity. The Palast is thoroughly contaminated with asbestos. The salvaged steel will go to Dubai to build the Burj Khalifa. Andë, I mean Winston, said that he used to go bowling there when he was a teenager in East Berlin. He's angry to see it disappear."

"I've never been there. Bowling? Winston is full of surprises."

He said, "I have a question. Everyone here calls him Andë except you and Gregorio. Why?"

"Old habit. We didn't know his real name when we first became friends. He always used his punk name, Winston Smith, like the protagonist of *1984*."

He smiled and said, "Perhaps I should read the book."

"It's not really necessary. Winston never did."

El laughed. "You're funny. I like that."

I said, "Don't forget to tip your waitress. I'll be here all week." El gave me a look of total incomprehension. I explained, "It's a stand up comedian's line. Forgive me."

El looked pleasantly confused as he drove past the Lustgarten. As if by some miracle, we found parking behind Humboldt University. El said, "I was going to drop you at the Pergamon Museum, but

I have enough time before my meeting to walk to the office from here. Is it okay?"

"Yes, thanks for the ride. Where would you like to meet?"

"I'll text you when I'm done. We can meet by the bridge in front of the museum, then go to the Bode. It's around the corner." We got out of the car, and before he left, kissed my cheeks three times and hugged me.

∞

At the museum, I sat on the steps of the Pergamon Altar and tried to stay awake. I watched the crowds pass by and remembered that the last time I was there, the place was full of Soviet soldiers on leave. They moved around in packs wearing gray overcoats and fur hats, with one of their number holding a cassette player aloft so they could all hear the audio tour in Russian. At the time, I wondered how many American soldiers were enjoying the Dahlem Museums, which were in their zone of occupation. Suddenly, a blonde toddler approached and started speaking gibberish to me. A minute later, a woman rushed over and smiled apologetically. She said to him, *Mein lieber, du solltest die Menschen respektieren.*

I said, "It's okay, he wasn't bothering me." At that instant, I realized that I understood what she was saying to her son, but I had no idea why. I attributed it to jet lag and lack of sleep.

I moved through the museum in a daze, until I stood in front of the immense Ishtar Gate, in such a beautiful state of preservation that it appeared to be a fake. Beside it was a sign acknowledging Iraq's claim of ownership to this ancient monument smuggled out of the Ottoman Empire by German archaeologists a hundred years before. As I wandered through the rest of the museum, I received a text from El. About twenty minutes later, I went to the coat check. El arrived at the bridge a few minutes late. We walked along the opposite side of the narrow channel of the river Spree and I asked, "How did your meeting go?"

He held up his hands in exasperation and said, "These administrators will do anything to ruin one's day. How was the museum?"

"Wonderful. Even though the Wall has come down, some things never change. The building still shakes a bit when a train goes by." He laughed, and I said, "It was lovely to see the Ishtar Gate again. There's a sign placed in front of it at the request of Iraq."

He shrugged. "Germany can have the gate. They have me, though I am not an antiquity. This country gave me a place to live and a free education. Why should I care about the modern state of Iraq? It killed three million of my people."

I was so shocked that I could think of nothing to say in response to El's statement, so I walked next to him in silence for a while. I said, "Gregorio told me you're Kurdish. I'm sorry I forgot."

"I come from a country that doesn't exist, because some English imbeciles who knew nothing but *The Arabian Nights* decided to draw a few arbitrary lines on a map of the Middle East. We have been dealing with the consequences ever since."

I asked, "Do you ever miss where you came from?"

"Not very much. I miss the sun and the heat. I grew up in a Christian neighborhood of Erbil in northern Iraq. I want to return, but only when it is safe again... if it is ever safe again." He paused. "I have a good life here."

I asked, "What sort of work do you do?"

He relaxed and said, "I do research on olfaction—the sense of smell—and emotional contagion, how emotions spread through groups of people. The current study is about empathy."

"That sounds interesting."

"It is, and it enables me to travel to meet my colleagues in Wien—a very beautiful city, but a little sleepy."

"That explains the Austrian cell phones." He smiled and nodded. "Speaking of sleep, I think we should head home before too long." We sat on the stone seats outside the Bode Museum, at the very tip of Museum Island.

El said, "Winston and Gregorio's building is not my home. I live close, at Rosa-Luxemburg-Platz. From there, I can walk to the Mitte campus of the hospital and these museums."

"I'd like to see your apartment."

He smiled, not acknowledging what could have been taken as a sexual proposition, and said, "Your friends have a much bigger place. Mine is *asketische*. I can't think of the English word." He stroked his beard and said, "Perhaps you would say 'austere.'"

I nodded. "I haven't seen much of the building yet, except my room and the kitchen and that imposing staircase. It's cavernous. I thought a vampire bat might come out of the attic."

He laughed. "The attic is where Winston paints. I'm not allowed to go there uninvited."

"Oh, Winston. Perhaps I can loosen him up a bit."

"I have tried. *He* is austere."

I said, "Well, I've known him since art school."

"Yes, he loves you a lot. I hope you know."

"I do. I've been a bad friend, not seeing him for a long time. I was so happy to see Gregorio in Los Angeles."

He leaned toward me. "He told me all about it. I wish I had been there, too."

"Oh yeah?"

"Without Gregorio, our household fell apart. I asked Winston, 'Who is this man seducing our lover?' Then Winston showed me your picture. You're more handsome in person, I think." I felt intoxicated in the presence of this man I had just met. I reached out and took his hand. He put his other hand, the one with the copper nail, on top of mine. He said, "If we're going to see more art, we should do it now. I prefer not to drive after six, when the traffic is worst."

We entered the Bode, a museum I didn't remember from my first visit to the city. Because most of its objects were sculptures rather than fragile paintings or works on paper, natural light—as much as there was in autumnal Berlin—flooded into the space. It was bright enough to inspire me to take a picture. I pulled out my camera and asked El to stand next to a sculpture called *St. Vitus in a Kettle*. The saint struck a pious pose, praying as he was about to be scalded to death, or possibly cooked and eaten by cannibals. El imitated the attitude of prayer, and we laughed. We moved on to see many fragmentary sculptures displayed on armatures in front of monochromatic panels, a modern context for works of art from the Middle Ages. We paused in front of a remarkable polychrome wood sculpture of Jesus by Hans Leinberger. The figure's naked feet were disproportionately large and his toes spread out sensually on the green grass at the base. I said, "This looks like it was carved by a foot fetishist."

El laughed uproariously. When he stopped, he said, "Look at the name of the sculpture."

"*Christus im Elend.*"

"Did you know I'm called Elend?" I nodded. "In Kurmanji it means the first light of dawn."

I asked, "What's Kurmanji?"

"It's one of the Kurdish languages. Most Kurds speak it, but there is also Sorani and Gorani."

"It's a lovely name."

He frowned. "In German, it means 'misery,' something I found out when my family came here in 1991. From that point onward, I asked people to call me El."

"Gregorio told me that your German is perfect."

He said, "I think in German, but my name always reminds me of the past." He paused. "I am not miserable, in case you wonder."

"No, you look happy." The moment I said this, El impulsively embraced me and kissed me on the mouth.

A guard came into the gallery and announced the closing of the museum in half an hour. El collected himself and said, "It's time to take you home." We left and walked to the car. Behind the wheel, El calmly navigated through the congestion around Friedrichstraße Station.

Surprised at how little traffic there was in the center of town, I asked, "Is it a holiday?"

"No, there are rarely traffic jams here. The trains and buses work extremely well. Someone once told me that Berlin was designed for eight million people, but only four million live here."

I said, "That's different from Los Angeles, which has about the same population, but feels as if it was designed for two million, at least during rush hour."

I soon lost my bearings in the city, the effect of being driven around in a car. As we left Mitte, he turned to me and asked, "Are you an artist, too?"

"In a manner of speaking."

"That's wonderful. Most of the people I know are scientists, When I met Gregorio, he gave me a passage to a new world." I reflected on my circle of acquaintances, mostly artists or teachers; I was excited to meet a scientist.

Knowing that the question was potentially embarrassing, I asked, "How did you meet Gregorio?"

The answer was simple: "At the gym." I nodded and didn't ask for more details.

Dinner was unexpected—sauerkraut and pork, a German dish in a house full of non-Germans—and delicious. At dinner I got a second wind and regaled El with school stories. Most were rather silly, but Winston and Gregorio were so happy to see me that they indulged my indiscretion. We stayed up late, and finally I announced my intention to go to bed. El looked disappointed. I decided to be indiscreet once more; I took him aside and whispered, "You can join me if you want."

I got ready for bed then lay there naked wondering if El would take me up on my offer. I was just about to jerk off and go to sleep when there was a knock at my door. I got up and opened it to see El wearing only his underwear and the crucifix he never took off. I was naked, and my cock was so hard it was throbbing. I let him in and he immediately knelt and started to suck me off. I nearly came. I pulled my cock out of his mouth and said, "Let's continue this on the bed."

He slipped off his briefs, and I saw his semi-hard penis jutting out from a bushy mass of pubic hair. He was uncircumcised, and had more foreskin than I had ever seen before. He noticed me staring and said, "It's not like the purple vest or the hair on my back. I can't take it off."

I hugged him tightly and our cocks rubbed against each other. "I love it."

We got into bed and started to kiss. He was so excited that he ejaculated. He then finished the blowjob he started, and I ejaculated in his mouth almost immediately. He came up for air and kissed me. When he caught his breath, he looked me in the eye and said seriously, "You can do anything you want with me." I reached down and started to finger his ass. He pulled my hand away and said, "For that I need to prepare."

"I understand. Do you like getting fisted?"

In the dim light of the bedroom I saw his eyes open wide in excitement. He said, "I want that, yes, but I have no experience. Please be kind to me."

I put my hand, the one that hadn't been playing with his ass, to his cheek, kissed him, and said, "You have nothing to worry about." He smiled and turned over. Within a minute, he was snoring at my side. Although I normally didn't cope very well with sharing my bed for the first time with a man, I was exhausted and soon fell into a deep sleep.

TWENTY-ONE

The next morning, I woke up alone and went into the kitchen to see my hosts lingering over breakfast. Winston said, "El went to the laboratory early today. He is disappointed that you are only visiting. He thought you might be moving in."

I blushed and said, "I have a life in Los Angeles."

He cut to the heart of the matter by asking, "How is your career as a producer, then?"

"I'm beginning to think there's no future in it."

"You are always welcome here. As you can see, there is plenty of room. We have a whole building to ourselves."

"It looks like a fortress from the outside."

Winston said, "An unfortunate necessity. When I came here, Ostkreuz was full of neo-Nazi skinheads and hardcore anarchists. Sometimes they fought each other in the street, behavior I enjoyed, because it meant they were not fighting me. This area used to be rather deserted, and they simply took what they wanted. Very dangerous for people who looked foreign, and even *Wessis*. I hacked my way through. I was forced to repel the intrusions of political losers and envious cunts. When I received money from selling paintings, I invested in security and renovations. I try not to leave the building empty for very long. The more people who live here, the safer it is, but the streets outside can still be unpleasant at times. Our life here is insular. Is that a word in English?" I nodded.

Gregorio said, "Some people in the neighborhood mistake me for an Indian, because I'm dark-skinned. They ask me where my turban is." He rolled his eyes.

I asked, "How do you manage?"

Winston smiled. "I let people believe that I am involved in organized crime, which is a common activity among my fellow Albanians. To the outside world, we are only fit to manage Italian restaurants and smuggle contraband. The anarchists see art handlers putting crates of paintings into trucks. They assume that it is some shady business deal, and they leave us alone. Why? Because they approve of capitalist accumulation as long as it is illicit." He struck a wild pose and mugged grotesquely, exclaiming, "Fuck the system, man!" Everyone laughed. He continued, "I use my Balkan origins as protection, like a magic amulet. Really, these people are children, playing the game of dissent in a rich capitalist country. No matter what their politics, they form their prejudices in their little 'scenes,' unaware that they are every bit as uncritical and conformist as the villagers who delivered their Jews to the ovens." He frowned in disgust.

I asked, "Am I in any danger here?"

"Not at all. If you stay longer, it would be amusing if you dressed less like an American. The local thugs might mistake you for a Russian. The conventional wisdom here has been that everyone rents or squats, only rich Russians buy real estate, and they do it with dirty money." He chuckled at the thought of me impersonating a small-time hood. "I can spread it around that you are a porn producer. I think this will impress them. Who knows? Perhaps you will be approached by skinheads who want to experiment sexually and become movie stars at the same time."

∞

That afternoon I went to Ostkreuz S-bahn. Gregorio told me that other stations were closer, but they were in the B zone, and if I walked a few minutes longer, I would pay a lower fare, because Ostkreuz was in the A zone. The station had a forlorn air, with broken fixtures and dirty signage. Weeds around the tracks had grown so high that they had almost become trees. There were few other passengers waiting at that time of day. The people on the train, coming from the direction of Ahrensfelde, appeared to be only reluctantly participating in the twenty-first century, from the looks of their hairstyles and clothing. I had been told that time moved differently in the East. Even years after the Wall came down, the East was poorer and lagged behind by Western standards. I was beginning to see what that remark meant. Gregorio told me to transfer to the U-bahn at Warschauer Straße, but I missed my stop and went all the way to Alexanderplatz. Thinking of Alfred Döblin, I expected something rather exciting in the neighborhood, but all I saw was an extensive maze of underground passageways full of people making connections to other lines in the system.

Much later than planned, I presented myself at the Pornofilmfestival office in Kreuzberg. I happened to arrive shortly after Jerry, who made his appearance as Eon McKai, alt.porn *auteur*. He looked like death warmed over and could barely speak. I had a quiet word with our colleague Malachi Ecks, who was also on the panel. He confirmed that Jerry had gone without speed for about twenty-four hours and was crashing. He had been using prescription pills over the years, but had recently started to top up his dose with street meth, never a large amount, but enough to cause a noticeable change in his behavior. He was at work on *Kill Girl Kill 4: The Maneaters*, but production had been temporarily suspended, because it was proving impossible for the editor to make sense of the footage. There was a tentative plan for Malachi to take over, but he had trouble grasping the scenario, most of which was in Jerry's head. Eon McKai had become such a reliable commercial entity that the producers trusted him to deliver releasable videos without much supervision. The whole enterprise seemed on the verge of collapse, and Malachi was at wit's end. The logical solution was to find speed in Berlin, but neither of them had been to the city before. Malachi said, "How hard can it be? I mean, the Axis powers invented amphetamine, didn't they? It must be everywhere."

I said, "I wouldn't suggest approaching the Germans with that line. I'll see what I can do." I searched the offices for the sluttiest, kinkiest gay guy I could find, one who had the embalmed look I had seen on Paul's face before he started working for Carmen's gallery. Malachi, as a man who was more or less straight and relatively sober, lacked the sort of intuition I had acquired from having sex with hundreds of anonymous men who might or might not be dangerous. Coming out of the toilet, I stumbled upon a man named Hans who seemed to fit the bill. I asked him, *Sprichst du Englisch*?

He rolled his eyes and asked, "What do you need?" I explained the situation, and he understood immediately. He asked when the speaking engagement was and said, "He should test his dose first. The speed here is different than in LA." I nodded in agreement, then introduced him to my friends. They went off to a nearby park.

∞

In the weak twilight, I took the train back to Ostkreuz. Gregorio asked about my brief excursion out of the house, and I told him what had transpired at the office. I added, "Did I ever tell you that Eon McKai is the porn name of your classmate Jerry?"

"Jerry's famous now? I'll be damned." He shook his head and asked, "Do you want to look at some of my work?"

I said, "Yes, please." Gregorio led me upstairs to a part of the building I hadn't seen before, threw open a door, and switched on a light. I was dazzled by what I saw. He had transformed the room to such an extent that there was absolutely no indication of where the walls and ceiling met. I only recognized the floor because I was standing on it. The installation looked like the explosion of a Christmas tree, with silver shards and bits of things that might have been tree branches and ornaments protruding at odd angles. Reflective planes created a space like a hall of mirrors. I said, "This is the best thing I've seen since a circus funhouse."

"Thanks. I'm in the process of documenting it. When I'm done, I'll rip all of this down and start over."

He led me down the hall and showed me the other studio where he did his photography. Hanging on its walls there were beautifully made black and white prints of details of the installation I had just seen. Each of them looked accomplished enough to be shown in a gallery. I asked, "Are you going to exhibit these?"

"No, I do them for myself."

I said, "You could have a career doing this."

"Yeah, could have, but won't. I see what a career does to Winston, and I say, 'No thank you.' He used to nag me about getting my work out there, but now he understands."

"Well, I can't say I've seen anything quite like it."

Gregorio looked at me and asked, "Do you know what the inspiration is?"

I shook my head and said, "Jack Smith's loft?"

"Good guess, but no. I was thinking about the Psycho Salon. It was so busy and disorienting and shiny. Do you remember visiting?"

"Of course, those were happy days."

He asked, "Whatever happened to John Boskovich?"

I said, "He died of a heart attack a couple of years ago."

"Oh, I had no idea."

"Los Angeles isn't what it used to be," I said with downcast eyes. "Maybe you saw that when you visited. There are definitely vacancies in the scene that haven't been filled. I don't have a lot of faith that they ever will be. Even Paul, our guide to the world of depravity, has settled down."

Gregorio motioned for me to sit on a stool, and he leaned against the wall. "Do you have many friends in LA?"

"Not really, and it's getting tougher to make new ones. That's what happens as we get older, I guess. Jim from Libros Revolución has moved to Pomona. He's teaching in prison. In a way, the best local friend I have is Carmen."

"That's pretty harsh."

"I don't know. I find her machinations rather amusing... from a certain distance. But yeah, there aren't a lot of people I can talk about art with. I call Frances all the time, but she's getting more and more difficult to reach. Rutgers asks a lot of her, and she's commuting to New Brunswick."

"What's Moira doing?"

"Still teaching in Chiapas. She has a husband and a daughter. If things work out, she'll probably never come back to Los Angeles."

He said, "I think I told you that Winston and I weren't getting along so well for a while. I had never felt so alone. He lives the same way he did in his grad school studio, but we have this huge building. He puts no effort into making the place a home. I'm lucky he flushes the toilet, brushes his teeth, and bathes. Everything else is a distraction from his work. The burden falls on me. Now that we have help around the house, it's better. I was so sick of the situation that I thought I'd try living with you. The only complication was El. I met him a few weeks before I came to Los Angeles, and we hit it off."

"Is Winston a part of the relationship with El?"

"Um..." Gregorio paused for a while. "Winston isn't very sexual anymore, he likes to watch. That was one of my complaints. Every so often, El manages to get a response from Winston. Who can explain these things?" He paused again. "In the years I've lived with him, I've noticed that Winston really gets off on power relations."

"BDSM?"

"No, more *Dangerous Liaisons*."

I asked, "What do you mean?"

"God, I may as well tell you. Almost from the beginning, Winston showed photos of you to El. He was planting a seed. He had a feeling that El was your type, and he found out that El definitely liked what he saw in the pictures."

"Winston had it right. I find El really sexy." I felt flustered admitting this to Gregorio.

He continued, "Well, it wasn't so simple. He had an agenda. You see, Winston wants you to move to Berlin, and he figured El was the perfect bait."

I rolled my eyes and said, "Winston missed his calling. He should have been a spy." I didn't know whether to be angry, flattered, or to dismiss the whole matter as a prank.

He said, "You were the only one who understood Winston's talent when he was in grad school. That's why he respects you so much. He does love you, but he's like an evil genius putting his plans into action. It doesn't matter if the project is a cycle of paintings or a drama that plays out between people. In this case, it's both. He makes paintings of El and me fucking. You should ask to see them. Maybe he'll want you to model for them, too. Anyway, Winston's gotten better at manipulating people since he started making money. And believe me, it's a lot of money."

"And I fell for his little scheme."

"Now you know what I live with."

I asked, "Does El know about all this?"

"El is a very smart man, but when it comes to human interactions, he's clueless. Winston sympathized and thought he'd help him out. If you hated El, it would have been a disaster."

I said, "Quite the contrary."

"Maybe El sees the manipulation and accepts it because he never had a regular boyfriend before he met me. It's a surprise, because he's attractive, but he doesn't seem to know it. Like me, he's into white guys, but he misunderstands them. Most of them want a good time with a big Middle Eastern guy, but they don't necessarily want to take the time to get to know him. He becomes emotionally attached, and his heart is broken. He's trying to build up defenses and not show his feelings so quickly. I think the formal way he dresses is a way to keep people at arm's length. Except us. He's been very affectionate. It was like a dam bursting." He paused and drifted off in a brief reverie, then said, "He's a little naïve, so be careful with him. I hope you won't hurt him."

"I have no intention of doing anything like that." I looked Gregorio in the eye and asked, "Do you mind that I slept with El?"

Gregorio said, "No, I don't own him. And anyway, you can have both of us in the same bed if you like. I'm open to it. Have you fisted him?"

I said, "I think progress will be slow."

"Really? He's so piggy, but I guess we all have our limits."

I went over to Gregorio and kissed him passionately on the lips. I looked in his eyes and said, "I've missed you." I felt his cock growing in his pants.

At that moment, there was a knock on the open door. "Hello, boys." It was El. "Is this a private party?"

I backed away from Gregorio and said, "No, we were just, um, talking."

"Please talk to me that way." He came up to me, caressed the side of my head, and said, "You should have let Goran cut your hair yesterday."

I asked, "Are you sure he didn't want to suck me off?" El laughed and declined to answer my question. I took hold of his hand and said, "I saw he has a copper fingernail, too. You two are members of a secret brotherhood, aren't you?"

El explained, "It is a secret, yes. At weddings in Iraq, single men dip their fingers in henna to signal their availability. Because some of us are permanently single, we use nail polish." He drew his hand away and said, "Kurdish men must be very careful, even in Europe, especially in Europe. It's best to be discreet."

I drew him close to me and kissed him on the lips. "In this house, you're encouraged to be indiscreet."

He looked intently at Gregorio and said, "You should have warned me. This charming man is a seducer." We all laughed.

"I think I'll start cooking dinner." Gregorio left to go to the kitchen, while El and I stayed in the studio.

∞

That night, I waited a long time for El to come to bed. When he did, he said, "I'm ready." We kissed, and I ran my hands down to his ass. He let me put a couple of fingers inside. His hole was already slick.

I fumbled around for a bottle of lube and spread it on my right hand. I said, "Get on all fours."

"No, I want to look into your eyes."

As he lay on his back, we continued kissing, and he took three fingers, then four. After a number of attempts, his hole didn't open any wider. I asked, "Do you have poppers?"

"No poppers." I nodded and tried again. I grazed his prostate with my knuckles, and he emitted a loud groan. I kissed him, and as I did so, I drew my fingers out of his ass as slowly as possible. He shook violently and grunted. I held him in my arms, and he continued to tremble. A few minutes later he said, "That was amazing."

"It's just the beginning." I smiled as I wiped off my hand with a towel.

He said, "Now I see why Gregorio didn't want to leave you. Do you want me to suck you? Do you want to come in my ass? Whatever you want."

I collapsed on the bed next to him. "Right now, I need to rest." I kissed his shoulder. When he calmed down, I asked, "Why don't you want to do poppers? They make everything easier."

He answered, "I can't lose my sense of smell. Remember my work. I wouldn't be a very good scientist if I ruined one of my investigative tools."

I said, "I can be patient. This will take a while."

"Then you must stay longer."

I said, "I'll see what I can do," and then fell asleep.

∞

The panel that brought me to Berlin took place in a former porn theater on the seedier end of Kreuzberg. Everyone was present: the directors Eon McKai and Malachi Ecks, performer Keiko, and me, the producer known as Hudson Wilcox. Eon had been able to obtain enough speed to keep him awake and alert, but he didn't find the correct dose. I assumed that he could act sensibly, but I quickly found out that this was an unrealistic expectation of someone addicted to a substance. Eon dominated the panel discussion completely. He jabbered non-stop, cutting off his colleagues when they tried to speak. Subtle hints that another topic aside from the production of his own body of work and the travails of the notoriety it brought him were completely ineffective. He rambled and skipped from one topic to another without finishing any single thought. At one point, Malachi made a sign reading "Cut his mic" and held it in front of him, but for some reason, no one acted on his suggestion. I attempted to talk over him, but he continued his discourse unabated as though no one else was in the room. The audience became restive, and spectators started leaving. Soon the auditorium was practically empty, and Eon failed to acknowledge this until it was too late. At last he stopped to take a breath, and by the time his fellow panelists spoke up, the festival organizers were making motions that the next screening would take place soon. We heard an impatient crowd outside every time someone opened the door. Each of us made a brief final statement for the sake of a recording, then the event was brought to a desultory conclusion. I felt relieved that I hadn't invited El, Gregorio, and Winston to the festival. Rather than attending the after-party, I immediately went back home to tell them that they had missed nothing.

TWENTY-TWO

El was spending every evening with us and sleeping in my bed. When he was willing, I would try to engage in some ass play. We kissed while I tried to put my hand in his ass; this was something I hadn't done before with a partner, and the two sensations together pleased El. It took several days to fit more than four fingers inside him, but what he was feeling encouraged him to keep trying. There was always a struggle at the point when the widest part of my hand entered his hole, but one night, very soon after the start of a session, I was able to go a bit farther. He was lying on his back. I saw a look of panic on his face, and I assured him, "You can do it." He inhaled deeply, and the rest of my hand slipped in. I asked him if he wanted me to pull out and he shook his head. His rectum was wide open. I slowly made a fist and left it inside him for a while. He writhed in ecstasy, and his eyes rolled back in his head. When he signaled that he'd had enough, I relaxed my hand and pulled it out as slowly as possible. He shook violently and groaned. When the spasms subsided, I asked him if he was in any pain. Once again he shook his head. He had lost the ability to speak. Shortly before falling asleep, he told me quietly, "That was the best sex I have ever had."

∞

Winston invited me to see his studio, which occupied the whole fourth floor of the building. The second floor contained Gregorio's studios, and on the opposite side of the staircase, a bedroom and bathroom that I had only seen briefly. The third floor contained the business offices of Andë Alia Studio, storage, and a couple of extra rooms. I was nearly winded by the time I reached the top floor, an attic with a trap door that closed it off from the rest of the building. Over the years, Gregorio and Winston had blocked off all but one wall of windows and installed skylights to provide indirect natural light. Winston had filled long stretches of the space with tables, bookshelves, palettes, easels, and an immense array of paints and brushes. The walls along the sides were hung with large sketches representing workers of various ages and ethnicities all marching toward something and gazing with excitement at objects on the horizon: the paintings in progress on the wall directly opposite the windows. These canvases had been worked with many layers of impasto, in the superficially chaotic yet controlled style characteristic of Andë Alia. One was a portrait of Benjamin Franklin apparently taken directly from a one hundred dollar bill; another came from a digital display of stock prices rising and falling; and a third was a view of a vault full of gold bullion. A forth canvas was blank. I turned around and said, "Amazing."

Winston chuckled and said, "There is no need to flatter the paintings, but yes, the space is very good." He turned on the stereo and played a record for me: the aria *Au font du temple saint*, a duet for baritone and tenor, from *The Pearl Fishers*, an opera we both loved in defiance of near-universal critical condescension. The music brought Winston to tears. When it was over, he could only say, "Robert Merrill and Jussi Björling."

I nodded and said, "Gregorio tells me you go to the opera often."

"We do. El is learning to appreciate this decadent Western art form, too. Germany mounts great productions. Attending opera performances is one of the pleasures I allow myself."

"No sex?" I asked.

"Seldom. This is unfortunate, because Gregorio is often horny, as you say in English. He has no doubt told you that I prefer to watch."

"He also said you paint his sex scenes with Elend."

Winston uncovered a table and let me look at a few studies. They resembled small scale variations on Francis Bacon's *The Wrestlers* (or *The Buggers*). I could recognize El and Gregorio in the wild brushstrokes and attacks of a palette knife that Winston used to make them. They were even less like images than his portrait paintings, and occupied a territory close to abstraction while strongly suggesting the union of two bodies. The paintings radiated an intensity that was lacking in the larger works in progress on the wall—the "official" works of Andë Alia. Winston said, "Do not tell me that these studies are better than the murals. I know this perfectly well. It is the problem that occupies all of my time these days."

I said, "John Singer Sargent had a similar problem. The studies he made of his boyfriends are much less refined than his portraits, and full of emotion."

"Yes, he painted public mural commissions that brought him fame and glory, but have come to look lifeless and pretentious. Now his male nudes are the only works anyone cares about." He shook his head as he pondered the cruelty of posterity.

I asked, "What's the project?"

"This is a full-scale cartoon of a mural cycle called *The Crowning of Labor* by John White Alexander. It decorates a grand staircase at the Carnegie Museum in Pittsburgh. These images on the side walls represent the last panels he completed, on the top floor."

I said, "I remember them. I went to the museum as a child."

"You are lucky. I must see the murals in person soon."

"They're in a part of the museum that few people see these days."

He said, "Alexander's work became unfashionable at the end of his life. He was a working class son of Pittsburgh who became a society painter. It is appropriate that you brought up Sargent, because in a way, Alexander was a less prestigious version of him. In the early twentieth century, Alexander's pretty paintings were obliterated by the arrival of Cubism, Futurism, all of the other isms. His fluent *beaux arts* style became academic in every sense of the word. He left the project at the Carnegie unfinished at the time of his death in 1915. There are few sketches, because he worked by painting directly on the canvas."

I looked around and asked, "Where are these figures supposed to be heading?"

He said, "The main theme of the mural cycle is that all higher human endeavors are based upon the labor of the masses, almost a Marxist idea. The lower floors show work in the steel mills, and on the next level, female spirits crown a bearded knight who levitates among the clouds. He is intended as an allegorical representation of labor, but he bears a strong resemblance to the captain of industry Andrew Carnegie. The climax of the cycle was to have been more allegorical figures: the muses of art, music, history, and science. Perhaps Alexander lost his nerve or the ability to envision a hopeful future. How can anyone paint such subjects? They are hopelessly abstract."

I said, "I would guess that someone trained to paint in a Socialist Realist style can provide an answer to that question."

He walked over to retrieve a book with reproductions of the murals, handed it to me, and said, "I have been asked to submit a proposal to finish *The Crowning of Labor*."

"Congratulations." I leafed through the book. I stopped at one page and said, "It's hard to see this stuff as anything but camp now."

He said, "Yes, it is what you would call a white elephant, an obsolete relic. I must find a way to reinvent this dated style. It is a challenge, because now *everything* in art looks dated. I have understood that a shift has taken place. In the capitalist West of one hundred years ago, the realm of culture predicted wider changes in society. But then society changed, and now contemporary art lags behind the latest breakthroughs in technology. I think art's new status as an asset class has transformed it into deeply conservative and empty formalism. A repellent turn of events. The stars of Sotheby's auctions will become white elephants in the near future. Perhaps they already are, and vested interests merely prop them up in the market. I am thoroughly implicated in this, but I must say that contemporary art fully deserves its obsolescence."

I chose not to respond to his bleak assessment and said, "Blank walls for a hundred years replaced by Andë Alia paintings. There'll be something to offend everyone in Pittsburgh."

He cleared his throat. "You tell the truth, my friend. I fear I will formulate a proposal doomed to be rejected. I have been experimenting with images associated with money and investments as the climax of the mural sequence. They are not as pretty as smoking factories, but what else would workers look at with so much interest today? A soccer match? In the present economic environment, finance is the highest level of aspiration. The promising graduates of elite universities no longer become artists, historians, scientists—they work for banks and brokerages, or become the politicians who stage manage the latest crimes of the financial industry. The proletariat has no chance, no future."

I said, "This sounds difficult to sell to a board of trustees."

"Regarding that, I have an idea. I need to write a proposal as well as many emails to the museum. My spoken English is adequate, but my written English is poor, as you know. I am unable to employ the proper euphemisms that will impress American arts administrators. You helped me when we were students, and perhaps you can help me now. I will pay you. It would be a real job."

I was nonplussed, and I asked, "Would the job require me to move to Berlin?"

"That would be best. There are unused rooms on the third floor, above our bedroom. You could take them and build whatever you need—a studio, a bedroom, perhaps a dungeon." He laughed. "You must climb the stairs to reach them, but that is good exercise." I was pleased that Winston tried to convince me to become a part of his household, but I was also a bit apprehensive. He said, "The need for your work is not immediate. You have time to consider the offer."

Winston paused for a long time while I looked closely at the works in progress. I said, "I think the danger of these paintings is that they might be ideas more than images. The criticism you raised in your email about my paintings applies to your work, too."

"Excellent point. Is it not always this way? We see our own problems in others."

"You're probably right."

He said, "If you want to learn how to make real paintings, I can show you."

"I know you're being generous, but it sounds so condescending."

He smirked and asked, "Is there a single person in Los Angeles willing to tell you the truth about your art?"

I thought about that for a moment but said only, "I've missed you so much. No one else calls me on my shit."

"I understand that as a 'no.'" We stood for a while without talking. He broke the silence by saying, "We should prepare for dinner. El will join us. He is a wonderful man."

"I'm discovering that."

"You have fucked him. You are still my friend who thinks with his cock."

"I admit we have played around." I blushed. Remembering what Gregorio had told me, I said, "But you knew this would happen all along."

"I know that you and Gregorio had an affair while he stayed with you. That is fine with me. Gregorio and El were having an affair. Why not be a threesome? You wanted one when we were students."

"With you," I said.

"I am no longer an active participant. I want to know everything and see everything, but not necessarily to be a part of it."

"That sounds severe."

"I have work to do and I do it well. This is not always pleasant. As an American who grew up watching television, you may not believe it, but artists are under no obligation to be likable people."

I laughed. "You seem to be proving your point."

I felt uncomfortable, and Winston, sensing this, tried a different approach. "Our friend El was a refugee, now he is an orphan. He has tried to be a part of the Berlin gay scene, but he does not fit in. This causes him pain. He is lonely. I want him to have love." With that, I saw that what Gregorio perceived as Winston manipulating his friends to serve his interests was something more altruistic. If his efforts happened to help him too, all the better.

I said, "I have no plans to break El's heart."

"Speaking of such things, be kind to Gregorio. He loves you very much, but he does not trust you."

I blushed again and asked, "What do you mean?"

"What is that man's name? Temo. A pretty face, but a waste of time. I knew that the moment I met him. Do you still see him?"

"No, that's over now. When he went missing, I was concerned. I developed feelings for him, but they weren't based on anything real. I always found him attractive, but since he came back into my life, I've been disillusioned."

He asked, "Are you fucking him?"

I said, "Temo moved to Mexico City recently."

Winston raised his voice. "What you must realize is that love is in front of you." I had nothing to say in response to this pronouncement. I was too proud to agree with him, however correct his observation was. "Let me tell you one more thing: if you fucked less often, you would have more time to make art."

"You always know how to get to the point, don't you?"

"I have merely developed an ability to tell the difference between the important and the trivial. You, my friend, are important to me. Gregorio and El are important."

"And your paintings?"

He sighed and said, "I try. With every painting, I want to learn something, and to surprise myself. My work is the reason I am on this earth. That, and providing for my loved ones."

"How are your mother and sister in Albania?"

He shook his head and said, "I bought them houses years ago with the first money I made from my paintings. I mean Gregorio and El... and you, if you will have us."

I stuttered, "Um, I don't know. I'd be uncomfortable living off you."

He scoffed, "You will be working here, performing a valuable service. The immigration authorities expect nothing less." He paused to think. "Let us stop speaking indirectly about the question. You are poor. A poor American artist must rely on the patronage of the rich. Do you realize that by depriving you of technical training, your education prepared you only to live off of people? The graduate program we attended was a glorified school for courtiers and prostitutes. I left the place as quickly as possible. For you, the important question is the choice of benefactors. Your friend Temo can buy you many times over. I was afraid that you would sell yourself to him. At least you avoided that pathetic fate. I ask you, what is the source of his money?"

"His family. They're a bunch of criminals."

"And you were in love with this man! Your cock is stupider than I thought. At least I made the money that supports this household myself. I do not give a shit about my auction prices, except that they make it possible for me to help the men I love." He looked at me with an expression as serious as any I had ever seen. "I do not expect you to relinquish your freedom. I am only offering you a new situation. At some point you will have to become serious about your artistic gifts. 'Adult video' as they call it is not a career for adults. Do you want to teach at a university that will drain you of your life's blood simply so you can pay a mortgage?"

I asked, "What about income from art sales?"

"Carmen might sell enough of your work to provide you with a livelihood, but artists with higher prices will be her main priorities. All galleries do this. They must in order to survive." Winston devastated in advance any counterargument I could make, and I was left with nothing to say. Rather than discussing the matter further, he changed the subject. "Soon I am having an exhibition at the Hamburger Kunsthalle. I will go to Hamburg tomorrow to visit the museum. I am out of town for a few days. I hope you will stay long enough for me to see you again."

"Absolutely. In the meantime, I'm going to enjoy myself with El and Gregorio."

"Exactly as I expected." He kissed me on both cheeks and led me to the trap door of his studio.

∞

We sat at the table in the kitchen while Gregorio finished preparing the evening meal, an Albanian specialty called *tavë kosi*, a type of quiche with lamb. El came in at the last minute, kissing all of us on the cheeks. He brought two bottles of *rakı* from a Turkish market. I had a feeling it would be a long night. My tolerance for alcohol was far less than my companions, and I struggled to keep up with the conversation. At one point, I said to El, "My friend Moira has a theory about television. She thinks that if you could smell as well as see and hear the evening news, the odors of battlefields would turn the audience against war permanently."

He said, "This has some truth in it, I'm sure. My sense of smell saved my life. In Kurdistan, I grew up in an atmosphere of chemical warfare. When I was a child, I was always the first to smell the approach of an unpleasant odor. I would quickly cover my face and hide in the cellar. We never suffered a direct hit, but I found out later that we were breathing the residue of gas attacks. The environment was poisoned, and I believe this killed my parents very slowly over time. So far I have survived." There was a long pause as he took a sip of his drink. "My research concerns the smell of fear, anxiety, happiness."

Drunk and oblivious, I said, "And sex."

Winston, as the most sober of the group, grumbled and turned the conversation back to the topic of war. The trial of Saddam Hussein was happening during those days, and both El and Winston were sure that he would be condemned to death. I was on the verge of making a hollow statement about human rights and the rule of law, when El summed things up categorically. He lifted his glass and said, "Let the son of a bitch burn in a hell of chlorine gas."

Further details of the night became somewhat hazy to me as I got progressively drunker, but I remembered Winston saying, "The end of the German Democratic Republic was a gigantic flea market. The leaders knew they were on their way out, and they stole whatever they could. Whole arsenals disappeared. It happened in Albania, and it happened here. They got rid of everything—public property sold for private gain."

I belched and asked, "Is that how you got this building?"

Winston raised his hand to quiet me and responded, "Not exactly. I assure you, it was a legal transfer of ownership."

El spoke up. "He's talking about war materiel of the German Democratic Republic. A massive amount was sold to Turkey, and the Turkish army used it to suppress Kurdish rebellion in the east. The collapse of the East German state therefore made possible an extermination campaign against the Kurds. One man's flea market is another man's genocide." He burst into tears.

Gregorio put his arm around El and said, "Please turn off the lights when you're done. I'm going to console our guest." The two of them started to kiss.

Winston also got up to leave and said, "I have a train to catch tomorrow morning."

I wasn't sure if I was invited to join them, so I did a few dishes and went to my own bed.

TWENTY-THREE

The next morning, I went into the kitchen to find something for my headache, and I saw Gregorio at the sink wearing nothing but a jock strap. It emphasized his shapely ass. I said, "Going to the gym has been a good investment. Your body is incredible." Hung over and horny, I experienced no problem as I had before with getting an erection in Gregorio's presence. I pulled down my pants and rubbed my cock against his ass. He opened up for me, and I started fucking him. I pounded him as he leaned against the kitchen counter until I was close to orgasm. I said, "I'm going to come."

He said, "Don't pull out." I shot a load inside him with a loud grunt.

At that moment, El came into the kitchen. I pulled my cock out of Gregorio and started to slink away in embarrassment, but El smiled at me and gestured for me to stay. He knelt in front of Gregorio's ass and started to eat it. After much moaning and slurping, El was satisfied that he had cleaned him up, and went over to me. He licked off my cock, then rose in front of me. His beard was full of cum. He asked, "Why don't you grow a beard?"

I kissed him and said, "Give me a month, and I will."

239

His face lit up, and he asked, "Will you stay that long?"

"I don't know."

He said, "You are a scoundrel, just as Winston warned me."

Gregorio laughed and said, "Men are such dirty things."

∞

After breakfast, El proposed that we visit the Gemäldegalerie, and Gregorio thought we should dress for the occasion. We climbed the stairs to the main bedroom, where my three friends had spent the night. The bed was big enough to accommodate all of them, but there was also another smaller bed off to one side. I asked about this, and Gregorio said, "Sometimes Winston likes to sleep alone."

"Even in the middle of an orgy, Winston wants to stay in his monk's cell."

Gregorio laughed. "Yeah, pretty much."

We took a shower together in a bathroom roughly the size of the bedroom where I slept. El masturbated to a climax, but he pinched the end of his long foreskin shut as he came. He told Gregorio to kneel down, then released a big wad of cum that flooded his mouth.

I said, "Nice trick."

El smiled, rinsed his cock, then left the shower. After he dried off, he opened a walk-in closet and started laying out articles of clothing on the bed. He said, "I will dress us all today."

Gregorio put on the sort of outfit that I would have worn: a simple pair of blue jeans, a t-shirt with no logo, and a leather jacket, with the fancy athletic shoes he favored. El wore a light blue shirt with narrow white stripes and a white collar, a red, white, and blue striped raw silk tie, a brown herringbone wool jacket, and a dark blue pocket square. He dressed me in a pair of his jeans, a light blue denim shirt, an ivory raw silk tie, a brown checkered wool vest with pockets, and a three-button suit jacket in a shade of blue dark enough to appear almost black. He placed a gray wool cap on my head, then puzzled over the choice of shoes. Finally he settled on a pair of cowboy boots that he had bought for Winston, but which were slightly too large for him. The whole ritual was suffused with erotic energy in a way that was sexier than the shower we took together. When we finished dressing, Gregorio gazed at us and said, "Wow, you two look like a couple," which made me blush and made El smile.

We each put on heavy overcoats and got into El's car. I asked him, "Do you ever take public transportation?"

"No, I prefer not to. In Prenzlauer Berg, I parked my car and left it for days in the same spot, walking around, taking trams and the U-bahn. Here, there are sometimes hassles with local boys. They wouldn't bother you, I think."

I said, "No, they leave me alone. If they do speak to me, it's always in German, and I never respond."

El said, "The older *Ossis* speak little English. If you stay, you must improve your German as soon as possible. I will help you."

Gregorio said, "I always take the trains. I wear track suits and look tough. It's playacting I learned from music videos, but the crazy thing is that it works. El's problem is that he's too nice."

I responded, "He is exactly nice enough." I turned to El and said, "When I start dressing like I'm in the Russian mafia, I'll protect you."

El laughed. "I prefer to drive, thank you."

∞

I had last seen the Gemäldegalerie when it was in Dahlem, with the Egyptian Museum and the Antiquities Museum, both of which had moved to Museum Island with their collections merged and rearranged. The outside of the new Gemäldegalerie at the Kulturforum suggested that the interior would be antiseptic, but I found it quieter and more comfortable than the galleries I remembered from the days of the Wall, and much more conveniently located, not far from the architectural atrocity that was Potsdamer Platz.

I found a map and headed straight for the Italian Baroque galleries. El and Gregorio followed me. We stood in front of a painting I had wanted to see for many years, Caravaggio's *Amor Vincit Omnia*. It was as I remembered it, but now bore a German title, discreetly placed on a narrow molding near the floor, *Amor als Sieger*. The three of us stood entranced by the picture of a winged youth exposing his naked, hairless crotch, standing amid a pile of musical instruments. None of us could think of anything to say, so we silently left to look at other works in the museum. On the way to see the Rembrandts, Gregorio whispered to me, "You know, if you lived here, you could look at that painting as often as you like. Just saying."

∞

In a city known for its night life, my favorite evening was spent with El and Gregorio watching opera videos in bathrobes. We sat in bed eating a bowl of popcorn as El cued up favorites from DVDs he had received from a fellow fan. It was an obsessive labor of love: every video available of the aria *Je crois entendre encore* from *The Pearl Fishers*. We heard great tenors such as Jussi Björling, Nicolai Gadda, Beniamino Gigli, and Alfredo Kraus, who was obviously the collector's favorite, since there were a half dozen versions by him alone. The part of Nadir, one of the best in Romantic opera, posed difficulties for a tenor. Everyone who tackled the aria was obliged to cheat a bit, for instance resorting to falsetto or singing louder than Bizet's score suggests. When the most challenging passage—sung very high and very softly—comes near the end, something I called the "holy shit" expression often appears on a tenor's face when he's unsure if he will actually make it through the piece without a vocal mishap.

There was an oddity at the end of the disc: a clip of uncertain origin featuring Kraus lip-syncing the aria. The scene resembled Jack Smith's never-finished film *Normal Love* transposed to a brackish lagoon. The video resurrects Bizet's crackpot Orientalism—the opera is set in Sri Lanka—as threadbare camp. It begins with a figure entirely shrouded in lurid green tulle making her way to a beach. She is unsure of her footing and moves clumsily. There is a dissolve to Kraus as Nadir, squatting at the side of the lagoon. He wears a blue-green turban, voluminous brown pants, and what appears to be a high-visibility orange worker's vest. In a wide shot, he is reduced to a bright speck beside a body of water as calm and unnatural as a flooded strip mine. The water is olive green and the sand, which has the consistency of mud, is black. The camera zooms in as he sings. The green lady turns to him, and he begins to walk toward her. His bare feet make slow progress in the muck strewn with wilted paper flowers. He must have wondered how he managed to get himself into such an undignified mess. He emotes in a close-up, with his back to the green lady, who is attempting to climb rocks in an outfit ill-suited to such athletics. Kraus, relieved that he is not singing but only mouthing the words, makes no alarmed face as the high notes come. The green lady continues walking to the ocean. The video left us speechless. We could only look at each other and laugh.

∞

After Winston's return from Hamburg, I was finally able to pry my speaker's fee from the festival. The director, who was disappointed at how the so-called panel discussion had turned out, gave me a dismissive look. I reminded him that I had tried to participate, but Jerry hadn't let me. He sighed and peeled four fifty Euro bills from a stack in his desk drawer then placed them in an envelope.

On my way home, I received a call from Jerry. He said, "I'm sorry I made a mess of the panel. Are you mad at me?"

"More concerned than anything. Are you okay?"

"No, I'm at the airport now. I'll go to rehab as soon as I get back to LA. I hate to admit it, but this latest binge is probably the end of Eon McKai's career. It was fun while it lasted."

I said, "It wasn't as bad as all that."

He exhaled loudly. "This was just the last in a whole bunch of fuck ups."

I asked, "Do you have any ideas about what you'll do next?"

"Probably another kind of porn, reality TV."

"I'm sure this call is costing a fortune in roaming charges, so all I'll say is good luck. Let me know if you need anything."

∞

On returning, I saw El, who had the day off. I told him I received some money and suggested we go shopping. He laughed and said, "You can borrow my clothes any time you want. I buy few things in shops; most of my clothes are made by Kurdish tailors. They fit you rather well." He caressed my cheek and said, "What you need is a haircut."

I agreed, and we went to Goran's shop in Kreuzberg. A dark shadow had formed on El's face in the last few days, and he asked for a shave. Once more he took off his shirt and exposed a torso that looked as though he was wearing a brown sweater. Goran carefully shaved El's neck and cheeks and gave him a hot towel afterward. He said something in Kurdish and motioned for me to sit in the chair. I submitted to the same treatment, which was so pleasurable that it gave me goose bumps. I relaxed and started to doze off. I awoke with a start as another man came into the shop. There was much hugging and kissing, and El introduced us. "This is Achmed."

The man was dressed just as stylishly as El. He had a beard that was blacker, denser, and longer than El's. "Achmed comes here every week. He must look his best. He'll run for the *Bundestag* one day." I looked at him blankly and he explained, "Our parliament." I shook Achmed's hand, which I noticed had a single copper fingernail. I smiled and nodded approvingly.

He asked, "When do you return to the United States?"

In good spirits, El said, "Never."

I looked at the calendar on the opposite wall and said. "Well, I just missed my return flight from Tegel. Maybe El is right."

Achmed said, "Then welcome to Berlin."

∞

On my last day in Berlin I asked Gregorio, "Why haven't I seen any of Winston's assistants?"

He said, "They work on the third floor, below his studio, and they take the back stairs. When you start using the empty rooms across from the offices, you'll see a lot of them." He caught himself and said, "I mean *if.*"

I smiled. "My taking up residence here is a foregone conclusion, isn't it?"

He shrugged and said, "Winston generally gets what he wants."

"What do you and El have to say about it?"

"We want you here more than Winston does."

I nodded. "I'll see what I can do. I have to work things out financially." I added, "I wonder if I'll ever see the sun again."

Winston, who had slipped into the kitchen without me noticing, said, "You have experienced enough sunshine for two lifetimes."

Gregorio added, "The summers are great here. You'll see."

That evening, we all helped with the cooking of a feast. There were Middle Eastern dishes with names I couldn't pronounce, and plenty of sweets for dessert. Since I would have to get up early the next morning to go to the airport, I avoided alcohol. The mood at dinner was low-key, almost mournful. At a quiet moment, I said, "I must come back. I spent so much time with you that I barely got to see the city."

El, who had hardly spoken a word all evening, announced, "After you leave, I'm moving in. Most of my things are here anyway. Goodbye Rosa-Luxemburg-Platz."

"Finally," Winston said. He turned to me. "He spends almost every night here. Why rent an empty apartment?"

El took my hand, looked me in the eye, and said, "I'll be using the bedroom where we slept. You'll know exactly where to find me when you return."

TWENTY-FOUR

Recovering from jet lag, I called my mother. I told her that I had visited Berlin and she responded blandly, "That's nice." She seemed distracted during the conversation, and I asked her if anything was wrong. She responded, "Nothing," and after a pause explained, "I've been dating a man."

"Oh, that's great. How long have you been seeing him?"

"It's been a few months now. I've moved in with him. You don't mind, do you?"

"Of course not. You should do what makes you happy."

"This makes me happy." The news that someone would be with my mother, who had lived alone for years, came as a huge relief to me. I had always feared that my time in Los Angeles would come to an end when she became unable to live alone and needed help, because there was no one else. Now she had someone to care for her, and for whom she could care. I suddenly felt free of the lingering sense of guilt and responsibility that cast a shadow over the independent life I had made for myself in California. She interrupted my thoughts by saying, "You should meet him."

"I will one day."

"I hope you can come home soon." My mother called the place where I grew up "home," even though I hadn't lived there in many years and had no intention of moving back.

Expecting a negative response, I asked, "Is it urgent?"

"Well, actually... I'm thinking of selling the house. I'm not using it, and the costs of maintaining it are real high. Before I sell, I want you to make sure I don't get rid of anything important to you."

"I'll check about a plane ticket, but for now, I have to take care of all the things I neglected while I was in Europe. I stayed longer than I expected."

My mother said, "Let me know when you're coming," and she gave me her boyfriend's address and phone number.

I said, "Mom, something strange happened to me there. I was in a museum and I heard a woman talking to her child. The funny thing was I understood what she was saying, but it was in German. I found myself understanding whole conversations when I was in Berlin."

"Well, your grandmother was a Berliner."

"I never knew where she was from."

She said, "I spent a lot of time in the hospital after you were born, and your grandmother took care of you. You two really bonded. I think you reminded her of her younger brother in Germany. He died when he was a child, and she always wanted another little boy to hold. She loved to babysit you. It wouldn't surprise me if she spoke German to you."

"I don't remember any of this."

"It was before you went to school, a long time ago."

I said, "The child couldn't have been more than three years old, and his mother was disciplining him. She said, 'My dear, you have to respect people.'"

My mother laughed. "I must have said the same thing to you many times. When you first learned to walk and talk, you were always approaching strangers in public. It was very sweet. You were gregarious and wanted to talk to everyone. Your grandmother must have worried that something bad was going to happen to you. Maybe she told you in German."

"I guess if I tried to learn German, it might not be so hard."

"Oh, I wouldn't know about that."

I said, "I was visiting my best friends from school. They moved to Berlin a few years ago, and they asked me to live with them. Would you be upset if I did that?"

She paused to think about it for a moment and said, "No, you should do what you want. You always do anyway." She sighed. "I never had a chance to go to foreign countries. I'm comfortable here at home. I won't hold you back. Your grandmother would be proud of you."

"I'm glad. Take care."

She said, "You too, dear. Let me know what you decide. Maybe I can visit you one day."

The thought of my mother among a bunch of fist fucking homosexuals in East Berlin came to my mind, and I could barely suppress a giggle. "Yes," I said, "That would be nice." I could count on one hand the number of times my mother had been more than a day's drive away from the place where she was born. I was unsure if she had ever been on an airplane. She had certainly never left the English speaking world. Perhaps sensing that there were some parts of my life as a single man that she preferred not to know about, my mother had never visited Los Angeles. As I hung up the phone, I thought about Graciela meeting her son's boyfriend (or whatever I was) and discovering what he did when he was away from her. This must have come as a shock. I didn't want to be responsible for my own mother having a heart attack.

∞

My friends in Berlin occupied most of my thoughts during those days. I couldn't deny the appeal of Winston's offer, though I resisted admitting he was correct in his assessment of my life in Los Angeles and my prospects for the future. Gregorio was flourishing in Berlin. He was not only in great physical shape, but he had matured emotionally. I marveled at his lack of selfishness in the face of El and me carrying on our affair. He wanted both of us to be happy, and he was secure enough that he didn't feel tempted to stir up drama out of jealousy. And then there was El. From the moment I landed in Los Angeles, I missed him. I found myself thinking about him constantly. I would often check my phone and calculate what time it was in Europe. I speculated about what he was doing at any given moment. I asked myself a litany of questions: Was he also thinking about me? Had he found any other men in Berlin? Would they usurp my place in his heart? I started calling Berlin at odd hours to leave messages. I didn't know El's email address, which would have given me a cheaper but less immediate way of reaching him. I wasn't sure what I would write to him, because I could hardly put what I was feeling into words. I had fallen into an obsession. I tried my best to keep it at bay and go through the motions of my daily routine, which had come to seem absolutely empty.

∞

I started logging porn footage again and prepared a set of four compilations, then sent the documents with an invoice to my contact at Larry Flynt Publications. I received the following response: "After this month, we will no longer be producing Tool Factory compilations, because LFP/Hustler Video has decided to concentrate exclusively on video-on-demand going forward. Thank you for all your great work for the company, and good luck with your future endeavors." DVDs were now officially an obsolete format in porn, and I would have to look for another job. I surveyed the traces of my career as a porn producer in the apartment: some DVDs, a large pile of window dubs, and a barely functioning VHS deck. I threw them out the next day in a moment of anger and frustration.

Later that week, I received a notice from my health insurance provider informing me that my premium would increase to $900 per month starting in January. That amount was more than my rent, and I had absolutely no idea how I was going to pay it. In the short term, I had sufficient money left over from the recent sales of my art, but in the long term, the only solution I could imagine was finding a regular job—something I hadn't had since the bookstore—in order to get health benefits. The alternative was never getting sick. A week later, my last paycheck arrived. I'd have to figure something out "going forward," to use the phrase from the lay-off email.

∞

I called Jim to see if he could give me a reference for job applications. He was happy to hear from me but said, "It's not the best time for job hunting. Everything is in upheaval. Technology has made a lot of employees redundant. The main growth sectors of the economy are finance and the prison system."

"Damn, I'm no mathematician. Are you suggesting I start working in corrections?"

"No, I'm only making an observation. I wish we were still at Libros Revolución, but bookstores are under threat, too. Any brick and mortar business has to get its shit together. These days life is fine as long as you happen to be a unit of financial capital, but actual human beings have a tough time of it. Offshore accounts are bigger than ever. Trillions of dollars are being laundered." He paused. "Things have changed so much. When I was in London, there were squats everywhere. I could live on almost nothing. Now those buildings are worth millions of pounds. I think money laundering is to blame." He chuckled. "Maybe you should be selling subprime mortgages. That market is booming. But you may have some moral qualms regarding *real* criminal behavior."

I asked, "What are you talking about?"

"Oh, the latest unregulated strategy for stealing from the poor and giving to the rich. It's probably better that you don't know. All I'll say is that reading the *Wall Street Journal* every morning puts me in the right mood to teach literature classes in prison."

I couldn't tell if Jim's statement was some kind of joke or not. It was absurd enough to be true. I asked, "What do you suggest I do?"

"Talk to the gallery. I enjoyed your exhibition. Did many of the paintings sell?"

"A couple did."

He said, "It beats having a regular job."

"That's for sure. I'm probably going to have a solo show only once every couple of years, though, so I'll have to be careful with my money. The market is fickle. There are no guarantees."

"There are no guarantees of anything in this life. I say you should do what you really want to do. It works for my brother, more often than not." He asked, "Ever hear from Bernie?"

"He sends me long emails. He traveled across the country and told some fascinating tales."

Jim said abruptly, "I think he was in love with you."

I asked, "Did he tell you that?"

"Not in so many words, but man, I heard it all the time. Every opinion you expressed, every question you asked would get reported back to me in breathless awe. I thought for sure you two were getting it on in the back room while I wasn't around."

I said, "We didn't have that kind of a relationship."

"That's a shame. I really want Bernie to be happy. He was frustrated in Los Angeles. I probably shouldn't tell you this, but..."

"Oh, now you must. Don't be a tease."

He continued, "I was at the counter with him once, and he excused himself to go to the toilet. He'd brought his laptop to work, and he left it open. He was logged on to a hookup site. It was practically under my nose, so I saw his personal ad or whatever you call it. He said he was a slave looking for a master. It made me wonder about you two, I must say."

"Hey, we just had friendly conversations. Back then, my heart belonged to our friend Temo."

He exhaled loudly. "Now that guy was *trouble*."

"Yeah, and it only took me about ten years to figure it out. Thanks again for your help with the rescue operation in El Centro."

"It's a shame you didn't give Bernie a chance. He would have been a lot more dependable as a partner."

I said, "Possibly, but dependability isn't very hot, is it? That's the problem. And I was complaining to him about Temo recently. I guess I put my foot in my mouth. I didn't mean to hurt him."

"We're all clueless when it comes to someone else's desires. I can't stand the women my brother dates, won't even talk about them with him. The feelings are mutual, I'm sure. Temo is handsome, but what a brat. I hate to say this, but I think if *you* got in any real trouble, he'd forget you existed. For the rich, poor people are just entertainment."

I said, "Speaking of entertainment, I was in Berlin recently, and I thought of Bernie. He could use a rich boyfriend. I bet there are plenty of likely candidates hanging out in Charlottenburg. Some old geezer who'd give him the punishment he so richly deserves would be just the thing."

"Maybe you should talk to him about it. I know he enjoys Berlin, but enjoyment and survival are two different things."

I said, "As a recent employee of the adult video industry, I'm well aware of that."

"Anyway, Bernie always loved working with you. He felt seen by you. I'm guessing he didn't feel that way very often. I don't know why, because the guy is incredibly smart."

"Not necessarily an advantage in this town's gay scene. Bernie's very good at hanging around and observing, taking note of small details and weaving them into stories. When it comes to casual conversations, he's pretty inept. Small talk stumps him. When he's around a man he finds attractive, it's a sorry spectacle. I've seen it. I think his main sexual outlet is sucking guys off in the shower at the gym." I asked, "Has he been in touch with you?"

"A few times. They're always interesting emails. I wish I had time to respond in kind."

I said, "I know what you mean. After I told him about my travails with Temo, he responded the next day with stories about a college friend who was profoundly mentally ill. He wanted to give me some useful advice, but it also occurred to me that there's a lot he's not telling us about himself."

Jim shrugged. "So what if his Catholic upbringing ruined him? People deal with worse. In all the hours we worked together, he never had a problem more serious than car trouble."

I said, 'Yeah. You know, about Temo, I remember something Bernie told me once: 'Never go out to dinner with a bunch of rich kids; they'll stick you with the check every time.'"

Jim laughed and said, "Sounds like him."

"Trying to help Temo was an expensive ordeal. He never talked about the time when he was... away. I think he must have spent some time in public hospitals, at the very least a few seventy-two hour involuntary holds."

"5150—happens to the best of us."

I said, "A shrink confided to me that he wasn't surprised at the state of Temo, because the public mental health system in California is completely broken; in fact, it's designed to fail. I've been told it's better in New York."

"Have you ever considered moving?"

"To New York? Never. I don't have serious career ambitions, or a trust fund. I suspect if I were starting out now, even Los Angeles would be too expensive. I have no idea what I'd do."

He said, "I never really left home, except for that period when I was a filmmaker. The problem is my hometown is pleasant enough that you find yourself staying forever. Pete and I have done all right. In a way, you're lucky that you're a recent arrival. You didn't get damaged by Los Angeles."

I protested, "Hey, not that recent. I've been here for almost twenty years. At least I think it's that long. So much time has slipped away that I'm not entirely sure."

"Well, you arrived as an adult, with your soul intact, and let's face it, your disillusionment with art school is a glamorous problem to have. What you say about public health here is true. It's great in theory, but a disaster if you actually have to rely on it. Same with education. Any shithead who can afford it sends his kids to private school. We're told that this is the best place in the world, despite the poverty, the racism and segregation, and a police force that's like the military of a Third World dictatorship. Now that I'm seeing the prison system, I understand the dysfunction of the 'California dream' better than ever. Education is fucked, the economy is rigged, real estate is obscene, and the whole shit sandwich is garnished with a generous helping of hypocrisy. 'Designed to fail' is right. It's as though California's state institutions were invented by socialists and run by libertarians." He paused to think. "My whole life I've dreamed about collective solutions to social problems, and our grand schemes have come to nothing. All I can advise you to do is save yourself." He asked, "Do you have any debt?"

"Not really."

"Then you're a free man. You can do anything."

I said, "Hmm, you may be right. Three friends have invited me to live with them in Berlin."

He said, "It would be a radical change of scenery, that's for sure. I say go for it."

∞

By coincidence, I received an email from Bernie later that day, the first since he had found an apartment in Brooklyn.

> My sublet (which, though illegal, is ostensibly for a long time) reminds me of moving to the Lower East Side in 1981. But now that kind of life happens in Brooklyn. Hart Crane lived near where I am now. I haven't done much exploration about where he, Walt Whitman, George Davis, et al lived. Some addresses no longer exist.

> It's a tiny place, with low ceilings and a cruddy bathroom and kitchenette. It could be worse—there are more recently renovated places in the building that have truly hideous overly-decorative cabinetry and detailing, and they're much more expensive—the people below me have the exact same set up and their rent is $2,700 a month. My rent is "below market rate," whatever magical formula is used to determine that. I like the place and feel cozy in it, and I'm trying to customize it for my condensed NYC needs—I don't know how or why anyone would pay "market rate" for this. I'm living basically as I did when I was twenty-two and working part-time for minimum wage at the Bleecker Street Cinema—I had a lot more fun then, too. But I do like my place.

> I'm across the street from the Brooklyn House of Detention, which looms above Boerum Hill as its tallest landmark. The jail is currently empty, scheduled to reopen in 2012. Evidently it was rumored that it would be turned into condos, a rumor that encouraged local real estate development, but the city

is "renovating" it with convict help because some buildings on Rikers Island have been condemned and there isn't enough room there. This area is the butt-end of downtown Brooklyn where all the grunge facilities are—jail, civil court, a storage facility for the MTA. It's also becoming thoroughly gentrified—mixing artisanal foods with bail bonds. Atlantic Avenue was a direct truck route from the now-defunct Brooklyn docks. There have been a lot of migratory elements in the area—it had been a transient Mohawk community coming from Quebec to work as steelworkers for several decades, and there are still elements of an Arabic neighborhood. There are amazing food stores—Lebanese, Syrian and Yemeni. The gentrification in the area is like a giant white-out of everything. Although no one has mentioned this that I know of, Atlantic Avenue, which I live on, functions as an unofficial racial divide—the downtown Brooklyn side is mostly black and it gets totally white on the Boerum Hill/Carroll Gardens side. My sense is that the black side is going to be pushed out soon. There is a brave new world of high rises planned for the periphery of the Fulton Street Mall, which is an older development.

Fulton Street has been occupied mostly by discount places and pawnshops, but about a quarter of the storefronts are empty. On Christmas I wandered around the pawnshops (all open), looking at the men's jewelry. I saw a lot of gangsta-style bling for men—*a lot*. I'm not used to seeing men's jewelry outnumber jewelry for women in displays. We don't see that at all in "Boring Hill."

Everything is a quick stroll—this is the most metropolitan urban area I've lived in, with conveniences and transportation all being readily at hand. I enjoy living here, even if I have to dodge pedigree children and dogs in the mornings on the sidewalk. I have yet to see my famed neighbor, the porn star Donnie Russo, who lives around the corner.

I wrote back to Bernie about my visit to Berlin, and said that I'd love to experience the city with him. As I typed, I pictured him being flogged by an old leather daddy in a sex club. I thought, perhaps I'll have an opportunity to see that scenario play out in real life one day.

TWENTY-FIVE

I knew I would have to return to Berlin, if only temporarily, but in the meantime, a trip to the Midwest was necessary. Since I would already be on the other side of the country, I planned to visit New York to see Frances and Bernie. Both were very happy that they would have a chance to see me, though only Frances lived in an apartment large enough to accommodate overnight guests. My mother told me that the house where I grew up was no longer in good repair, as she had neglected it while living with her boyfriend. She said, "You should stay at his house. It's a nice place, and there's plenty of room." I was reluctant to accept the hospitality of a man I had never met, but I had little choice in the matter.

∞

I arrived in my hometown late one December night. My mother was at the airport to meet me, and she brought her boyfriend. He looked older than her and in less than perfect health. He extended his hand to give me a hearty businessman's handshake and said, "Hello, nice to meet you. I'm Bob." He spoke in brief phrases, and every time he wished to say something, he brought his left hand up to his throat to close a hole left by a tracheotomy. He explained, "I thought you two should have some time alone, but your mom insisted I come along." He struggled with long utterances, and I appreciated not only what he said, but the effort he expended to say it. My mother looked at him lovingly.

On the way to Bob's house, I noticed that driving was a cooperative effort between the two of them, with my mother checking to see if any cars were coming every time he made a turn. The house was on a lake, and in the morning I would be able to see a view of it from the guest bedroom.

At breakfast the next day, I sat with my mother alone while Bob took his daily walk. She said, "You can borrow my car today. Take whatever you want from the house."

"It won't be a lot, only things I can fit in my suitcase or mail home. It seems like you're abandoning the house."

She shrugged. "I'm going to sell it 'as-is.' I can't cope with all the repairs."

I asked, "Do you have plans to marry Bob?"

"Heavens no. He wants me to, but I don't really want anything to change."

'I'm asking because if you get rid of your house, where will you live after Bob dies? Does he have children?"

"Why are you talking about such morbid things? You just met him, and now you're thinking about his death." Once she calmed down, she said, "He has a daughter. She's very nice."

"I'm sure she is, but if you aren't married to Bob, she'll inherit the house unless you're listed as his heir in the will, or the will gives you the right to live in the house for the rest of your life."

She said, "I don't want to talk about this."

"And I don't want you to be homeless."

With a sense of finality, she said, "I'm sure he's arranged everything so I'll be okay."

"I'm sorry. I was just concerned."

"I guess now that I have Bob, you can leave the country without a second thought."

I blushed and said, "That's not how I see it. And I haven't made any decisions about where I'm living. I may be in Los Angeles for the rest of my life."

Changing the subject, she asked, "What do you want to do while you're here?"

"I'm not sure how much I can do. In a couple of days, I'm flying to New York to visit friends."

My mother looked down, and tears started to spill down her cheeks. "I hope I get to spend some time with you."

"Let's have a nice dinner tonight."

She wiped her face and said, "That would be good. Bob is such a decent man. I hope you can get to know him."

∞

The ranch style house where I grew up hadn't been occupied in a long time, and it was so stuffy that I opened all the windows to let in cold fresh air. I took a look around and noticed nothing seriously damaged, and no vermin invading the place. I looked in the closets and under the beds for anything I might have forgotten in my move to California. I found very little: a sketchbook containing drawings and notes for a film I never made; a few pictures taken in a college photography class; and most potentially embarrassing (and useful), a stash of porn magazines from the 1980s. I took one last look at the house where I had spent my childhood and a few excruciating months of my adulthood. It was smaller than I remembered, much smaller than Bob's house. The lot on which it had been built was larger than normal for the area—over an acre—so I guessed that it would be purchased for the land and torn down. The last physical traces of my past would thus be obliterated. Instead of feeling sad, I felt liberated, as though nothing held me back from pursuing the future I chose.

I turned on a faucet in the kitchen to pour myself a glass of water, but I thought better of it when I smelled a sulfurous odor coming from the tap. I had heard from my mother that fracking had been taking place in the region, and effluent from the process had fouled the well water. I found a small plastic bottle of water in the refrigerator. Then I placed my possessions in a grocery bag, shut all the windows, washed my hands, and left the place where I was raised forever.

It was late afternoon, and I decided to take a drive around my hometown in the dying sunlight. The industrial wasteland I remembered from my youth had disappeared, replaced by another type of landscape: a bland, quiet space of big box stores and generic office buildings. It wasn't at all clear how the residents of the town supported themselves, but industrial labor seemed to have no role in the economy.

In a rundown area of the neighboring city, I found a gay bar called Expressions, which looked like a 1990s-style replacement of the old gay bar I patronized from time to time during my young adulthood. I walked in to see a line of serious alcoholics at the bar drinking before dinner. As I ordered a ginger ale, I saw someone I recognized coming out of the men's room. I said, "Andrew?"

He turned with a start and came toward me. The man I had fucked and almost fisted many years before still had the same sunny, mischievous demeanor, but he had gained a bit of weight and grown a full beard. He hugged me and said, "What the hell are you doing here?"

"Let's sit down." I ordered a drink for him, and we made our way to a table well away from the other patrons.

He leaned toward me and said, "You're a sight for sore eyes. You look just the same."

I said, "Thanks. I rarely visit family. It's been years and years. I think about you sometimes."

"Same."

I asked, "Have you been living here all along?"

"No, I moved to Oregon for a while."

"Did you like it?"

"I loved it. There's so much nature. Great hiking. And Oregon has a decent state healthcare system. I was able to get my HIV meds for free." He asked, "Where have you been living?"

"Los Angeles."

"That's great. Have you become a famous filmmaker?"

I laughed. "Not at all, but I was producing gay porn compilations for Larry Flynt until recently."

"Exciting."

"Not as much as you might think."

He said, "Still, you got out. That's an achievement in itself. Do you think you'll ever move back home?"

"Los Angeles is my home. I have rent control, so I sometimes think the only way I'll leave my apartment for good is in a body bag."

He laughed. "I had it pretty good in Oregon, but you know, the guys in Eugene are a bunch of wimps, so passive-aggressive. Hardly any of them are into fisting."

I said simply, "Damn."

"I moved back to take care of my dad, who isn't doing so well."

"I'm sorry." After a moment's thought, I said, "So you can't host?"

"No."

I frowned. "Neither can I. I'm staying with my mom and her boyfriend."

"Sounds complicated."

I said, "Only a little. Today I had to grab whatever possessions I want to keep from my mother's house, because she's going to sell it. The place is a dump."

He laughed. "Aren't all the houses around here?"

"Well, the boyfriend is rich, so mom is comfortable now."

"Married for money. Good for her."

I asked, "Have you been doing any fisting?"

"Yeah, I'm totally vers now that I'm a daddy—fisting and getting fisted. Not a huge number of partners around, but I do okay. We all sort of look out for each other."

"Good."

"It is." He paused. "When we hooked up, I was desperate to leave town. But you know, it's not so bad here, as long as you have a circle of friends."

I nodded. "I think that's true anywhere. I'm glad you've found a community. You're looking well."

"Thanks. Maybe the next time you're in town, I'll be renting my own place again, and we can have ourselves a time."

"I'd like that. I'm afraid I have to go to dinner with the family now." We kissed each other on the cheeks and embraced, and I left the bar. I had a feeling I'd never return.

∞

I took the only non-stop flight from the local airport to New York, and landed at LaGuardia late. I made it to Washington Heights shortly before nine at night. Frances welcomed me, fed me dinner, and asked for the latest gossip. I gave her the fullest account I could of my recent trip to Berlin. She said, "You must have had a hell of a lot of sex."

I laughed. "Enough." After a pause, I said, "I think I'm going back to Berlin soon. Gregorio and Winston have asked me to live with them."

"Wow, if you do that, you have to invite me to visit you some time. Berlin has thirty lesbian bars, and they're all calling my name." She asked, "Are you going to live happily ever after?"

"Maybe so. They have a new addition to their household, a guy named Elend. He's lovely."

"Darling, I'd love to paint a portrait of the three of you again."

I said, "And now there are four."

"Beautiful."

I asked, "How has teaching been going?"

"Well, I taught adjunct for a long time, and, except for the salary, it was a good thing. I could be the demonstrative, inappropriate punk, a naughty devil pervert, because there's no responsibility to the institution. When I got the tenure track job, I decided to behave as I always do, because in my department, there's a bunch of interesting painters who try not to kill each other's practices. Why not?"

"Do you think the job has taken over your life?"

"I'm having just as many shows and have just as much of a social life as I've always had, so I don't think that's true. I'm running around all over the place. Maybe I'm getting better at multitasking. I don't have time to do things like shop, but I never did anyway."

The next day we rode the subway to Chelsea, a trip that lasted about a half hour. I marveled at the convenience compared to Los Angeles, where a walk around the neighborhood could easily take that long. Frances was committed to doing the rounds at galleries every Saturday, and though I found it rather exhausting, she seemed to be energized by the ritual. She saw many friends on the street, and knew several of the artists with shows on view. She had become a woman about town, and it was clear that she had made exactly the right decision in moving back to New York.

∞

On Sunday, we went to visit Bernie in Brooklyn. The trip took about an hour. When he opened his door, he seemed rather flustered. He let us in, and we immediately understood why. The inside of the apartment was crammed with boxes and piles of books. Bernie got himself ready as quickly as he could, as we waited uncomfortably in the tiny open space available to us. We went out and took a short walk, during which I got disoriented, because I had never been to the neighborhood before. We entered a drab bar that appeared to be a leftover from a previous era. We sat at a small table, and Bernie said, "I'm still in the process of emptying my storage facility here, because I can't afford it plus my 'below market rate' apartment. I've been working two jobs. I'm trying not to turn my apartment into a version of the storage space, with a bed as an afterthought. I guess I failed." He looked down at his beer in despair.

Attempting to change the mood, I said, "I used *The Black Diaries* for making art, and I really appreciated it."

It was as though I had said nothing. He continued, "I haven't seen most of this stuff for at least ten years, and my needs have changed a lot since then. There are books I still can't locate, which worries me somewhat. There's certainly an excess."

The word "excess" made Frances laugh, and she apologized.

He shrugged. "Many of the books can go, but one of the realizations I've had about New York is that most of my collection comes from used bookstores that no longer exist. The amazing range of what could be found in those places can't exist these days, either." He sighed and said, "I've never felt so much like a relic."

I asked, "What have you been doing for work?"

He took a big sip of beer and said, "Teaching again at ICP, and assisting a photo dealer on the Upper East Side. She's an over-the-top version of a WASP. I don't understand her at all. She doesn't seem to sweat or ever use the toilet." We all laughed at this.

At that point, a tall, stocky Latino man came in and positioned himself at the bar in Bernie's line of sight. I saw him, too, but from an angle, while Frances's back was to him. Unnoticed by the other patrons, he began to adjust his crotch until the bulge in his pants swelled considerably. He then went to the men's room, and after a beat, Bernie excused himself to join him.

Oblivious, Frances said, "Bernie seems like he's struggling these days."

"Yeah, but he's always struggling. I feel bad for him. He's so ill-prepared for the world he's forced to live in." I described the emails Bernie had sent me over the last few months, and I said how much I missed him.

After a few minutes, I saw the man from the men's room make a hasty exit, and a short while later, Bernie returned to the table looking a bit disheveled. His hair stood up at odd angles, but Frances, who rarely used a brush herself, didn't notice. She had seen nothing of the sexual scene that played out behind her back. I wondered if Bernie gave guys blow jobs at this bar often, if the management was aware of this—the place didn't appear to be a gay bar—and if the man whose cock he'd just sucked was a total stranger or one of his "regulars."

Frances interrupted my thoughts by announcing to Bernie, "I'd like to paint your portrait."

He perked up and said, "People have done photographic portraits galore, but never a painting. I'd be honored."

She asked, "Do you mind if it's in the nude?"

He looked even more tickled and said, "No. All those hours I spend at the gym will be immortalized."

Frances and Bernie exchanged phone numbers and discussed their schedules. Both of them seemed ridiculously overcommitted. I felt like a true Los Angeles layabout, working a bare minimum to survive. I didn't let myself think about the porn job I had just lost. Frances looked at her watch and said, "We should get going. It's a long trip back home, and I'm thawing out a roast for tonight." She asked Bernie, "Would you like to come over?"

Bernie hemmed and hawed, not disclosing what his plans were, and made meek apologetic noises. I hoped he had another sex date lined up for that evening, but I knew that he would never tell me if he did. I raised what was left of the beer in my glass and said, "Next year, in Berlin."

When we rose to leave the bar, Bernie hugged me and burst into tears. He held me for a long time, and a wet spot formed on my shirt. Finally, he backed away from me and said, "See you."

On the subway ride to Washington Heights, Frances said, "Bernie is great. They don't make 'em like that anymore. I can't wait to paint him."

"Normally he's an amazing conversationalist, but he can only talk about certain things." I didn't mention the men's room blow job, but said, "His sexual experiences are completely bracketed off from the rest of his life, and he never seems to have any intimate relationships."

"That's sad."

"From a certain point of view, but it works for him. He has great friends who are like his family. In the end, it doesn't matter very much whether those relationships lead to sex." I said this as much to convince myself that my lack of sexual interest in Bernie was not a problem as to explain him to Frances. "He's organized his life pretty well. It only gets painful when he falls in love."

"Like with you?"

"Yeah, that was a little awkward, wasn't it?" I sighed. "I really care about the guy, but romance was never going to happen. I don't think anyone should feel sorry for him. Why bring assumptions to other people's sex lives? He's probably going to get flogged and brutalized tonight, and he'll love every minute of it. Who cares whether that fits in with some suburban ideal of marriage?" After a silence, I asked, "Speaking of marriage, do you have a girlfriend now?"

She said, "I thought you'd never ask. Her name is Lucy. We met at a bar called Metropolitan. She was wearing this really cute hat, and I thought she kind of looked like Diane Keaton. I asked her, 'You're not Diane Keaton, are you?' She thought I was crazy. I wasn't like, Oh, I'm really attracted to that person. I found her unique in a way.

The whole time, I was thinking about this painting that I was really pissed off about. I hadn't finished it, so I left while Lucy was in the bathroom. Then we met again at this party that Nicole Eisenman and AL Steiner threw called Ridykeulous. Lucy passed out on the dance floor because the power went out and the music stopped. So I gave her mouth-to-mouth resuscitation. It was our first kiss. We've been together ever since."

I said, "That sounds romantic."

"Your life is full of romance, too, isn't it?"

I blushed and said, "I'm working on it." I had been thinking of my friends Elend, Gregorio, and Winston during the whole conversation, and perhaps this had been obvious from the expression on my face.

She put her arm around me and said, "I hope you find what you're looking for."

TWENTY-SIX

After my return to Los Angeles, I arranged to have lunch with Raúl during the day on New Year's Eve. He was in town to visit family and to work for the Lutheran Church. I arrived at the restaurant near Sunset Junction to find him wearing a priest's collar and a crucifix. I kissed him and asked, "Do you need any poppers or lube? I want to walk into Circus of Books with you dressed like that."

He laughed and said, "Actually I do. The sex shops in Phoenix are shit." After this exchange, the question of whether we would have sex again hung over the conversation, and I decided to tell him that I was considering moving away. He looked disappointed and commented, "Lots of fisting in Berlin."

I said, "That seems to be the main thing my friends know about the place." I asked, "How do you think I should tell Daniel?"

"I'm not sure. He's not your boyfriend."

"He says I'm the best he's ever had, but in the blink of an eye, he gets a dozen old white men to fist him. And he's hooked up with most of my friends, too."

Raúl shook his head. "He does love his drama. Hey, have you seen the news lately?"

"No, what?"

"The US executed Saddam Hussein yesterday. Hanged by the neck until dead. Not like that's going to solve their problems."

"Wow. I have a Kurdish friend who's probably celebrating right now."

He said, "I'm celebrating, too, but for different reasons, I'm sure. Have you noticed that the US has stopped fucking with every other country in the Western Hemisphere?" I thought about this while he continued, "American foreign policy is so preoccupied with war in the Middle East that there's no time or money to meddle in the politics of our neighbors to the south."

"Yeah, when I was growing up, the 'CIA-backed coup' was a commonplace."

"Not anymore. The shit show in Iraq has forced the motherfuckers to leave us alone. It's a new day in Latin America."

I asked, "Do you think you'll move back there?"

"Sometimes I'm tempted, but I have a boyfriend and a job." He held up the crucifix around his neck.

I said, "Whatever happens, good luck."

"You too, my friend."

"If I move to Berlin, you should come to see us. I bet my friends would enjoy meeting you."

"I'll keep it in mind." Before we parted, we kissed and he said, "I love you."

I responded, "I love you, too."

As he left, I reflected on the time I had spent in Los Angeles meeting men and fisting them. I thought, these years haven't been wasted, because I've made one true friend.

That evening I called Daniel. There was a New Year's Eve party happening at his house, and he barely heard me over the noise. His only response to the news that I might be leaving Los Angeles was, "Have a good time. I'll miss you." I had worried about his reaction for nothing.

∞

I scheduled a meeting with Carmen and Paul at Blanco Projects' new space in West Hollywood as soon as the staff returned from the holidays. It wasn't far away from the route of the Beverly Boulevard bus, so it took only about forty-five minutes to get there. The gallery would open in a matter of weeks, and renovations were nearly complete. There were a couple of new employees milling around, looking like younger versions of Carmen in less expensive clothes. Carmen herself wore the most extraordinary outfit I had ever seen on her: a long off-white skirt with very thin pleats and a bright white blouse made of a stretch fabric; what I could only describe as a miniature curtain rod was affixed to a cord around her neck, and in front of her breasts hung a small fuchsia lamé jacket and an artificial red rose. I thought that if this was a daily work outfit for her, she would have no trouble whatsoever making an impression in the art world. Her only problem would be upstaging the artworks she showed. Dressed in a trim black turtleneck and light wool pants also in black, Paul had returned to his all-business demeanor. I hugged both of them and said to Carmen, "The gallery looks amazing, and so do you. I'm sure collectors will be eating out of your hand in no time."

Carmen said, "I'm excited. I hope you'll join us for the opening of our first exhibition at the end of the month."

"Of course."

Paul turned away to deal with a question at the front desk. Carmen asked, "Have you been making any new work?"

"Things have been in flux. It's been difficult to find the calm I need to paint."

We moved to the viewing room, a lounge where sales could be finalized in comfort. We sat on Barcelona chairs under a large painting by one of Carmen's new artists. I was positioned with my back to it. Paul brought bottles of mineral water and joined us. He said, "We've been concerned about you. There's some doubt as to whether you're really committed to making paintings over the long term."

"It's true that I don't see myself primarily as a painter. I make art, and paintings are what I'm doing now. I suppose that makes the work tough to sell."

Carmen said, "That's why I respect you. There are lots of painters, and there will always be collectors for them, but someone who has a unique project, one that seems perverse in the present market, this is more rare."

"I must say I was surprised you even gave me an exhibition."

She said, "If every show is a surefire commercial success, it gets a bit oppressive. There has to be variety in a gallery's program."

Paul glanced over at Carmen with a questioning look, and she nodded. He said, "There's some news. We've managed to place another piece. A visitor from Europe bought one of your Marx paintings." He fiddled with his BlackBerry for a moment. "The pink one, 'Here we ascend from earth to heaven.' He thought it might have been a passage from Agnes Martin's writings, but when he found out the actual source, he was still interested. Bless those German collectors."

"That's great," I said with a smile.

He continued, "We should be able to cut you a check by the end of this week."

Carmen said, "To be frank, I didn't expect to sell anything from your show. Three sales so far have been a nice surprise. I'm eager to see what you do next. We need to find collectors with curiosity to support your work. There's shockingly little curiosity around these days."

Paul asked, "Are you planning to do more painting soon?"

I said, "So about that, I've been laid off from my porn industry job. There isn't much keeping me in Los Angeles anymore. The artists you work with can live anywhere, so I'm moving to Berlin."

Carmen sat upright. "Oh?"

I continued, "I thought I'd discuss it with you. As you know, I'm close to Winston, or Andë, as the art world knows him. The thing is, he offered me a job. He's negotiating his first commission from an American museum, and he needs me to handle the correspondence. Our old friend has become something of a cultural institution in his adopted country."

Paul dropped the catty tone he normally adopted with me and said, "Yes, his auction prices are very strong these days, but there have been no American exhibitions since immediately after art school. Gagosian mounted a show for him, but I believe that was in London. He couldn't understand why Winston paints everything himself by hand, because it slows up production. Good old Larry. Anyway, no one has developed much of a market for his work in the US yet." He squirmed at the thought of someone whose price point was considerably higher than the other painters in the gallery.

I imagined that Carmen was scheming how she might make use of my connection to the great Andë Alia to snag him for Blanco Projects, thereby getting a jump on the blue-chip galleries in New York. "This is all very interesting," she said with an enigmatic smile.

"Winston and Gregorio own a large building in East Berlin, and there's plenty of room for me to have a studio there. I'm looking forward to continuing our conversations about art."

Carmen said, "I think you should do it, and the money from this latest sale will help you move."

"That's what I was thinking. I came here to talk about finances, and my question was answered before I had to ask."

Paul said, "It's a sign that this is meant to happen."

Carmen asked, "When do you plan to leave?"

"Possibly as early as the end of the month. If I stay around much longer, I might get sucked into the sort of job that would keep me from making art. It's now or never." A second later, Carmen received a call that she had to take.

Paul said, "I have a good feeling about this. Los Angeles has been getting too bland for the likes of you." I had expected him to say "the likes of us," but he no longer considered himself to be a bohemian.

Carmen returned, and when Paul excused himself to attend to another matter, she said to me confidentially, "I've always wanted to see Berlin. It's where my family is from." She took my arm and walked me to the door. "Perhaps you'll make something happen, and that will give me a good excuse to travel to Berlin on business."

I said, "I'll see what I can do." Then we kissed each other on both cheeks and I left.

As I walked to Beverly Boulevard, I felt an excitement I hadn't experienced since I first started art school. I didn't go to the gallery with the intention of discussing emigration, yet somehow saying it out loud to Carmen and Paul made it real for me. On the bus back home, I texted Gregorio, "I'm moving to Berlin." Within minutes, he texted back, "Hooray!" It must have been after dinner there, so I sent one more text: "Tell the boys." He responded, "I already have."

∞

I called Moira in Chiapas and told her the news. She was delighted that I had finally managed to break the spell Temo had cast over me. I told her, "I didn't think about him once while I was in Berlin, except when Winston brought him up."

She said, "I'm sure he's finding willing victims in Mexico as we speak. That is, if his mother ever lets him out of the house."

I asked, "How is your family?"

"Flor is talking now. She's trilingual. Some children with three native languages are frustrated and confused before they learn the difference between them and can make themselves understood. Others talk all the time, in three languages simultaneously, to whomever will listen. I'm happy to say that Flor is the latter kind of child. Everyone is charmed by her."

"Are you and Miguel teaching?"

"Yes, a new school, the Intercultural University of Chiapas, was founded this year. For now it's just a big sign with the president's name on it, but one day soon, it'll be a real college with instruction in Mayan languages and Spanish. We've been working with other instructors to develop a model curriculum, and classes begin off campus in about nine months."

"That's great."

"I feel as though all my work is coming to fruition. Some of my former students will be instructors at the university. I'm so happy I'm here."

∞

I spent about two weeks winding up my affairs in Los Angeles. My life was simpler than most because I didn't own much of anything. I paid off my credit card debt and closed my bank account. I informed the building manager of my forwarding information, gave him some money for postage, and took his email address. I told him that I had an apartment full of furniture and no place to put it. He said not to worry, because he could find a tenant for a furnished apartment. After he inspected the place, I got most of my security deposit back.

A couple of days before my flight, I received my last piece of mail in Los Angeles. El sent me a postcard from the Pergamon Museum with an image of the Ishtar Gate. It read, "I have moved in with Gregorio and Winston and taken your bed. It is cold without you.

When are you returning? We need you here." I put the card in the suitcase I was packing for the trip. I carefully wrapped up my most valuable possession, the portrait of Enver Hoxha I received as a gift at the end of art school. I would take it with me as carry-on luggage.

∞

The flight took off late from LAX, but the pilot assured us that he could make up that time riding the jet stream. I unexpectedly fell into a deep sleep not long after take off. I was exhausted from the preparations for the move, and at last I could relax. I awoke in time to eat breakfast as the plane passed over the North Sea. As we came closer to our destination, I saw endless flat, snowy fields, not all that different from the landscape of the American Midwest that I had left long before. Rather than reassuring me, it brought on a wave of panic. I didn't really know Berlin, as I had barely left Winston and Gregorio's during my visit; I wasn't sure I could live with Elend, whom I had known only briefly; my German was essentially baby talk; and it had been many years since I had experienced a winter with snow and ice for months on end.

We landed at Tegel on time, and I passed through the official corridors quickly. I didn't have much company, since few tourists came to Germany at the end of January. I entered the terminal, and whatever panic I felt dissipated. I saw the three men I loved waiting for me, and I thought to myself, This is my new family.